125 Best
Gluten-Free
Bread Machine
Recipes

For Paula

Enjoy

Heather L Butt

Donna J Washburn

125 Best
Gluten-Free
Bread Machine
Recipes

Donna Washburn and Heather Butt

Robert
ROSE

For complete cataloguing information, see page 253.

Disclaimer
The recipes in this book have been carefully tested by our kitchen and our tasters. To the best of our knowledge, they are safe and nutritious for ordinary use and users. For those people with food or other allergies, or who have special food requirements or health issues, please read the suggested contents of each recipe carefully and determine whether or not they may create a problem for you. All recipes are used at the risk of the consumer. Consumers should always consult their bread machine manufacturer's manual for recommended procedures and cooking times.

We cannot be responsible for any hazards, loss or damage that may occur as a result of any recipe use.

For those with special needs, allergies, requirements or health problems, in the event of any doubt, please contact your medical adviser prior to the use of any recipe.

Editor: Sue Sumeraj
Recipe Editor and Tester: Jennifer MacKenzie
Proofreader: Sheila Wawanash
Indexer: Gillian Watts
Design and Production: Kevin Cockburn/PageWave Graphics Inc.
Photography: Colin Ericson
Food Styling: Kathryn Robertson and Kate Bush
Prop Styling: Charlene Ericson

Cover image: Sun-Dried Tomato Rice Loaf (page 92), Cranberry Wild Rice Loaf (page 90) and Teff Bread (page 60)

We acknowledge the financial support of the Government of Canada through the Book Publishing Industry Development Program (BPIDP) for our publishing activities.

Published by Robert Rose Inc.
120 Eglinton Avenue East, Suite 800, Toronto, Ontario, Canada M4P 1E2
Tel: (416) 322-6552 Fax: (416) 322-6936

Mixed Sources
Product group from well-managed forests, controlled sources and recycled wood or fiber
www.fsc.org Cert no. SW-COC-000952
© 1996 Forest Stewardship Council

FSC

Printed and bound in Canada

1 2 3 4 5 6 7 8 9 TCP 18 17 16 15 14 13 12 11 10

To our special celiac friends, who, over the years,
have brought purpose and joy to our lives.

Contents

Acknowledgments

This book has had the support and assistance of many people from its inception to the final reality. We want to thank those who helped us along the way.

Our thanks to the following people and companies for supplying products for recipe development: Doug Yuen of Dainty Foods for brown rice flour and rice bran; George Birinyi Jr. of Grain Process Enterprises Ltd. for potato starch, tapioca starch, sorghum flour, amaranth flour, whole bean flour, chickpea flour, pea flour and quinoa flour; Howard Selig of Valley Flaxflour Ltd. for flax flour and flaxseed, both brown and golden; Margaret Hudson of Burnbrae Farms Ltd. for Naturegg Simply Whites and Break Free liquid eggs; Egg Farmers of Ontario for whole-shell eggs; Michel Dion of Lallamand Inc. for Eagle Instaferm® yeast; Beth Armour and Tracy Perry of Cream Hill Estates Ltd. for oat flour and rolled oats (Beth also gets our thanks for giving us permission to share the Oat Groat Crust recipe, which she originally developed); Seaton Smith Family of Gluten-Free Oats Company for old-fashioned rolled oats; FarmPure Foods Inc. for Only Oats™ for oat bran, oat flour, oat flakes and steel-cut pearls; CanolaInfo and Canbra Foods Ltd. for Canola Harvest canola oil, HiLo spray and baking/waffle spray (also to Dorothy Long of CanolaInfo for permission to share recipes originally developed for them); Best Cooking Pulses for organic pea fiber, whole yellow pea flour and chickpea flour; Northern Quinoa Corp. for quinoa flour; and Workinesh Spice Blends Inc. for teff flour.

Thank you to the many manufacturers of bread machines who continue to supply our test kitchen with the latest models: Applica, Salton/Toastmaster Inc., Breadman, Cuisinart, Oster, Black & Decker and Zojirushi. Thanks to Hamilton Beach Brands for the food processor.

A huge thank you to Orma McDougall, and to the members of the Brockville chapter of the Canadian Celiac Association and the members of our focus group, who faithfully and tirelessly tasted gluten-free products from the beginning to the end of recipe development. Your comments, suggestions and critical analysis were invaluable and helped make this a better book.

We want to express our appreciation to photographer Colin Erricson, food stylist Cathy Robertson and prop stylist Charlene Erricson. Thank you for making the photographs of our gluten-free recipes look delicious. Once again, we enjoyed baking for the photo shoot.

Bob Dees, our publisher, Marian Jarkovich, Sales and Marketing Manager, National Retail Accounts, and Nina McCreath, International Sales and Marketing at Robert Rose Inc., deserve special thanks for their ongoing support.

To Kevin Cockburn of PageWave Graphics, thank you for working through this cookbook's design, layout and production. Thanks also to Sue Sumeraj, our editor.

Thank you to our families: Heather's husband, our sons, our daughters-in-law and our grandchildren. You help bring balance to our lives when we get too focused on our work.

Finally, to you who must follow a gluten-free diet, we sincerely hope these recipes help make your life easier and more enjoyable. We developed them with you in mind.

— *Donna and Heather*

Introduction

We are frequently asked to speak at international celiac conferences and support groups. Our favorite topic is bread machine baking, using the more nutritious flours, of course. Over the last few years, we have spoken about bread machine baking and advanced baking techniques at the GIG in Richmond, Virginia, a special workshop for TWEGIG (The West End Gluten Intolerance Group) in Virginia and the Canadian Celiac Conference in beautiful Victoria, British Columbia, among others. We've enjoyed our hands-on day-long workshops with celiac children and their parents at the Hospital for Sick Children in Toronto, Ontario. Each time we speak at a conference, we are inundated with questions about bread baking. Your many emails about bread machine baking confirmed the need for this book. Talking with our publisher, Bob Dees, we realized a need for a whole cookbook of gluten-free bread machine recipes.

Manufacturers are constantly releasing new bread machine models. Even though some of the recipes in this book were published in our earlier gluten-free cookbooks, they have all been retested in the new bread machines; most required minor adjustments in some ingredients. Because some cycles no longer exist with the new machines and newer cycles have been introduced, we also had to change the method for all gluten-free loaves prepared in the bread machine. We have given detailed instructions on using the Dough and Bake cycles, as well as the new Gluten-Free Cycle available on some machines.

Everyone who visits our test kitchen is amazed by the number of bread machines we have. Often, half a dozen machines are on the go, at different stages. In the late afternoon, you'll find us measuring, evaluating and tasting what we made that day. We make minor adjustments to the recipes and the ingredients go back into the machines the next day, until we get perfect-looking and perfect-tasting loaves. As we work, we are constantly thinking of tips to pass on to you.

A member of our local celiac chapter spent a morning with us as we developed recipes for this book, which led us to consider conducting hands-on workshops on bread machine baking in our test kitchen. Everyone we speak to gives us positive feedback on this idea. Please contact us if you are interested in taking part in one of these workshops.

Whenever we are getting ready to head out to an event, we reminisce about past conferences and wonder which of our celiac friends will be there. So many of you hold such precious memories for us! Keep in touch. We love your emails and letters, as they give us much-appreciated feedback. We know you must find time in your busy lives to write, and your questions and comments are important to us.

Donna J. Washburn, P.H.Ec., and Heather L. Butt, P.H.Ec.
Quality Professional Services
1104 Burnside Drive
Brockville, Ontario K6V 5T1
Phone/fax: (613) 923-2116
Email: bread@ripnet.com
Website: www.bestbreadrecipes.com

Speaking Our Language:
Are We All on the Same Page?

- "GF" means "gluten-free," such as GF sour cream, GF oat bran, etc., when both gluten-free and gluten-containing products are available. We recommend that you read package labels every time you purchase a GF product. Manufacturers frequently change the ingredients.

- In developing our recipes, we used large eggs, liquid honey, light (fancy) molasses, bread machine (instant) yeast, unsweetened fruit juice (not fruit drinks) and salted butter. We know you'll get the same great results if you bake with these, but expect slightly different results if you make substitutions.

- We tested with 2%, 1% or nonfat milk, yogurt and sour cream, but our recipes will work with other fat levels.

- Unless otherwise stated in the recipe or your bread machine manual, eggs and dairy products are used cold from the refrigerator.

- All foods that require washing are washed before preparation. Foods such as oranges, bananas and garlic are peeled, but fresh apples and apricots are not (unless specified).

- If the preparation method (chopped, melted, diced, sliced) is listed before the food, it means that you prepare the food before measuring. If it is listed after the food, measure first, then prepare. Examples are "melted butter" vs. "butter, melted"; "ground flaxseed" vs. "flaxseed, ground"; and "cooked wild rice" vs. "wild rice, cooked."

- If in doubt about a food term, a piece of equipment or a specific recipe technique, refer to the glossaries, located on pages 230 to 240.

Using Your Bread Machine for Gluten-Free Baking

We have worked with many different brands and models of bread machines over the years, and we enjoy the challenges presented by the fact that each is so individual. Some bread machines on the market today have a longer and more vigorous knead than others, which results in slightly different loaves from the same recipe. We baked eight loaves in eight different bread machines using the White Bread mix, and got eight different results. The manual for your bread machine will help you become familiar with your make and model. Read it before you attempt to bake a loaf of bread: happy baking depends on it.

When purchasing a new bread machine, make sure it has at least one of the following choices: both a Dough Cycle and a Bake Cycle; a Programmable Cycle; or a dedicated Gluten-Free Cycle. Neither the 58-minute nor the 70-minute Rapid cycles are long enough to rise and bake loaves successfully. The old 2-Hour Rapid Cycle works well, but this machine is no longer available. If you are using an older bread machine that doesn't have any of these options, try baking the loaves using a Basic, White or Sweet Cycle.

The recipes in this book were developed for 1½-lb (750 g) or 2-lb (1 kg) bread machines with either one or two kneading blades. These are the only ones you will have success with. The larger-capacity bread machines (those that bake 2½-lb/1.25 kg or 3-lb/1.5 kg loaves) are too large to properly knead the amount of dough in our recipes.

Getting to Know Your Bread Machine

Before you bake your first gluten-free loaf, it is important to become familiar with your bread machine, since models vary so much. Here's what we recommend. Standing in front of your machine, manual in hand, fill the baking pan with 1 inch (2.5 cm) of water. Observe and record the digital readout for the beginning of each operation as you determine the answers to the following questions.

Does the manual recommend warming the liquids and eggs?

Some machines advise warming liquids to between 80°F and 90°F (27°C and 32°C) if you're using the Dough Cycle, or to between 110°F and 115°F (43°C and 46°C) if you're using the Gluten-Free Cycle. In addition, some suggest warming eggs to room temperature (see the Techniques Glossary, page 238.)

Does it have a Preheat Cycle? If so, how long is it?

Some machines start immediately, while others delay up to 25 minutes. Write the length of the Preheat Cycle on a label and stick it to your bread machine.

How long is the mixing stage?

Some machines mix for 1 to 2 minutes, others for up to 4 minutes. Write how long the mixing stage takes on the label you stuck to your bread machine when answering the previous question.

How long does the kneading take? Is it constant or intermittent?

The kneading stage varies from to 15 to 35 minutes. Add this information to the label you stuck to the bread machine. With an intermittent knead, it is difficult to know when the machine is finished kneading and is beginning the rise cycle. When you're making dough that won't be baked in the machine, we suggest removing it as soon as the kneading portion of the cycle is complete, simply because doing so speeds up the bread-baking process. If you forget and the machine finishes the cycle, don't worry about it.

Does the machine alert me when it's time to remove the kneading blade?

Most bread machines have an audible signal that tells you when to remove the blade. If yours doesn't, remove it at the end of the long knead (unless you're using the Programmable Cycle; see page 17).

At the end of the Dough Cycle, does the machine shut off automatically or stay on?

Look for a flashing colon, which will tell you it is still on.

Is the time for the Bake Cycle preset?

Some machines have the baking time preset to 10 minutes and you'll need to set it by 10-minute intervals. Others are preset to 90 minutes and need to be adjusted to 60 minutes. To adjust the time, move the timer arrows up or down.

Can the Bake Cycle be immediately set for more time at the end of the cycle?

Before turning the machine off, take the internal temperature of the loaf with an instant-read thermometer. It should be 200°F (100°C). If it's below 180°F (85°C), you'll need to reset the Bake Cycle and check the internal temperature every 10 minutes.

Can the baking time for the Gluten-Free Cycle be extended?

If not, turn on the Bake Cycle and check the internal temperature every 10 minutes.

Does the machine have a Keep Warm Cycle? How long is it?

Most machines have a 1-hour Keep Warm Cycle, which is a handy feature if the bread is between 180°F (85°C) and 200°F (100°C) after 60 minutes on the Bake Cycle. Simply leave the machine on the Keep Warm Cycle until the bread reaches 200°F (100°C).

Baking Bread

To use the Dough Cycle, then the Bake Cycle

Select the Dough Cycle first. Remove the kneading blade at the end of the long knead, then allow the cycle to finish. Immediately select the Bake Cycle, setting it to 350°F or 360°F (180°C or 185°C) for 60 minutes. Allow the Bake Cycle to finish.

It is important to get to know your own bread machine. For instance, we have one that is a lot hotter than the rest, and we find that we have to lower the baking temperature; however, with other machines of the same make and model, the loaf bakes with a thin, tender crust. In most machines, the default temperature is 350°F (180°C). Check your manual to learn how to change time and temperature.

To use the dedicated Gluten-Free Cycle

If an information box appears below a recipe, read it first. For many loaves, we had to increase the liquid in the recipe to make it work for this cycle. In addition, some ingredients, including liquids and eggs, needed to be warmed, not used directly from the refrigerator. (See the Techniques Glossary, page 238, for information on safely warming eggs). Select the Gluten-Free Cycle, removing the kneading blade when the machine signals or at the end of the long knead. Consult your manual for the timing of this signal. Removing the paddle prevents over-kneading and collapse of the top crust.

To use the Programmable Cycle

Read your owner's manual to learn how to set the Programmable Cycle. Select a short knead of 2 minutes (the machine stirs slowly, allowing for the addition of dry ingredients). Then set a knead of 20 minutes, then a rise of 70 minutes and a 60-minute Bake Cycle at 350°F (180°C). When prompted, set all other cycles to 0, eliminating the extra cycles. There's no need to remove the paddle. You only need to program the machine once, as it will remember your settings until you change them.

Tips for Successful Gluten-Free Bread Machine Baking

- Read through the recipe before beginning, then gather the equipment and ingredients and wash anything that needs it.
- We selected specific flour combinations for individual recipes based on the desired texture and flavor of the final product. Rather than using a standard mix of flours, we like to vary the proportions of flours and starches so that each recipe is unique. Unless mentioned as a variation, we have not tested other GF flours in the recipes. Substituting other flours may adversely affect the results.
- Select either metric or imperial measures and stick to your choice for the entire recipe.
- Gluten-free recipes can be temperamental, so be sure to measure all ingredients accurately. Even an extra tablespoon (15 mL) of water in a baked product can cause the recipe to fail. Use a clear, graduated liquid measuring cup for all liquids. Place it on a flat surface and read it at eye level.
- Select the correct dry measures. For example, when the recipe calls for ¾ cup, use a ½-cup measure and a ¼-cup measure (for 175 mL, use a 125 mL measure and a 50 mL measure). Use the "spoon lightly, heap and level once" method of measuring for accuracy and perfect products. Use measuring spoons, not kitchen cutlery, for small amounts. There are also sets of long-handled, narrow spoons made especially to fit into spice jars. These are accurate and fun to use.
- Remove the baking pan from the bread machine when adding ingredients. Do not measure over the bread pan.
- Gluten-free flours and starches must be well mixed or sifted together before they are slowly added to liquids, as they have a fine, powder-like consistency and lump easily.
- If your bread machine has a Preheat Cycle, keep the top down until mixing starts, so the heat does not escape. As soon as the liquids begin to mix, add the dry ingredients, scraping the corners, sides and bottom of the baking pan and the kneading blade while adding. Watch that the rubber spatula does not get caught under the rotating blade. Continue scraping until no dry ingredients remain and dough is well mixed. Some machines require more "help" mixing than others.

- The consistency of the dough is closer to a cake batter than the traditional yeast dough ball. You should see the motion of the kneading blade turning. The mixing mark of the kneading blade remains on top of the dough. Some doughs are thicker than others, but do not adjust by adding more liquid or dry ingredients.
- The kneading blade needs to be removed at the end of the long knead to prevent the collapse of the final loaf. However, some bread machines knead intermittently rather than continuously, so the first few times you use a new machine, listen carefully for the sounds of the different cycles. Make notes of the times the cycles change. We note the times for start of mixing and end of long knead right on the machine. Use either a label or permanent marker to write them on the machine. Then set an auxiliary timer for the time the kneading finishes and the rising starts. This will alert you to when to remove the kneading blade. The dough is sticky, so rinse the rubber spatula and your hand with cold water before removing the blade. Smooth the top of the loaf quickly.
- Some bread machines and some recipes bake darker-colored crusts than others. If you find certain loaves are too dark, next time set the Bake Cycle temperature lower. When baking on a Gluten-Free Cycle, a Basic Cycle or a 2-Hour Rapid Cycle, select a lighter crust setting, if possible.
- At the end of the baking cycle, before turning the machine off, take the temperature of the loaf using an instant-read thermometer. It should read 200°F (100°C). If it's between 180°F (85°C) and 200°F (100°C), leave the machine on the Keep Warm Cycle until the loaf is baked. If it's below 180°F (85°C), turn on the Bake Cycle and check the internal temperature every 10 minutes. (Some bread machines are automatically set for 60 minutes; others need to be set by 10-minute intervals.)
- Slice the cooled baked loaf with an electric knife or bread knife with a serrated blade. Place one or two slices in individual plastic bags, then place bags in a larger resealable bag. Freeze for up to 3 weeks. Remove a slice or two at a time.

Using an Instant-Read Thermometer

When we bake gluten-free, it is important to use a thermometer to test foods for doneness, as it is more difficult to tell when they are baked: the outside of the bread or cake may look browned enough when the inside is still raw. The indicators you may be used to looking for when baking with wheat may not be reliable, as gluten-free foods often have a different appearance. A thermometer is the only accurate way to be sure the food is done.

Purchasing

The best thermometer for this purpose is a bimetallic stemmed thermometer often called an instant-read or chef's thermometer. It has a round head at the top, a long metal stem and a pointed end that senses the temperature. There are both digital and dial versions available. Check the temperature range to be sure it covers the temperatures you need. Instant-read thermometers are widely available in department stores, some grocery stores, specialty shops and big-box stores, and can also be purchased online.

Use

To test baked goods for doneness, insert the thermometer into the center of the product. Gluten-free baked goods, whether breads, cakes or muffins, are baked at 200°F (100°C). Do not leave the thermometer in the product during baking, as the plastic cover will melt, ruining the thermometer.

To test for doneness in meats, insert the metal stem halfway or at least 2 inches (5 cm) into the product, making sure you do not touch the pan, bone or fat. (Some of the newer thermometers only need to be inserted to a depth of $3/4$ inch/2 cm, so check the manufacturer's instructions.) With thin cuts, it may be necessary to insert the stem horizontally. Meatballs can be stacked.

Clean the probe thoroughly after each use and store the thermometer in the plastic sleeve that came with it. Some of the more expensive ones (but not all) are dishwasher-safe. Read the manufacturer's instructions.

How to Calibrate Your Thermometer

It is important to make sure your thermometer is reading temperatures accurately, so you'll want to test it periodically. There are two ways of doing this and either will work, though we prefer the boiling-water method.

- **Boiling-water method:** Bring a pot of water to a boil. Insert the thermometer probe into the boiling water, making sure it doesn't touch the pot. It should read 212°F or 100°C. (Be careful not to burn yourself on the steam; we hold the thermometer with needle-nose pliers.)
- **Ice-water method:** Fill a container with crushed ice and cold water (mostly ice; just use water to fill the gaps). Insert the thermometer probe into the center of the ice water, making sure it doesn't touch the container. It should read 32°F or 0°C.

If the temperature reading is not exact, hold the calibration nut (found right under the round head) with a wrench and rotate the head until it reads the correct number of degrees.

The Gluten-Free Bread Machine Pantry

Great bread depends on choosing the right ingredients and measuring them accurately. Here's a guide to the most important ingredients you'll be using for the recipes in this book. Additional details can be found in the Ingredient Glossary (page 231).

Flours, Grains and Starches

- **Amaranth flour** is very fine and has a light cream color and a pleasant, nutty taste. Because of its high moisture content, use it in combination with other flours. It produces loafs that are moist and dense, but added starch helps to lighten the texture. The grain of the bread is more open, the texture not as silky and the crumb color slightly darker than wheat flour breads. Amaranth flour tends to form a crust on the outside of a loaf during baking, sealing the outside before the bread is completely cooked on the inside, so use the smallest amount of liquid you can and allow for slightly longer baking times than you might otherwise. Products with amaranth baked in the oven tend to brown quickly and may need to be tented with foil during the last third of the baking time.
- **Buckwheat flour** is very fine, with a unique, strong, musty, slightly sour, slightly nutty flavor. Buckwheat flour tends to make baked goods heavier and give them a distinctive, stronger taste.
- **Cornmeal** has larger granules than regular GF flour and can be yellow, white, red or blue. Although these varieties are slightly different in texture and flavor, one can be substituted for the other. The coarser the grind, the more granular the texture of the finished product and the more intense the corn flavor. Cornmeal is sometimes used to dust a greased pan, which helps keep the product from sticking to the pan and gives the crust extra crunch and a hint of flavor.
- **Cracked flaxseed** is not sold in stores but can be prepared at home: use a coffee grinder to crack the outer coating of the seed slightly, resulting in pieces of different sizes and textures. Add cracked flaxseed to yeast breads for extra crunch. Cracked flaxseed is easier to digest than whole flaxseed.
- **Ground flaxseed** is sold as flax flour, milled flaxseed or sprouted flax flour. All forms of ground flaxseed are

interchangeable in recipes. You can prepare your own by grinding whole flaxseed to a gold to medium brown powder with slightly darker flecks.

- **Millet** is not a true grain but is closely related to corn and sorghum. It is yellow or white, small and round, with a mild, delicate, corn-like flavor and a texture much like that of brown rice. Millet takes on the flavor of whatever it is cooked with and adds a crunchy texture.

- **Nut flours and meals** are made from very finely ground nuts, such as almonds, hazelnuts and pecans. They are not as smooth or as fine as grain flours. They can be purchased, or you can grind them yourself (see the Techniques Glossary, page 240). Almond, hazelnut and pecan nut meals or flours are interchangeable in recipes.

- **Potato flour** is made from the whole potato, including the skin. Because it has been cooked, it absorbs large amounts of water. Potato flour is much denser and heavier than potato starch and has a definite potato flavor. It is not used like other flours in baking, as it would absorb too much liquid and make the product gummy, but small amounts can be used to hold the product together. We rarely use potato flour (with the exception of Banana Raisin Sticky Buns, page 212), but we frequently use potato starch (see below, under Starches).

- **Quinoa flour** is finely ground and tan-colored, with a strong, slightly nutty flavor. Because of its strong flavor, use it in small amounts. Bread made with quinoa has a tender, moist crumb and good keeping qualities.

- **Sorghum flour** ranges in color from a gray-tan to eggshell white, and the grinds vary from coarse (stone-ground) to very fine. Because its flavor is neutral, it absorbs other flavors well. The most wheat-like of all GF flours, it is the best general-purpose flour, giving bread a warm, creamy color.

- **Starches**, such as arrowroot starch, cornstarch, potato starch and tapioca starch, help doughs bind better, cause breads to rise higher and lighten the finished product. Potato starch lumps easily and must be sifted frequently. Potato starch is often confused with potato flour, but one cannot be substituted for the other

- **Teff flour** milled from brown teff has a sweet, nutty flavor, while flour from white teff is milder. Teff flour has excellent baking qualities.

Legume Flours

Legumes include beans, peas, lentils and peanuts. They are also called pulses.

- All **bean flours** are interchangeable in recipes. We used whole bean (Romano) flour in our recipes, but you can substitute any of the following: fava bean flour, chickpea (garbanzo bean) flour, garfava flour (sold as garbanzo-fava bean flour in Canada), white (navy) bean flour or pinto bean flour.
- **Pea flour** (either yellow or green) can be substituted for any bean flour. Green pea flour has a sweeter flavor than yellow pea flour. Pea flours keep baked products softer longer and improve dough made in a bread machine.
- **Soy flour** (soya flour) is available in full-fat (natural), low-fat and defatted versions. The higher the fat content, the deeper the color. Soy flour has a strong odor when wet that disappears with baking. It adds rich color, fine texture, a pleasant nutty flavor, tenderness and moistness to breads. Products containing soy flour bake faster and tend to brown quickly, so the baking time may need to be shortened. If you're baking bread in the oven, lowering the oven temperature or tenting the bread with foil partway through the baking time also helps.

GF Oats
- **GF rolled oats** (oatmeal) are available in a variety of sizes, from large-flake to quick-cooking. Any of these can be used in gluten-free breads; instant oats, however, are not suitable for a bread machine.
- **GF oat flour** is made from finely ground groats, which contain much of the bran. Oat flour makes bread moist and more crumbly, but it stays fresh longer than bread baked with wheat flour.
- **GF oat bran** is the outer layer of the oat groat. It provides a distinctive texture and a rich, nutty flavor. When used in bread, it increases the fiber content. Breads may also be dusted with oat bran before they are baked, to create a flavorful topping.

Rice Flours
- **Brown rice flour** is milled from the whole grain. It is only a shade darker than white rice flour and has a mild, nutty flavor. Brown rice flour results in bread with a grainy texture and a fine, dry crumb.
- **Rice bran** and **rice polish** are the two outer parts of the rice kernel, removed during milling for white rice flour. When bran and polish are added in small amounts to recipes, the fiber content is increased. They are interchangeable in recipes.
- **Sweet rice flour** (glutinous rice flour) contains more starch than brown rice flour. We use it to dust baking pans or our fingers for easier handling of sticky dough.

Other Ingredients

Fats

Fat gives the crust its tenderness and the loaf its softness. It also helps to retain moisture, which keeps the loaf from going stale too quickly. The type of fat used is a matter of preference and can include vegetable oil, butter, shortening or margarine. (Your choice may have some effect on the loaf, however.) Do not use low-calorie margarine, as its high water content will affect the size and texture of the loaf.

Cheese and egg yolk contribute to the fat in some recipes. When measuring shredded cheese, do not pack. Weight is a more accurate measure than volume. If desired, small cubes of cheese can replace shredded, since cheese melts during baking.

Salt

While we have used only small amounts of salt in our recipes, the salt is necessary, since it controls the yeast's activity and prevents the loaf from over-rising and collapsing. Breads made without salt are very bland and over-risen. Do not omit the salt, even if you are on a low-sodium diet.

Sugars

Sugar provides food for the yeast and adds flavor to the dough. Granulated sugar, packed brown sugar, liquid honey, pure maple syrup, corn syrup and light (fancy) molasses can be used interchangeably, though the results will vary slightly in color, flavor and texture.

Aspartame-based sugar substitutes can be used, but not those based on saccharin. Substitute an equal amount for the sugar in the recipe. Loaves will be lighter in color than when sugar is used.

Xanthan Gum

Xanthan gum is a natural carbohydrate made from a microscopic organism called *Xanthomonas campestris*. It is produced from the fermentation of glucose. It helps prevent baked goods from crumbling, gives them greater volume, improves their texture and extends their shelf life. Do not omit xanthan gum from a recipe.

Xanthan gum can be purchased at health food stores, online or where you purchase other gluten-free ingredients. Before working with xanthan gum, be sure to wipe counters and containers with a dry cloth. When it comes in contact with water, it becomes slippery, slimy and almost impossible to wipe up.

Guar gum is also gluten-free, but it may act as a laxative in some people. It can be substituted for xanthan gum in an equal amount.

Yeast

Yeast converts the carbohydrates in flour and sugar to produce the carbon dioxide gas that causes dough to rise. The recipes in this cookbook were developed using bread machine (instant) yeast. We always recommend using the type of yeast called for in the recipe. Bread machine (instant) yeast is a very active strain of yeast that can be added directly to the bread machine without the need for pre-activating.

The expiry date on a package of yeast indicates that it should be opened before that date and used within a two-month period. Yeast should be kept in an airtight container in the freezer, and there's no need to defrost before measuring. Do not transfer yeast from one container to another; exposing it to air can shorten its life.

Perform this test for freshness if you suspect yeast has become less active: Dissolve 1 tsp (5 mL) granulated sugar in $\frac{1}{2}$ cup (125 mL) lukewarm water. Add 2 tsp (10 mL) yeast and stir gently. In 10 minutes, the mixture should have a strong yeasty smell and be foamy. If it doesn't, the yeast is too old — time to buy fresh yeast!

The Basics

White Bread

**MAKES 15 SLICES
(1 per serving)**

*We know you'll enjoy
this moist, all-purpose
yeast bread, whether
for sandwiches or
to accompany your
favorite salad.*

Tips

To ensure success, see
page 15 for information
on using your bread
machine and page 18 for
general tips on bread
machine baking.

Remember to thoroughly
mix the dry ingredients
before adding them to
the liquids — they are
powder-fine and could
clump together.

Use any leftovers to
make bread crumbs (see
the Techniques Glossary,
page 237.

2¼ cups	brown rice flour	550 mL
⅔ cup	potato starch	150 mL
⅓ cup	tapioca starch	75 mL
¼ cup	nonfat dry milk or skim milk powder	60 mL
¼ cup	granulated sugar	60 mL
2½ tsp	xanthan gum	12 mL
1¼ tsp	bread machine or instant yeast	6 mL
1¾ tsp	salt	8 mL
1¼ cups	water	300 mL
¼ cup	vegetable oil	60 mL
1 tsp	cider vinegar	5 mL
2	eggs, lightly beaten	2
2	egg whites, lightly beaten	2

1. In a large bowl or plastic bag, combine brown rice flour, potato starch, tapioca starch, dry milk, sugar, xanthan gum, yeast and salt; mix well and set aside.
2. Pour water, oil and vinegar into the bread machine baking pan. Add eggs and egg whites.
3. Select the **Dough Cycle**. As the bread machine is mixing, gradually add the dry ingredients, scraping bottom and sides of pan with a rubber spatula. Try to incorporate all the dry ingredients within 1 to 2 minutes. When the mixing and kneading are complete, remove the kneading blade, leaving the bread pan in the bread machine. Quickly smooth the top of the loaf. Allow the cycle to finish. Turn off the bread machine.
4. Select the **Bake Cycle**. Set time to 60 minutes and temperature to 350°F (180°C). Allow the cycle to finish. Do not turn machine off before taking the internal temperature of the loaf with an instant-read thermometer. It should be 200°F (100°C). If it's between 180°F (85°C) and 200°F (100°C), leave machine on the **Keep Warm Cycle** until baked. If it's below 180°F (85°C), turn on the **Bake Cycle** and check the internal temperature every 10 minutes. (Some bread machines are automatically set for 60 minutes; others need to be set by 10-minute intervals.)
5. Once the loaf has reached 200°F (100°C), remove it from the pan immediately and let cool completely on a rack.

NUTRITIONAL VALUES per serving	
Calories	177
Fat, total	5 g
Fat, saturated	1 g
Cholesterol	25 mg
Sodium	295 mg
Carbohydrate	30 g
Fiber	2 g
Protein	3 g
Calcium	22 mg
Iron	1 mg

Variation

Add 1¼ cups (300 mL) milk instead of the water and nonfat dry milk or skim milk powder.

Gluten-Free Cycle

If your bread machine has a Gluten-Free Cycle, you will need to make these adjustments:

1. Warm the water to between 110°F and 115°F (43°C and 46°C).

2. Warm the eggs and egg whites (see the Techniques Glossary, page 238).

3. Follow the recipe instructions, but select the **Gluten-Free Cycle** rather than the Dough Cycle and Bake Cycle.

4. At the end of the Gluten-Free Cycle, take the temperature of the loaf using an instant-read thermometer. It is baked at 200°F (100°C). If it's between 180°F (85°C) and 200°F (100°C), leave machine on the **Keep Warm Cycle** until baked. If it's below 180°F (85°C), turn on the **Bake Cycle** and check the internal temperature every 10 minutes. (Some bread machines are automatically set for 60 minutes; others need to be set by 10-minute intervals.)

Grandma's Brown Bread

The perfect sandwich bread! Just add shaved roast beef, a leaf of romaine and a hint of mustard. It carries well for a tasty lunch.

Tip

To ensure success, see page 15 for information on using your bread machine and page 18 for general tips on bread machine baking.

1½ cups	brown rice flour	375 mL
1 cup	sorghum flour	250 mL
⅓ cup	cornstarch	75 mL
½ cup	rice bran	125 mL
1 tbsp	xanthan gum	15 mL
1½ tsp	bread machine or instant yeast	7 mL
1¼ tsp	salt	6 mL
1¼ cups	water	300 mL
2 tbsp	vegetable oil	30 mL
2 tbsp	liquid honey	30 mL
2 tbsp	light (fancy) molasses	30 mL
1 tsp	cider vinegar	5 mL
2	eggs, lightly beaten	2
2	egg whites, lightly beaten	2

1. In a large bowl or plastic bag, combine brown rice flour, sorghum flour, cornstarch, rice bran, xanthan gum, yeast and salt; mix well and set aside.

2. Pour water, oil, honey, molasses and vinegar into the bread machine baking pan. Add eggs and egg whites.

3. Select the **Dough Cycle**. As the bread machine is mixing, gradually add the dry ingredients, scraping bottom and sides of pan with a rubber spatula. Try to incorporate all the dry ingredients within 1 to 2 minutes. When the mixing and kneading are complete, remove the kneading blade, leaving the bread pan in the bread machine. Quickly smooth the top of the loaf. Allow the cycle to finish. Turn off the bread machine.

4. Select the **Bake Cycle**. Set time to 60 minutes and temperature to 350°F (180°C). Allow the cycle to finish. Do not turn machine off before taking the internal temperature of the loaf with an instant-read thermometer. It should be 200°F (100°C). If it's between 180°F (85°C) and 200°F (100°C), leave machine on the **Keep Warm Cycle** until baked. If it's below 180°F (85°C), turn on the **Bake Cycle** and check the internal temperature every 10 minutes. (Some bread machines are automatically set for 60 minutes; others need to be set by 10-minute intervals.)

5. Once the loaf has reached 200°F (100°C), remove it from the pan immediately and let cool completely on a rack.

NUTRITIONAL VALUES
per serving

Calories	162
Fat, total	4 g
Fat, saturated	1 g
Cholesterol	25 mg
Sodium	212 mg
Carbohydrate	28 g
Fiber	2 g
Protein	4 g
Calcium	14 mg
Iron	2 mg

Variations

For a milder flavor, increase the honey to ¼ cup (60 mL) and omit the molasses.

Substitute GF oat bran for the rice bran.

Gluten-Free Cycle

If your bread machine has a Gluten-Free Cycle, you will need to make these adjustments:

1. Warm the water to between 110°F and 115°F (43°C and 46°C).

2. Warm the eggs and egg whites (see the Techniques Glossary, page 238).

3. Follow the recipe instructions, but select the **Gluten-Free Cycle** rather than the Dough Cycle and Bake Cycle.

4. At the end of the Gluten-Free Cycle, take the temperature of the loaf using an instant-read thermometer. It is baked at 200°F (100°C). If it's between 180°F (85°C) and 200°F (100°C), leave machine on the **Keep Warm Cycle** until baked. If it's below 180°F (85°C), turn on the **Bake Cycle** and check the internal temperature every 10 minutes. (Some bread machines are automatically set for 60 minutes; others need to be set by 10-minute intervals.)

Brown Sandwich Bread

MAKES 15 SLICES
(1 per serving)

◆ **A CANOLAINFO RECIPE**

*For those who want a
rich, golden, wholesome,
nutritious sandwich
bread to carry for lunch,
this is your loaf.*

Tips

To ensure success, see
page 15 for information on
using your bread machine
and page 18 for general tips
on bread machine baking.

Pea flour, like soy flour, has
a distinctive odor when wet
that disappears with baking.

1¼ cups	sorghum flour	300 mL
1 cup	pea flour	250 mL
½ cup	tapioca starch	125 mL
⅓ cup	rice bran	75 mL
2 tbsp	packed brown sugar	30 mL
1 tbsp	xanthan gum	15 mL
2 tsp	bread machine or instant yeast	10 mL
1½ tsp	salt	7 mL
1⅔ cups	water	400 mL
2 tbsp	vegetable oil	30 mL
2 tbsp	light (fancy) molasses	30 mL
1 tsp	cider vinegar	5 mL
2	eggs, lightly beaten	2
2	egg whites, lightly beaten	2

1. In a large bowl or plastic bag, combine sorghum flour, pea flour, tapioca starch, rice bran, brown sugar, xanthan gum, yeast and salt; mix well and set aside.

2. Pour water, oil, molasses and vinegar into the bread machine baking pan. Add eggs and egg whites.

3. Select the **Dough Cycle**. As the bread machine is mixing, gradually add the dry ingredients, scraping bottom and sides of pan with a rubber spatula. Try to incorporate all the dry ingredients within 1 to 2 minutes. When the mixing and kneading are complete, remove the kneading blade, leaving the bread pan in the bread machine. Quickly smooth the top of the loaf. Allow the cycle to finish. Turn off the bread machine.

4. Select the **Bake Cycle**. Set time to 60 minutes and temperature to 350°F (180°C). Allow the cycle to finish. Do not turn machine off before taking the internal temperature of the loaf with an instant-read thermometer. It should be 200°F (100°C). If it's between 180°F (85°C) and 200°F (100°C), leave machine on the **Keep Warm Cycle** until baked. If it's below 180°F (85°C), turn on the **Bake Cycle** and check the internal temperature every 10 minutes. (Some bread machines are automatically set for 60 minutes; others need to be set by 10-minute intervals.)

5. Once the loaf has reached 200°F (100°C), remove it from the pan immediately and let cool completely on a rack.

NUTRITIONAL VALUES
per serving

Calories	136
Fat, total	3 g
Fat, saturated	0 g
Cholesterol	25 mg
Sodium	251 mg
Carbohydrate	23 g
Fiber	3 g
Protein	5 g
Calcium	20 mg
Iron	2 mg

Variations

Any type of bean flour can be substituted for the pea flour.

Substitute GF oat bran for the rice bran.

For a slightly sweeter flavor, substitute liquid honey or packed brown sugar for the molasses.

Gluten-Free Cycle

If your bread machine has a Gluten-Free Cycle, you will need to make these adjustments:

1. Warm the water to between 110°F and 115°F (43°C and 46°C).

2. Warm the eggs and egg whites (see the Techniques Glossary, page 238).

3. Follow the recipe instructions, but select the **Gluten-Free Cycle** rather than the Dough Cycle and Bake Cycle.

4. At the end of the Gluten-Free Cycle, take the temperature of the loaf using an instant-read thermometer. It is baked at 200°F (100°C). If it's between 180°F (85°C) and 200°F (100°C), leave machine on the **Keep Warm Cycle** until baked. If it's below 180°F (85°C), turn on the **Bake Cycle** and check the internal temperature every 10 minutes. (Some bread machines are automatically set for 60 minutes; others need to be set by 10-minute intervals.)

Egg-Free, Corn-Free, Dairy-Free, Soy-Free Brown Bread

**MAKES 15 SLICES
(1 per serving)**

Though shorter than some loaves, this is the perfect sandwich bread for those who must eliminate eggs, corn dairy and/or soy from their diet. It carries well for a tasty lunch.

Tips

To ensure success, see page 15 for information on using your bread machine and page 18 for general tips on bread machine baking.

Slice this or any bread with an electric knife for thin, even sandwich slices.

1/3 cup	flax flour or ground flaxseed	75 mL
1/3 cup	warm water	75 mL
1 1/2 cups	brown rice flour	375 mL
3/4 cup	sorghum flour	175 mL
1/2 cup	rice bran	125 mL
1/4 cup	tapioca starch	60 mL
1 tbsp	xanthan gum	15 mL
1 1/2 tsp	bread machine or instant yeast	7 mL
1 1/4 tsp	salt	6 mL
1 1/4 cups	water	300 mL
3 tbsp	vegetable oil	45 mL
3 tbsp	liquid honey	45 mL
1 tbsp	light (fancy) molasses	15 mL
1 tsp	cider vinegar	5 mL

1. In a small bowl or measuring cup, combine flax flour and warm water; set aside for 5 minutes.
2. In a large bowl or plastic bag, combine brown rice flour, sorghum flour, rice bran, tapioca starch, xanthan gum, yeast and salt; mix well and set aside.
3. Pour water, oil, honey, molasses and vinegar into the bread machine baking pan. Add flax flour mixture.
4. Select the **Dough Cycle**. As the bread machine is mixing, gradually add the dry ingredients, scraping bottom and sides of pan with a rubber spatula. Try to incorporate all the dry ingredients within 1 to 2 minutes. When the mixing and kneading are complete, remove the kneading blade, leaving the bread pan in the bread machine. Quickly smooth the top of the loaf. Allow the cycle to finish. Turn off the bread machine.

NUTRITIONAL VALUES
per serving

Calories	161
Fat, total	5 g
Fat, saturated	1 g
Cholesterol	0 mg
Sodium	198 mg
Carbohydrate	27 g
Fiber	3 g
Protein	3 g
Calcium	15 mg
Iron	2 mg

Variations

Make 1 dozen dinner rolls by following the method in Egg-Free, Corn-Free, Dairy-Free, Soy-Free White Dinner Rolls (page 139).

For a milder-flavored bread, omit the molasses and add 2 tbsp (30 mL) packed brown sugar with the tapioca starch.

The rice bran can be replaced by an equal amount of oat bran or brown or white rice flour.

5. Select the **Bake Cycle**. Set time to 60 minutes and temperature to 350°F (180°C). Allow the cycle to finish. Do not turn machine off before taking the internal temperature of the loaf with an instant-read thermometer. It should be 200°F (100°C). If it's between 180°F (85°C) and 200°F (100°C), leave machine on the **Keep Warm Cycle** until baked. If it's below 180°F (85°C), turn on the **Bake Cycle** and check the internal temperature every 10 minutes. (Some bread machines are automatically set for 60 minutes; others need to be set by 10-minute intervals.)

6. Once the loaf has reached 200°F (100°C), remove it from the pan immediately and let cool completely on a rack.

Gluten-Free Cycle

If your bread machine has a Gluten-Free Cycle, you will need to make these adjustments:

1. Warm the water to between 110°F and 115°F (43°C and 46°C).

2. Follow the recipe instructions, but select the **Gluten-Free Cycle** rather than the Dough Cycle and Bake Cycle.

3. At the end of the Gluten-Free Cycle, take the temperature of the loaf using an instant-read thermometer. It is baked at 200°F (100°C). If it's between 180°F (85°C) and 200°F (100°C), leave machine on the **Keep Warm Cycle** until baked. If it's below 180°F (85°C), turn on the **Bake Cycle** and check the internal temperature every 10 minutes. (Some bread machines are automatically set for 60 minutes; others need to be set by 10-minute intervals.)

Pumpernickel Loaf

With all the hearty flavor of traditional pumpernickel, this version is great for sandwiches. Try it filled with sliced turkey, accompanied by a crisp garlic dill pickle.

Tips

To ensure success, see page 15 for information on using your bread machine and page 18 for general tips on bread machine baking.

Thoroughly mix the dry ingredients before adding them to the liquids — they are powder-fine and could clump together.

1 cup	whole bean flour	250 mL
1 cup	yellow pea flour	250 mL
2/3 cup	potato starch	150 mL
1/3 cup	tapioca starch	75 mL
3 tbsp	packed brown sugar	45 mL
2½ tsp	xanthan gum	12 mL
1½ tsp	bread machine or instant yeast	7 mL
1½ tsp	salt	7 mL
1 tbsp	instant coffee granules	15 mL
1 tbsp	unsweetened cocoa powder	15 mL
½ tsp	ground ginger	2 mL
1⅔ cups	water	400 mL
2 tbsp	vegetable oil	30 mL
3 tbsp	light (fancy) molasses	45 mL
1 tsp	cider vinegar	5 mL
3	eggs, lightly beaten	3

1. In a large bowl or plastic bag, combine whole bean flour, yellow pea flour, potato starch, tapioca starch, brown sugar, xanthan gum, yeast, salt, coffee granules, cocoa and ginger; mix well and set aside.

2. Pour water, oil, molasses and vinegar into the bread machine baking pan. Add eggs.

3. Select the **Dough Cycle**. As the bread machine is mixing, gradually add the dry ingredients, scraping bottom and sides of pan with a rubber spatula. Try to incorporate all the dry ingredients within 1 to 2 minutes. When the mixing and kneading are complete, remove the kneading blade, leaving the bread pan in the bread machine. Quickly smooth the top of the loaf. Allow the cycle to finish. Turn off the bread machine.

NUTRITIONAL VALUES
per serving

Calories	126
Fat, total	3 g
Fat, saturated	0 g
Cholesterol	37 mg
Sodium	249 mg
Carbohydrate	21 g
Fiber	2 g
Protein	4 g
Calcium	27 mg
Iron	1 mg

If yellow pea flour is unavailable, use chickpea (garbanzo bean) flour.

For a milder flavor, omit the coffee and cocoa powder.

4. Select the **Bake Cycle**. Set time to 60 minutes and temperature to 350°F (180°C). Allow the cycle to finish. Do not turn machine off before taking the internal temperature of the loaf with an instant-read thermometer. It should be 200°F (100°C). If it's between 180°F (85°C) and 200°F (100°C), leave machine on the **Keep Warm Cycle** until baked. If it's below 180°F (85°C), turn on the **Bake Cycle** and check the internal temperature every 10 minutes. (Some bread machines are automatically set for 60 minutes; others need to be set by 10-minute intervals.)

5. Once the loaf has reached 200°F (100°C), remove it from the pan immediately and let cool completely on a rack.

Gluten-Free Cycle

If your bread machine has a Gluten-Free Cycle, you will need to make these adjustments:

1. Warm the water to between 110°F and 115°F (43°C and 46°C).

2. Warm the eggs (see the Techniques Glossary, page 238).

3. Follow the recipe instructions, but select the **Gluten-Free Cycle** rather than the Dough Cycle and Bake Cycle.

4. At the end of the Gluten-Free Cycle, take the temperature of the loaf using an instant-read thermometer. It is baked at 200°F (100°C). If it's between 180°F (85°C) and 200°F (100°C), leave machine on the **Keep Warm Cycle** until baked. If it's below 180°F (85°C), turn on the **Bake Cycle** and check the internal temperature every 10 minutes. (Some bread machines are automatically set for 60 minutes; others need to be set by 10-minute intervals.)

Cinnamon Raisin Bread

Enjoy a toasted slice or two of this deep golden loaf for breakfast — it's the perfect snack when served with a cup of hot cocoa.

Tips

To ensure success, see page 15 for information on using your bread machine and page 18 for general tips on bread machine baking.

Thoroughly mix the dry ingredients before adding them to the liquids — they are powder-fine and can clump together.

1¾ cups	brown rice flour	425 mL
½ cup	potato starch	125 mL
¼ cup	tapioca starch	60 mL
½ cup	granulated sugar	125 mL
¼ cup	nonfat dry milk or skim milk powder	60 mL
1 tbsp	xanthan gum	15 mL
1½ tsp	bread machine or instant yeast	7 mL
1¼ tsp	salt	6 mL
1 tbsp	ground cinnamon	15 mL
1½ cups	raisins	375 mL
1 cup	water	250 mL
2 tbsp	vegetable oil	30 mL
2 tsp	cider vinegar	10 mL
2	eggs, lightly beaten	2
2	egg whites, lightly beaten	2

1. In a large bowl or plastic bag, combine brown rice flour, potato starch, tapioca starch, sugar, dry milk, xanthan gum, yeast, salt, cinnamon and raisins; mix well and set aside.

2. Pour water, oil and vinegar into the bread machine baking pan. Add eggs and egg whites.

3. Select the **Dough Cycle**. As the bread machine is mixing, gradually add the dry ingredients, scraping bottom and sides of pan with a rubber spatula. Try to incorporate all the dry ingredients within 1 to 2 minutes. When the mixing and kneading are complete, remove the kneading blade, leaving the bread pan in the bread machine. Quickly smooth the top of the loaf. Allow the cycle to finish. Turn off the bread machine.

4. Select the **Bake Cycle**. Set time to 60 minutes and temperature to 350°F (180°C). Allow the cycle to finish. Do not turn machine off before taking the internal temperature of the loaf with an instant-read thermometer. It should be 200°F (100°C). If it's between 180°F (85°C) and 200°F (100°C), leave machine on the **Keep Warm Cycle** until baked. If it's below 180°F (85°C), turn on the **Bake Cycle** and check the internal temperature every 10 minutes. (Some bread machines are automatically set for 60 minutes; others need to be set by 10-minute intervals.)

NUTRITIONAL VALUES per serving	
Calories	190
Fat, total	3 g
Fat, saturated	1 g
Cholesterol	25 mg
Sodium	219 mg
Carbohydrate	40 g
Fiber	2 g
Protein	3 g
Calcium	35 mg
Iron	1 mg

5. Once the loaf has reached 200°F (100°C), remove it from the pan immediately and let cool completely on a rack.

Gluten-Free Cycle

If your bread machine has a Gluten-Free Cycle, you will need to make these adjustments:

1. Warm the water to between 110°F and 115°F (43°C and 46°C).

2. Warm the eggs and egg whites (see the Techniques Glossary, page 238).

3. Follow the recipe instructions, but select the **Gluten-Free Cycle** rather than the Dough Cycle and Bake Cycle.

4. At the end of the Gluten-Free Cycle, take the temperature of the loaf using an instant-read thermometer. It is baked at 200°F (100°C). If it's between 180°F (85°C) and 200°F (100°C), leave machine on the **Keep Warm Cycle** until baked. If it's below 180°F (85°C), turn on the **Bake Cycle** and check the internal temperature every 10 minutes. (Some bread machines are automatically set for 60 minutes; others need to be set by 10-minute intervals.)

Nutmeg Loaf

MAKES 15 SLICES
(1 per serving)

Flecks of brown nutmeg stand out against the white background in this tangy-sweet loaf. The aroma will have you slicing it hot.

Tips

To ensure success, see page 15 for information on using your bread machine and page 18 for general tips on bread machine baking.

For the best flavor, use freshly grated nutmeg. Use about half as much as you would purchased ground nutmeg.

1¾ cups	brown rice flour	425 mL
½ cup	quinoa flour	125 mL
⅓ cup	arrowroot starch	75 mL
¼ cup	tapioca starch	60 mL
⅓ cup	granulated sugar	75 mL
1 tbsp	xanthan gum	15 mL
1½ tsp	bread machine or instant yeast	7 mL
1¼ tsp	salt	6 mL
2 tsp	ground nutmeg	10 mL
¾ cup	water	175 mL
½ cup	plain yogurt	125 mL
¼ cup	vegetable oil	60 mL
2	eggs, lightly beaten	2
2	egg whites, lightly beaten	2

1. In a large bowl or plastic bag, combine brown rice flour, quinoa flour, arrowroot starch, tapioca starch, sugar, xanthan gum, yeast, salt and nutmeg; mix well and set aside.

2. Pour water, yogurt and oil into the bread machine baking pan. Add eggs and egg whites.

3. Select the **Dough Cycle**. As the bread machine is mixing, gradually add the dry ingredients, scraping bottom and sides of pan with a rubber spatula. Try to incorporate all the dry ingredients within 1 to 2 minutes. When the mixing and kneading are complete, remove the kneading blade, leaving the bread pan in the bread machine. Quickly smooth the top of the loaf. Allow the cycle to finish. Turn off the bread machine.

4. Select the **Bake Cycle**. Set time to 60 minutes and temperature to 350°F (180°C). Allow the cycle to finish. Do not turn machine off before taking the internal temperature of the loaf with an instant-read thermometer. It should be 200°F (100°C). If it's between 180°F (85°C) and 200°F (100°C), leave machine on the **Keep Warm Cycle** until baked. If it's below 180°F (85°C), turn on the **Bake Cycle** and check the internal temperature every 10 minutes. (Some bread machines are automatically set for 60 minutes; others need to be set by 10-minute intervals.)

5. Once the loaf has reached 200°F (100°C), remove it from the pan immediately and let cool completely on a rack.

NUTRITIONAL VALUES	
per serving	
Calories	170
Fat, total	5 g
Fat, saturated	1 g
Cholesterol	25 mg
Sodium	218 mg
Carbohydrate	27 g
Fiber	2 g
Protein	4 g
Calcium	24 mg
Iron	1 mg

Variations

If you cannot tolerate quinoa, or it is not available, increase the brown rice flour by ⅓ cup (75 mL).

Vanilla yogurt or GF sour cream can replace the plain yogurt. Read the label carefully, because some contain wheat starch.

Gluten-Free Cycle

If your bread machine has a Gluten-Free Cycle, you will need to make these adjustments:

1. Warm the water to between 110°F and 115°F (43°C and 46°C).

2. Warm the eggs and egg whites (see the Techniques Glossary, page 238).

3. Follow the recipe instructions, but select the **Gluten-Free Cycle** rather than the Dough Cycle and Bake Cycle.

4. At the end of the Gluten-Free Cycle, take the temperature of the loaf using an instant-read thermometer. It is baked at 200°F (100°C). If it's between 180°F (85°C) and 200°F (100°C), leave machine on the **Keep Warm Cycle** until baked. If it's below 180°F (85°C), turn on the **Bake Cycle** and check the internal temperature every 10 minutes. (Some bread machines are automatically set for 60 minutes; others need to be set by 10-minute intervals.)

Italian Herb Bread

The fragrant aroma of this loaf makes waiting for it to bake extremely difficult. Serve this zesty herb bread with any course — soup, salad or entrée.

Tips

To ensure success, see page 15 for information on using your bread machine and page 18 for general tips on bread machine baking.

This is an excellent loaf for making croutons (see pages 223–225) and bread crumbs. See the Techniques Glossary, page 237, for information about bread crumbs. Use the crumbs to make a stuffing or dressing for beef, pork or poultry.

NUTRITIONAL VALUES per serving	
Calories	157
Fat, total	6 g
Fat, saturated	1 g
Cholesterol	25 mg
Sodium	243 mg
Carbohydrate	24 g
Fiber	2 g
Protein	3 g
Calcium	55 mg
Iron	3 mg

1½ cups	sorghum flour	375 mL
¾ cup	whole bean flour	175 mL
½ cup	potato starch	125 mL
¼ cup	tapioca starch	60 mL
⅓ cup	granulated sugar	75 mL
1 tbsp	xanthan gum	15 mL
1½ tsp	bread machine or instant yeast	7 mL
1½ tsp	salt	7 mL
½ cup	snipped fresh parsley	125 mL
1 tbsp	ground dried marjoram	15 mL
1 tbsp	ground dried thyme	15 mL
1¼ cups	water	300 mL
⅓ cup	vegetable oil	75 mL
1 tsp	cider vinegar	5 mL
2	eggs, lightly beaten	2

1. In a large bowl or plastic bag, combine sorghum flour, whole bean flour, potato starch, tapioca starch, sugar, xanthan gum, yeast, salt, parsley, marjoram and thyme; mix well and set aside.

2. Pour water, oil and vinegar into the bread machine baking pan. Add eggs.

3. Select the **Dough Cycle**. As the bread machine is mixing, gradually add the dry ingredients, scraping bottom and sides of pan with a rubber spatula. Try to incorporate all the dry ingredients within 1 to 2 minutes. When the mixing and kneading are complete, remove the kneading blade, leaving the bread pan in the bread machine. Quickly smooth the top of the loaf. Allow the cycle to finish. Turn off the bread machine.

4. Select the **Bake Cycle**. Set time to 60 minutes and temperature to 350°F (180°C). Allow the cycle to finish. Do not turn machine off before taking the internal temperature of the loaf with an instant-read thermometer. It should be 200°F (100°C). If it's between 180°F (85°C) and 200°F (100°C), leave machine on the **Keep Warm Cycle** until baked. If it's below 180°F (85°C), turn on the **Bake Cycle** and check the internal temperature every 10 minutes. (Some bread machines are automatically set for 60 minutes; others need to be set by 10-minute intervals.)

Variations

Substitute triple the amount of snipped fresh marjoram and thyme for the dried. See the Techniques Glossary, page 241, for information about working with fresh herbs.

5. Once the loaf has reached 200°F (100°C), remove it from the pan immediately and let cool completely on a rack.

Gluten-Free Cycle

If your bread machine has a Gluten-Free Cycle, you will need to make these adjustments:

1. Warm the water to between 110°F and 115°F (43°C and 46°C).

2. Warm the eggs (see the Techniques Glossary, page 238).

3. Follow the recipe instructions, but select the **Gluten Free Cycle** rather than the Dough Cycle and Bake Cycle.

4. At the end of the Gluten-Free Cycle, take the temperature of the loaf using an instant-read thermometer. It is baked at 200°F (100°C). If it's between 180°F (85°C) and 200°F (100°C), leave machine on the **Keep Warm Cycle** until baked. If it's below 180°F (85°C), turn on the **Bake Cycle** and check the internal temperature every 10 minutes. (Some bread machines are automatically set for 60 minutes; others need to be set by 10-minute intervals.)

Herbed Hearth Bread

Instead of slicing this loaf, split it in half horizontally and fill with your favorite sandwich filling.

Tips

To ensure success, see page 15 for information on using your bread machine and page 18 for general tips on bread machine baking.

Use an electric or serrated knife to thickly slice into wedges.

Variations

Omit the oregano and parsley for a plain Jane hearth bread.

Substitute basil, dill, marjoram or thyme for the oregano.

NUTRITIONAL VALUES
per serving

Calories	138
Fat, total	3 g
Fat, saturated	0 g
Cholesterol	0 mg
Sodium	303 mg
Carbohydrate	25 g
Fiber	2 g
Protein	3 g
Calcium	26 mg
Iron	2 mg

◆ **8-inch (20 cm) round baking pan, lightly greased and sprinkled with cornmeal**

1½ cups	brown rice flour	375 mL
½ cup	amaranth flour	125 mL
⅔ cup	potato starch	150 mL
1 tbsp	granulated sugar	15 mL
2 tsp	xanthan gum	10 mL
1 tbsp	bread machine or instant yeast	15 mL
1½ tsp	salt	7 mL
½ cup	snipped fresh oregano	75 mL
½ cup	snipped fresh parsley	75 mL
1½ cups	water	375 mL
2 tbsp	extra virgin olive oil	30 mL
2 tsp	cider vinegar	10 mL
2	egg whites, lightly beaten	2

1. In a large bowl or plastic bag, combine brown rice flour, amaranth flour, potato starch, sugar, xanthan gum, yeast, salt, oregano and parsley; mix well and set aside.

2. Pour water, olive oil and vinegar into the bread machine baking pan. Add egg whites.

3. Select the **Dough Cycle**. As the bread machine is mixing, gradually add the dry ingredients, scraping bottom and sides of pan with a rubber spatula. Try to incorporate all the dry ingredients within 1 to 2 minutes. Stop bread machine as soon as the kneading portion of the cycle is complete. Do not let bread machine finish the cycle.

4. Spoon the dough onto prepared pan, leaving the top rough. Let rise, uncovered, in a warm, draft-free place for 60 minutes. Meanwhile, preheat oven to 375°F (190°C).

5. Bake for 30 to 33 minutes or until internal temperature of loaf registers 200°F (100°C) on an instant-read thermometer. Remove from the pan immediately and let cool completely on a rack.

Crusty French Baguette

**MAKES TWO
12-INCH (30 CM)
LOAVES, 12 SLICES
EACH
(1 per serving)**

You'll be amazed by this one — a crusty loaf with a typical French bread texture.

Tips

To ensure success, see page 15 for information on using your bread machine and page 18 for general tips on bread machine baking.

See the Equipment Glossary, page 230, for information about baguette pans.

Store this bread loosely covered in a paper bag to maintain the crisp crust.

Use an electric or serrated knife to thickly slice these loaves on the diagonal.

NUTRITIONAL VALUES per serving	
Calories	57
Fat, total	0 g
Fat, saturated	0 g
Cholesterol	0 mg
Sodium	151 mg
Carbohydrate	13 g
Fiber	1 g
Protein	1 g
Calcium	2 mg
Iron	0 mg

◆ **Baguette pan or baking sheet, lightly greased, then lined with parchment paper and sprinkled with cornmeal**

2 cups	brown rice flour	500 mL
⅔ cup	potato starch	150 mL
2 tsp	granulated sugar	10 mL
2 tsp	xanthan gum	10 mL
2 tsp	bread machine or instant yeast	10 mL
1½ tsp	salt	7 mL
1½ cups	water	375 mL
2 tsp	cider vinegar	10 mL
2	egg whites, lightly beaten	2

1. In a large bowl or plastic bag, combine brown rice flour, potato starch, sugar, xanthan gum, yeast and salt; mix well and set aside.

2. Pour water and vinegar into the bread machine baking pan. Add egg whites.

3. Select the **Dough Cycle**. As the bread machine is mixing, gradually add the dry ingredients, scraping bottom and sides of pan with a rubber spatula. Try to incorporate all the dry ingredients within 1 to 2 minutes. Stop bread machine as soon as the kneading portion of the cycle is complete. Do not let bread machine finish the cycle.

4. Divide dough in half and form each half into the shape of a baguette. Place parallel to each other in prepared pan, at least 3 inches (7.5 cm) apart. Using the edge of a moistened rubber spatula or a sharp knife, draw 3 or 4 diagonal lines, ¼ inch (0.5 cm) deep, across the top of each loaf. Let rise, uncovered, in a warm, draft-free place for 60 minutes. Meanwhile, preheat oven to 425°F (220°C).

5. Bake for 20 to 23 minutes or until internal temperature of loaf registers 200°F (100°C) on an instant-read thermometer. Remove from the pan immediately and let cool completely on a rack.

Tomato Basil Bruschetta

Enjoy the late-summer crop of fresh tomatoes with fresh basil from your garden in this delicious topping.

Tips

Choose a meaty tomato, such as San Marzano.

To snip basil, place the leaves in a cup and cut with kitchen shears. Pack tightly to measure.

Variations

For a milder flavor, use half basil and half parsley.

Substitute an equal amount of oregano or thyme for the basil.

◆ Preheat broiler

1	Crusty French Baguette (see page 45), diagonally sliced 1 inch (2.5 cm) thick, toasted on 1 side	1
4	plum (Roma) tomatoes, chopped	4
2	cloves garlic, minced	2
1/4 cup	snipped fresh parsley	60 mL
2 tbsp	snipped fresh basil	30 mL
2 tbsp	extra virgin olive oil	30 mL
3/4 cup	shredded mozzarella cheese	175 mL

1. Place baguette slices, toasted side down, on a baking sheet. In a bowl, combine tomatoes, garlic, parsley, basil and oil. Spread on baguette slices and sprinkle with cheese.
2. Toast under preheated broiler for 1 to 2 minutes, just until cheese melts.

NUTRITIONAL VALUES
per serving

Calories	162
Fat, total	4 g
Fat, saturated	1 g
Cholesterol	4 mg
Sodium	339 mg
Carbohydrate	28 g
Fiber	2 g
Protein	4 g
Calcium	55 mg
Iron	1 mg

Roasted Red Pepper and Shrimp Bruschetta

MAKES 12 SLICES
(1 per serving)

Bright red peppers, piled high on each bruschetta slice, will whet the appetite of the guests at your barbecue. The balsamic vinegar gives this colorful topping a rich, fruity character.

Tips

See the Techniques Glossary, page 237, for information on roasting bell peppers.

Add in roasted yellow and orange bell peppers for a lively color combination.

4	roasted red bell peppers, chopped	4
2	cloves garlic, minced	2
½ cup	snipped fresh parsley	125 mL
2 tbsp	balsamic vinegar	30 mL
2 tsp	extra virgin olive oil	10 mL
	Freshly ground white pepper	
1	Crusty French Baguette (see page 45), diagonally sliced 1 inch (2.5 cm) thick, toasted on 1 side	1
48	cooked salad shrimp	48

1. In a bowl, combine roasted peppers, garlic, parsley, vinegar and oil; stir gently. Season to taste with pepper. Heap mixture onto untoasted side of baguette slices. Top each with 4 shrimp.

NUTRITIONAL VALUES per serving	
Calories	148
Fat, total	3 g
Fat, saturated	0 g
Cholesterol	9 mg
Sodium	322 mg
Carbohydrate	29 g
Fiber	2 g
Protein	4 g
Calcium	17 mg
Iron	1 mg

Mozzarella Toast

MAKES 12 SLICES
(1 per serving)

*Here's a tasty bread
to serve with chili the
next time you invite the
gang over.*

Tip

Preheat the broiler for 8 to
10 minutes to quickly melt
cheese rather than bake it.

Variation

Try a Havarti and goat
cheese combination in place
of the mozzarella and grill
on the barbecue.

◆ **Preheat broiler**

1	Crusty French Baguette (see page 45), diagonally sliced 1 inch (2.5 cm) thick, toasted on 1 side	1
6	anchovy fillets, minced	6
2	cloves garlic, minced	2
2 tbsp	snipped fresh cilantro	30 mL
⅓ cup	softened butter	75 mL
¾ cup	shredded mozzarella cheese	175 mL

1. Place baguette slices, toasted side down, on a baking sheet. In a bowl, combine anchovies, garlic, cilantro and butter. Spread on baguette slices and sprinkle with cheese.
2. Toast under preheated broiler for 1 to 2 minutes, just until cheese melts.

NUTRITIONAL VALUES per serving	
Calories	178
Fat, total	7 g
Fat, saturated	4 g
Cholesterol	18 mg
Sodium	386 mg
Carbohydrate	26 g
Fiber	1 g
Protein	4 g
Calcium	55 mg
Iron	0 mg

Hearty Grains, Seeds and Nuts

Whole-Grain Amaranth Bread

This soft-textured, creamy, honey-colored bread is so delicious you won't even suspect how nutritious it is.

Tips

To ensure success, see page 15 for information on using your bread machine and page 18 for general tips on bread machine baking.

Substitute ¼ cup (60 mL) liquid egg whites for the 2 egg whites.

Store amaranth grain in an airtight container in the refrigerator for up to 6 months.

Amaranth is high in fiber, iron and calcium and lower in sodium than most grains.

1¼ cups	brown rice flour	300 mL
¾ cup	amaranth flour	175 mL
½ cup	potato starch	125 mL
½ cup	amaranth grain	125 mL
1 tbsp	xanthan gum	15 mL
1½ tsp	bread machine or instant yeast	7 mL
1½ tsp	salt	7 mL
2 tbsp	grated orange zest	30 mL
1 cup	water	250 mL
¼ cup	vegetable oil	60 mL
¼ cup	liquid honey	60 mL
2 tsp	cider vinegar	10 mL
2	eggs, lightly beaten	2
2	egg whites, lightly beaten	2

1. In a large bowl or plastic bag, combine brown rice flour, amaranth flour, potato starch, amaranth grain, xanthan gum, yeast, salt and orange zest; mix well and set aside.

2. Pour water, oil, honey and vinegar into the bread machine baking pan. Add eggs and egg whites.

3. Select the **Dough Cycle**. As the bread machine is mixing, gradually add the dry ingredients, scraping bottom and sides of pan with a rubber spatula. Try to incorporate all the dry ingredients within 1 to 2 minutes. When the mixing and kneading are complete, remove the kneading blade, leaving the bread pan in the bread machine. Quickly smooth the top of the loaf. Allow the cycle to finish. Turn off the bread machine.

4. Select the **Bake Cycle**. Set time to 60 minutes and temperature to 350°F (180°C). Allow the cycle to finish. Do not turn machine off before taking the internal temperature of the loaf with an instant-read thermometer. It should be 200°F (100°C). If it's between 180°F (85°C) and 200°F (100°C), leave machine on the **Keep Warm Cycle** until baked. If it's below 180°F (85°C), turn on the **Bake Cycle** and check the internal temperature every 10 minutes. (Some bread machines are automatically set for 60 minutes; others need to be set by 10-minute intervals.)

5. Once the loaf has reached 200°F (100°C), remove it from the pan immediately and let cool completely on a rack.

NUTRITIONAL VALUES per serving	
Calories	165
Fat, total	5 g
Fat, saturated	1 g
Cholesterol	25 mg
Sodium	250 mg
Carbohydrate	26 g
Fiber	2 g
Protein	4 g
Calcium	22 mg
Iron	2 mg

Variation

Substitute lemon zest for the orange zest.

Gluten-Free Cycle

If your bread machine has a Gluten-Free Cycle, you will need to make these adjustments:

1. Warm the water to between 110°F and 115°F (43°C and 46°C).

2. Warm the eggs and egg whites (see the Techniques Glossary, page 238).

3. Follow the recipe instructions, but select the **Gluten-Free Cycle** rather than the Dough Cycle and Bake Cycle.

4. At the end of the Gluten-Free Cycle, take the temperature of the loaf using an instant-read thermometer. It is baked at 200°F (100°C). If it's between 180°F (85°C) and 200°F (100°C), leave machine on the **Keep Warm Cycle** until baked. If it's below 180°F (85°C), turn on the **Bake Cycle** and check the internal temperature every 10 minutes. (Some bread machines are automatically set for 60 minutes; others need to be set by 10-minute intervals.)

Henk's Flax Bread

*Henk Rietveld of
Huntsville, Ontario,
suggested using the flax
flour in this loaf, which
makes a white bread
with a lovely warm color.
It's delicious thinly sliced
and toasted.*

Tips

To ensure success, see
page 15 for information
on using your bread machine
and page 18 for general tips
on bread machine baking.

For information on
cracking flaxseeds, see
the Techniques Glossary,
page 238.

We tried this bread with
sprouted flax powder, flax
meal and ground flaxseed
in place of the flax flour. All
yielded acceptable loaves.

NUTRITIONAL VALUES
per serving

Calories	176
Fat, total	7 g
Fat, saturated	1 g
Cholesterol	25 mg
Sodium	261 mg
Carbohydrate	26 g
Fiber	2 g
Protein	4 g
Calcium	42 mg
Iron	1 mg

1⅓ cups	brown rice flour	325 mL
⅓ cup	flax flour	75 mL
⅔ cup	potato starch	150 mL
⅓ cup	cornstarch	75 mL
⅓ cup	cracked flaxseed	75 mL
⅓ cup	nonfat dry milk or skim milk powder	75 mL
2½ tsp	xanthan gum	12 mL
1¼ tsp	bread machine or instant yeast	6 mL
1½ tsp	salt	7 mL
1¼ cups	water	300 mL
¼ cup	vegetable oil	60 mL
¼ cup	liquid honey	60 mL
2 tsp	cider vinegar	10 mL
2	eggs, lightly beaten	2
2	egg whites, lightly beaten	2

1. In a large bowl or plastic bag, combine brown rice flour, flax flour, potato starch, cornstarch, flaxseed, dry milk, xanthan gum, yeast and salt; mix well and set aside.
2. Pour water, oil, honey and vinegar into the bread machine baking pan. Add eggs and egg whites.
3. Select the **Dough Cycle**. As the bread machine is mixing, gradually add the dry ingredients, scraping bottom and sides of pan with a rubber spatula. Try to incorporate all the dry ingredients within 1 to 2 minutes. When the mixing and kneading are complete, remove the kneading blade, leaving the bread pan in the bread machine. Quickly smooth the top of the loaf. Allow the cycle to finish. Turn off the bread machine.
4. Select the **Bake Cycle**. Set time to 60 minutes and temperature to 350°F (180°C). Allow the cycle to finish. Do not turn machine off before taking the internal temperature of the loaf with an instant-read thermometer. It should be 200°F (100°C). If it's between 180°F (85°C) and 200°F (100°C), leave machine on the **Keep Warm Cycle** until baked. If it's below 180°F (85°C), turn on the **Bake Cycle** and check the internal temperature every 10 minutes. (Some bread machines are automatically set for 60 minutes; others need to be set by 10-minute intervals.)

Variations

Substitute raw hemp powder for the flax flour and Hemp Hearts for the flaxseed.

Substitute an equal amount of packed brown sugar for the honey.

Substitute millet seed for half of the flaxseed.

5. Once the loaf has reached 200°F (100°C), remove it from the pan immediately and let cool completely on a rack.

Gluten-Free Cycle

If your bread machine has a Gluten-Free Cycle, you will need to make these adjustments:

1. Warm the water to between 110°F and 115°F (43°C and 46°C).

2. Warm the eggs and egg whites (see the Techniques Glossary, page 238).

3. Follow the recipe instructions, but select the **Gluten-Free Cycle** rather than the Dough Cycle and Bake Cycle.

4. At the end of the Gluten-Free Cycle, take the temperature of the loaf using an instant-read thermometer. It is baked at 200°F (100°C). If it's between 180°F (85°C) and 200°F (100°C), leave machine on the **Keep Warm Cycle** until baked. If it's below 180°F (85°C), turn on the **Bake Cycle** and check the internal temperature every 10 minutes. (Some bread machines are automatically set for 60 minutes; others need to be set by 10-minute intervals.)

Sunflower Flax Bread

*Looking for something
different for your morning
toast? Try this crunchy,
nutty loaf.*

Tips

To ensure success, see
page 15 for information
on using your bread
machine and page 18 for
general tips on bread
machine baking.

For information on
cracking flaxseed, see
the Techniques Glossary,
page 238.

We tried this bread with
sprouted flax powder, flax
meal and ground flaxseed
in place of the flax flour. All
yielded acceptable loaves.

¾ cup	sorghum flour	175 mL
⅔ cup	amaranth flour	150 mL
⅓ cup	flax flour	75 mL
⅔ cup	potato starch	150 mL
⅓ cup	cornstarch	75 mL
¼ cup	granulated sugar	60 mL
2½ tsp	xanthan gum	12 mL
2 tsp	bread machine or instant yeast	10 mL
1½ tsp	salt	7 mL
½ cup	cracked flaxseed	125 mL
½ cup	unsalted raw sunflower seeds	125 mL
1¼ cups	water	300 mL
3 tbsp	vegetable oil	45 mL
2 tsp	cider vinegar	10 mL
2	eggs, lightly beaten	2
2	egg whites, lightly beaten	2

1. In a large bowl or plastic bag, combine sorghum flour, amaranth flour, flax flour, potato starch, cornstarch, sugar, xanthan gum, yeast, salt, flaxseed and sunflower seeds; mix well and set aside.

2. Pour water, oil and vinegar into the bread machine baking pan. Add eggs and egg whites.

3. Select the **Dough Cycle**. As the bread machine is mixing, gradually add the dry ingredients, scraping bottom and sides of pan with a rubber spatula. Try to incorporate all the dry ingredients within 1 to 2 minutes. When the mixing and kneading are complete, remove the kneading blade, leaving the bread pan in the bread machine. Quickly smooth the top of the loaf. Allow the cycle to finish. Turn off the bread machine.

4. Select the **Bake Cycle**. Set time to 60 minutes and temperature to 350°F (180°C). Allow the cycle to finish. Do not turn machine off before taking the internal temperature of the loaf with an instant-read thermometer. It should be 200°F (100°C). If it's between 180°F (85°C) and 200°F (100°C), leave machine on the **Keep Warm Cycle** until baked. If it's below 180°F (85°C), turn on the **Bake Cycle** and check the internal temperature every 10 minutes. (Some bread machines are automatically set for 60 minutes; others need to be set by 10-minute intervals.)

NUTRITIONAL VALUES
per serving

Calories	186
Fat, total	9 g
Fat, saturated	1 g
Cholesterol	25 mg
Sodium	251 mg
Carbohydrate	23 g
Fiber	4 g
Protein	5 g
Calcium	36 mg
Iron	2 mg

Substitute raw hemp powder for the flax flour and Hemp Hearts for the flaxseed.

5. Once the loaf has reached 200°F (100°C), remove it from the pan immediately and let cool completely on a rack.

Gluten-Free Cycle

If your bread machine has a Gluten-Free Cycle, you will need to make these adjustments:

1. Warm the water to between 110°F and 115°F (43°C and 46°C).

2. Warm the eggs and egg whites (see the Techniques Glossary, page 238).

3. Follow the recipe instructions, but select the **Gluten-Free Cycle** rather than the Dough Cycle and Bake Cycle.

4. At the end of the Gluten-Free Cycle, take the temperature of the loaf using an instant-read thermometer. It is baked at 200°F (100°C). If it's between 180°F (85°C) and 200°F (100°C), leave machine on the **Keep Warm Cycle** until baked. If it's below 180°F (85°C), turn on the **Bake Cycle** and check the internal temperature every 10 minutes. (Some bread machines are automatically set for 60 minutes; others need to be set by 10-minute intervals.)

Egg-Free, Corn-Free, Dairy-Free, Soy-Free Flax Bread

Though shorter than some loaves, this is the perfect sandwich bread for those who must eliminate eggs, corn, dairy and/or soy from their diet. It carries well, for a tasty lunch.

Tips

To ensure success, see page 15 for information on using your bread machine and page 18 for general tips on bread machine baking.

Slice this or any bread with an electric knife for thin, even sandwich slices.

1/3 cup	flax flour or ground flaxseed	75 mL
1/2 cup	warm water	125 mL
2 cups	brown rice flour	500 mL
1/3 cup	almond flour	75 mL
1/2 cup	potato starch	125 mL
1/4 cup	tapioca starch	60 mL
1/3 cup	cracked flaxseed	75 mL
2 tbsp	granulated sugar	30 mL
2 1/2 tsp	xanthan gum	12 mL
1 1/2 tsp	bread machine or instant yeast	7 mL
1 1/2 tsp	salt	7 mL
1 2/3 cups	water	400 mL
2 tbsp	vegetable oil	30 mL
2 tsp	cider vinegar	10 mL

1. In a small bowl or measuring cup, combine flax flour and water; set aside for 5 minutes.

2. In a large bowl or plastic bag, combine brown rice flour, almond flour, potato starch, tapioca starch, flaxseed, sugar, xanthan gum, yeast and salt; mix well and set aside.

3. Pour water, oil and vinegar into the bread machine baking pan. Add the flax flour mixture.

4. Select the **Dough Cycle**. As the bread machine is mixing, gradually add the dry ingredients, scraping bottom and sides of pan with a rubber spatula. Try to incorporate all the dry ingredients within 1 to 2 minutes. When the mixing and kneading are complete, remove the kneading blade, leaving the bread pan in the bread machine. Quickly smooth the top of the loaf. Allow the cycle to finish. Turn off the bread machine.

NUTRITIONAL VALUES
per serving

Calories	166
Fat, total	6 g
Fat, saturated	1 g
Cholesterol	0 mg
Sodium	238 mg
Carbohydrate	26 g
Fiber	3 g
Protein	4 g
Calcium	25 mg
Iron	1 mg

5. Select the **Bake Cycle**. Set time to 60 minutes and temperature to 350°F (180°C). Allow the cycle to finish. Do not turn machine off before taking the internal temperature of the loaf with an instant-read thermometer. It should be 200°F (100°C). If it's between 180°F (85°C) and 200°F (100°C), leave machine on the **Keep Warm Cycle** until baked. If it's below 180°F (85°C), turn on the **Bake Cycle** and check the internal temperature every 10 minutes. (Some bread machines are automatically set for 60 minutes; others need to be set by 10-minute intervals.)

6. Once the loaf has reached 200°F (100°C), remove it from the pan immediately and let cool completely on a rack.

Gluten-Free Cycle

If your bread machine has a Gluten-Free Cycle, you will need to make these adjustments:

1. Warm the water for the bread machine to between 110°F and 115°F (43°C and 46°C).

2. Follow the recipe instructions, but select the **Gluten-Free Cycle** rather than the Dough Cycle and Bake Cycle.

3. At the end of the Gluten-Free Cycle, take the temperature of the loaf using an instant-read thermometer. It is baked at 200°F (100°C). If it's between 180°F (85°C) and 200°F (100°C), leave machine on the **Keep Warm Cycle** until baked. If it's below 180°F (85°C), turn on the **Bake Cycle** and check the internal temperature every 10 minutes. (Some bread machines are automatically set for 60 minutes; others need to be set by 10-minute intervals.)

Mock Rye Loaf

This is the perfect loaf for making delicious sandwiches from leftover roast beef. Just add a little mustard.

Tip

To ensure success, see page 15 for information on using your bread machine and page 18 for general tips on bread machine baking.

1 cup	sorghum flour	250 mL
¾ cup	whole bean flour	175 mL
½ cup	quinoa flour	125 mL
½ cup	tapioca starch	125 mL
¼ cup	packed brown sugar	60 mL
1 tbsp	xanthan gum	15 mL
1¼ tsp	bread machine or instant yeast	6 mL
1¼ tsp	salt	6 mL
2 tbsp	caraway seeds	30 mL
1¼ cups	water	300 mL
2 tbsp	vegetable oil	30 mL
1 tsp	cider vinegar	5 mL
2	eggs, lightly beaten	2
2	egg whites, lightly beaten	2

1. In a large bowl or plastic bag, combine sorghum flour, whole bean flour, quinoa flour, tapioca starch, brown sugar, xanthan gum, yeast, salt and caraway seeds; mix well and set aside.

2. Pour water, oil and vinegar into the bread machine baking pan. Add eggs and egg whites.

3. Select the **Dough Cycle**. As the bread machine is mixing, gradually add the dry ingredients, scraping bottom and sides of pan with a rubber spatula. Try to incorporate all the dry ingredients within 1 to 2 minutes. When the mixing and kneading are complete, remove the kneading blade, leaving the bread pan in the bread machine. Quickly smooth the top of the loaf. Allow the cycle to finish. Turn off the bread machine.

4. Select the **Bake Cycle**. Set time to 60 minutes and temperature to 350°F (180°C). Allow the cycle to finish. Do not turn machine off before taking the internal temperature of the loaf with an instant-read thermometer. It should be 200°F (100°C). If it's between 180°F (85°C) and 200°F (100°C), leave machine on the **Keep Warm Cycle** until baked. If it's below 180°F (85°C), turn on the **Bake Cycle** and check the internal temperature every 10 minutes. (Some bread machines are automatically set for 60 minutes; others need to be set by 10-minute intervals.)

NUTRITIONAL VALUES per serving	
Calories	119
Fat, total	3 g
Fat, saturated	0 g
Cholesterol	25 mg
Sodium	212 mg
Carbohydrate	20 g
Fiber	2 g
Protein	4 g
Calcium	21 mg
Iron	1 mg

Tips

Thoroughly mix the dry ingredients before adding them to the liquids — they are powder-fine and could clump together.

Slice this or any bread with an electric knife for thin, even sandwich slices.

5. Once the loaf has reached 200°F (100°C), remove it from the pan immediately and let cool completely on a rack.

Gluten-Free Cycle

If your bread machine has a Gluten-Free Cycle, you will need to make these adjustments:

1. Warm the water to between 110°F and 115°F (43°C and 46°C).

2. Warm the eggs and egg whites (see the Techniques Glossary, page 238).

3. Follow the recipe instructions, but select the **Gluten-Free Cycle** rather than the Dough Cycle and Bake Cycle.

4. At the end of the Gluten-Free Cycle, take the temperature of the loaf using an instant-read thermometer. It is baked at 200°F (100°C). If it's between 180°F (85°C) and 200°F (100°C), leave machine on the **Keep Warm Cycle** until baked. If it's below 180°F (85°C), turn on the **Bake Cycle** and check the internal temperature every 10 minutes. (Some bread machines are automatically set for 60 minutes; others need to be set by 10-minute intervals.)

Teff Bread

MAKES 15 SLICES
(1 per serving)

*Teff, a powerhouse
of nutrition, makes a
delicious bread.*

Tips

To ensure success, see
page 15 for information
on using your bread
machine and page 18 for
general tips on bread
machine baking.

See the Techniques
Glossary, page 238, for
information on grinding
flaxseed.

You can use ½ cup (125 mL)
liquid whole eggs and
¼ cup (60 mL) liquid egg
whites, if you prefer.

¾ cup	brown rice flour	175 mL
¾ cup	teff flour	175 mL
½ cup	GF oat flour	125 mL
½ cup	potato starch	125 mL
¼ cup	teff grain	60 mL
2 tbsp	ground flaxseed	30 mL
1 tbsp	xanthan gum	15 mL
2 tsp	bread machine or instant yeast	10 mL
1½ tsp	salt	7 mL
2 tbsp	grated orange zest	30 mL
⅔ cup	dried blueberries	150 mL
1¼ cups	water	300 mL
¼ cup	vegetable oil	60 mL
¼ cup	liquid honey	60 mL
2 tsp	cider vinegar	10 mL
2	eggs, lightly beaten	2
2	egg whites, lightly beaten	2

1. In a large bowl or plastic bag, combine brown rice flour, teff flour, oat flour, potato starch, teff grain, flaxseed, xanthan gum, yeast, salt, orange zest and blueberries; mix well and set aside.
2. Pour water, oil, honey and vinegar into the bread machine baking pan. Add eggs and egg whites.
3. Select the **Dough Cycle**. As the bread machine is mixing, gradually add the dry ingredients, scraping bottom and sides of pan with a rubber spatula. Try to incorporate all the dry ingredients within 1 to 2 minutes. When the mixing and kneading are complete, remove the kneading blade, leaving the bread pan in the bread machine. Quickly smooth the top of the loaf. Allow the cycle to finish. Turn off the bread machine.

NUTRITIONAL VALUES per serving	
Calories	179
Fat, total	6 g
Fat, saturated	1 g
Cholesterol	25 mg
Sodium	251 mg
Carbohydrate	29 g
Fiber	3 g
Protein	4 g
Calcium	36 mg
Iron	2 mg

Variations

If you can't find teff grain, substitute ¼ cup (60 mL) poppy seeds or amaranth grain.

Substitute raisins or dried cranberries for the dried blueberries.

4. Select the **Bake Cycle**. Set time to 60 minutes and temperature to 350°F (180°C). Allow the cycle to finish. Do not turn machine off before taking the internal temperature of the loaf with an instant-read thermometer. It should be 200°F (100°C). If it's between 180°F (85°C) and 200°F (100°C), leave machine on the **Keep Warm Cycle** until baked. If it's below 180°F (85°C), turn on the **Bake Cycle** and check the internal temperature every 10 minutes. (Some bread machines are automatically set for 60 minutes; others need to be set by 10-minute intervals.)

5. Once the loaf has reached 200°F (100°C), remove it from the pan immediately and let cool completely on a rack.

Gluten-Free Cycle

If your bread machine has a Gluten-Free Cycle, you will need to make these adjustments:

1. Warm the water to between 110°F and 115°F (43°C and 46°C).

2. Warm the eggs and egg whites (see the Techniques Glossary, page 238).

3. Follow the recipe instructions, but select the **Gluten-Free Cycle** rather than the Dough Cycle and Bake Cycle.

4. At the end of the Gluten-Free Cycle, take the temperature of the loaf using an instant-read thermometer. It is baked at 200°F (100°C). If it's between 180°F (85°C) and 200°F (100°C), leave machine on the **Keep Warm Cycle** until baked. If it's below 180°F (85°C), turn on the **Bake Cycle** and check the internal temperature every 10 minutes. (Some bread machines are automatically set for 60 minutes; others need to be set by 10-minute intervals.)

Ancient Grains Bread

Here's a quartet of healthy grains — sorghum, amaranth, cornmeal and quinoa — combined in a soft-textured, nutritious loaf that's perfect for sandwiches.

Tip

To ensure success, see page 15 for information on using your bread machine and page 18 for general tips on bread machine baking.

1 cup	sorghum flour	250 mL
¾ cup	amaranth flour	175 mL
¾ cup	cornmeal	175 mL
¼ cup	quinoa flour	60 mL
½ cup	tapioca starch	125 mL
⅓ cup	packed brown sugar	75 mL
1 tbsp	xanthan gum	15 mL
¾ tsp	bread machine or instant yeast	3 mL
1½ tsp	salt	7 mL
1¼ cups	water	300 mL
2 tbsp	vegetable oil	30 mL
1 tsp	cider vinegar	5 mL
2	eggs, lightly beaten	2
2	egg whites, lightly beaten	2

1. In a large bowl or plastic bag, combine sorghum flour, amaranth flour, cornmeal, quinoa flour, tapioca starch, brown sugar, xanthan gum, yeast and salt; mix well and set aside.

2. Pour water, oil and vinegar into the bread machine baking pan. Add eggs and egg whites.

3. Select the **Dough Cycle**. As the bread machine is mixing, gradually add the dry ingredients, scraping bottom and sides of pan with a rubber spatula. Try to incorporate all the dry ingredients within 1 to 2 minutes. When the mixing and kneading are complete, remove the kneading blade, leaving the bread pan in the bread machine. Quickly smooth the top of the loaf. Allow the cycle to finish. Turn off the bread machine.

4. Select the **Bake Cycle**. Set time to 60 minutes and temperature to 350°F (180°C). Allow the cycle to finish. Do not turn machine off before taking the internal temperature of the loaf with an instant-read thermometer. It should be 200°F (100°C). If it's between 180°F (85°C) and 200°F (100°C), leave machine on the **Keep Warm Cycle** until baked. If it's below 180°F (85°C), turn on the **Bake Cycle** and check the internal temperature every 10 minutes. (Some bread machines are automatically set for 60 minutes; others need to be set by 10-minute intervals.)

NUTRITIONAL VALUES per serving	
Calories	151
Fat, total	3 g
Fat, saturated	0 g
Cholesterol	25 mg
Sodium	252 mg
Carbohydrate	27 g
Fiber	2 g
Protein	4 g
Calcium	21 mg
Iron	2 mg

You can use ½ cup (125 mL) liquid whole eggs and ¼ cup (60 mL) liquid egg whites, if you prefer.

5. Once the loaf has reached 200°F (100°C), remove it from the pan immediately and let cool completely on a rack.

To make this recipe egg-free: Omit eggs and egg whites from the recipe. Add 4 tsp (20 mL) powdered egg replacer with the dry ingredients. Increase yeast to 2 tsp (10 mL). Increase water by ¼ cup (60 mL). This flavorful egg-free loaf is shorter than some.

Gluten-Free Cycle

If your bread machine has a Gluten-Free Cycle, you will need to make these adjustments:

1. Warm the water to between 110°F and 115°F (43°C and 46°C).

2. Warm the eggs and egg whites (see the Techniques Glossary, page 238).

3. Follow the recipe instructions, but select the **Gluten-Free Cycle** rather than the Dough Cycle and Bake Cycle.

4. At the end of the Gluten-Free Cycle, take the temperature of the loaf using an instant-read thermometer. It is baked at 200°F (100°C). If it's between 180°F (85°C) and 200°F (100°C), leave machine on the **Keep Warm Cycle** until baked. If it's below 180°F (85°C), turn on the **Bake Cycle** and check the internal temperature every 10 minutes. (Some bread machines are automatically set for 60 minutes; others need to be set by 10-minute intervals.)

Historic Grains Bread

This loaf takes our Ancient Grains Bread (page 62) one step further, with five healthy grains represented: sorghum, amaranth, quinoa, flaxseed and millet seeds.

Tips

To ensure success, see page 15 for information on using your bread machine and page 18 for general tips on bread machine baking.

See the Techniques Glossary, page 238, for information on cracking flaxseed.

You can use ½ cup (125 mL) liquid whole eggs and ¼ cup (60 mL) liquid egg whites, if you prefer.

NUTRITIONAL VALUES per serving	
Calories	164
Fat, total	5 g
Fat, saturated	1 g
Cholesterol	25 mg
Sodium	211 mg
Carbohydrate	26 g
Fiber	3 g
Protein	5 g
Calcium	32 mg
Iron	3 mg

1¼ cups	sorghum flour	300 mL
1 cup	amaranth flour	250 mL
¼ cup	quinoa flour	60 mL
½ cup	cracked brown flaxseed	125 mL
¼ cup	millet seeds	60 mL
½ cup	tapioca starch	125 mL
1 tbsp	xanthan gum	15 mL
1¼ tsp	bread machine or instant yeast	6 mL
1¼ tsp	salt	6 mL
1¼ cups	water	300 mL
¼ cup	liquid honey	60 mL
2 tbsp	vegetable oil	30 mL
1 tsp	cider vinegar	5 mL
2	eggs, lightly beaten	2
2	egg whites, lightly beaten	2

1. In a large bowl or plastic bag, combine sorghum flour, amaranth flour, quinoa flour, flaxseed, millet seeds, tapioca starch, xanthan gum, yeast and salt; mix well and set aside.

2. Pour water, honey, oil and vinegar into the bread machine baking pan. Add eggs and egg whites.

3. Select the **Dough Cycle**. As the bread machine is mixing, gradually add the dry ingredients, scraping bottom and sides of pan with a rubber spatula. Try to incorporate all the dry ingredients within 1 to 2 minutes. When the mixing and kneading are complete, remove the kneading blade, leaving the bread pan in the bread machine. Quickly smooth the top of the loaf. Allow the cycle to finish. Turn off the bread machine.

4. Select the **Bake Cycle**. Set time to 60 minutes and temperature to 350°F (180°C). Allow the cycle to finish. Do not turn machine off before taking the internal temperature of the loaf with an instant-read thermometer. It should be 200°F (100°C). If it's between 180°F (85°C) and 200°F (100°C), leave machine on the **Keep Warm Cycle** until baked. If it's below 180°F (85°C), turn on the **Bake Cycle** and check the internal temperature every 10 minutes. (Some bread machines are automatically set for 60 minutes; others need to be set by 10-minute intervals.)

Variations

Substitute golden flaxseed for the brown.

Substitute amaranth grain or whole flaxseed for the millet seeds.

5. Once the loaf has reached 200°F (100°C), remove it from the pan immediately and let cool completely on a rack.

Gluten-Free Cycle

If your bread machine has a Gluten-Free Cycle, you will need to make these adjustments:

1. Warm the water to between 110°F and 115°F (43°C and 46°C).
2. Warm the eggs and egg whites (see the Techniques Glossary, page 238).
3. Follow the recipe instructions, but select the **Gluten-Free Cycle** rather than the Dough Cycle and Bake Cycle.
4. At the end of the Gluten-Free Cycle, take the temperature of the loaf using an instant-read thermometer. It is baked at 200°F (100°C). If it's between 180°F (85°C) and 200°F (100°C), leave machine on the **Keep Warm Cycle** until baked. If it's below 180°F (85°C), turn on the **Bake Cycle** and check the internal temperature every 10 minutes. (Some bread machines are automatically set for 60 minutes; others need to be set by 10-minute intervals.)

Triple-Seed Brown Bread

A sandwich bread with a rich color and added crunch — what a treat!

Tips

To ensure success, see page 15 for information on using your bread machine and page 18 for general tips on bread machine baking.

You can purchase buttermilk powder in bulk stores and health food stores.

Toasting the seeds gives them a nuttier flavor. For instructions, see the Techniques Glossary, page 240.

1¼ cups	sorghum flour	300 mL
⅔ cup	whole bean flour	150 mL
⅓ cup	tapioca starch	75 mL
⅓ cup	rice bran	75 mL
⅓ cup	buttermilk powder	75 mL
1 tbsp	xanthan gum	15 mL
1½ tsp	bread machine or instant yeast	7 mL
1¼ tsp	salt	6 mL
⅓ cup	unsalted green pumpkin seeds, toasted	75 mL
⅓ cup	unsalted raw sunflower seeds, toasted	75 mL
¼ cup	sesame seeds, toasted	60 mL
1¼ cups	water	300 mL
2 tbsp	vegetable oil	30 mL
2 tbsp	liquid honey	30 mL
2 tbsp	light (fancy) molasses	30 mL
1 tsp	cider vinegar	5 mL
3	eggs, lightly beaten	3

1. In a large bowl or plastic bag, combine sorghum flour, whole bean flour, tapioca starch, rice bran, buttermilk powder, xanthan gum, yeast, salt, pumpkin seeds, sunflower seeds and sesame seeds; mix well and set aside.

2. Pour water, oil, honey, molasses and vinegar into the bread machine baking pan. Add eggs.

3. Select the **Dough Cycle**. As the bread machine is mixing, gradually add the dry ingredients, scraping bottom and sides of pan with a rubber spatula. Try to incorporate all the dry ingredients within 1 to 2 minutes. When the mixing and kneading are complete, remove the kneading blade, leaving the bread pan in the bread machine. Quickly smooth the top of the loaf. Allow the cycle to finish. Turn off the bread machine.

NUTRITIONAL VALUES
per serving

Calories	163
Fat, total	8 g
Fat, saturated	1 g
Cholesterol	38 mg
Sodium	211 mg
Carbohydrate	20 g
Fiber	2 g
Protein	5 g
Calcium	52 mg
Iron	2 mg

Variations

For a milder bread, substitute packed brown sugar for the molasses.

Substitute brown rice flour, raw hemp powder or flaxseed meal for the rice bran.

Replace the sesame seeds with cracked flaxseed, Hemp Hearts or poppy seeds.

4. Select the **Bake Cycle**. Set time to 60 minutes and temperature to 350°F (180°C). Allow the cycle to finish. Do not turn machine off before taking the internal temperature of the loaf with an instant-read thermometer. It should be 200°F (100°C). If it's between 180°F (85°C) and 200°F (100°C), leave machine on the **Keep Warm Cycle** until baked. If it's below 180°F (85°C), turn on the **Bake Cycle** and check the internal temperature every 10 minutes. (Some bread machines are automatically set for 60 minutes; others need to be set by 10-minute intervals.)

5. Once the loaf has reached 200°F (100°C), remove it from the pan immediately and let cool completely on a rack.

Gluten-Free Cycle

If your bread machine has a Gluten-Free Cycle, you will need to make these adjustments:

1. Warm the water to between 110°F and 115°F (43°C and 46°C).

2. Warm the eggs (see the Techniques Glossary, page 238).

3. Follow the recipe instructions, but select the **Gluten-Free Cycle** rather than the Dough Cycle and Bake Cycle.

4. At the end of the Gluten-Free Cycle, take the temperature of the loaf using an instant-read thermometer. It is baked at 200°F (100°C). If it's between 180°F (85°C) and 200°F (100°C), leave machine on the **Keep Warm Cycle** until baked. If it's below 180°F (85°C), turn on the **Bake Cycle** and check the internal temperature every 10 minutes. (Some bread machines are automatically set for 60 minutes; others need to be set by 10-minute intervals.)

Lemon Millet Bread

This rich, golden loaf is studded with white dots of millet. The refreshing addition of lemon makes it a real taste treat.

Tips

To ensure success, see page 15 for information on using your bread machine and page 18 for general tips on bread machine baking.

No need to cook the millet seeds — they soften enough during baking to provide an interesting crunch.

1½ cups	amaranth flour	375 mL
1¼ cups	brown rice flour	300 mL
⅓ cup	tapioca starch	75 mL
½ cup	millet seeds	125 mL
1 tbsp	xanthan gum	15 mL
1½ tsp	bread machine or instant yeast	7 mL
1¼ tsp	salt	6 mL
2 tbsp	grated lemon zest	30 mL
1 cup	water	250 mL
⅓ cup	freshly squeezed lemon juice	75 mL
¼ cup	liquid honey	60 mL
2 tbsp	vegetable oil	30 mL
2	eggs, lightly beaten	2
2	egg whites, lightly beaten	2

1. In a large bowl or plastic bag, combine amaranth flour, brown rice flour, tapioca starch, millet seeds, xanthan gum, yeast, salt and lemon zest; mix well and set aside.

2. Pour water, lemon juice, honey and oil into the bread machine baking pan. Add eggs and egg whites.

3. Select the **Dough Cycle**. As the bread machine is mixing, gradually add the dry ingredients, scraping bottom and sides of pan with a rubber spatula. Try to incorporate all the dry ingredients within 1 to 2 minutes. When the mixing and kneading are complete, remove the kneading blade, leaving the bread pan in the bread machine. Quickly smooth the top of the loaf. Allow the cycle to finish. Turn off the bread machine.

4. Select the **Bake Cycle**. Set time to 60 minutes and temperature to 350°F (180°C). Allow the cycle to finish. Do not turn machine off before taking the internal temperature of the loaf with an instant-read thermometer. It should be 200°F (100°C). If it's between 180°F (85°C) and 200°F (100°C), leave machine on the **Keep Warm Cycle** until baked. If it's below 180°F (85°C), turn on the **Bake Cycle** and check the internal temperature every 10 minutes. (Some bread machines are automatically set for 60 minutes; others need to be set by 10-minute intervals.)

NUTRITIONAL VALUES per serving	
Calories	176
Fat, total	4 g
Fat, saturated	0 g
Cholesterol	25 mg
Sodium	211 mg
Carbohydrate	31 g
Fiber	3 g
Protein	5 g
Calcium	24 mg
Iron	4 mg

Variation

Substitute orange zest and juice for the lemon.

5. Once the loaf has reached 200°F (100°C), remove it from the pan immediately and let cool completely on a rack.

Gluten-Free Cycle

If your bread machine has a Gluten-Free Cycle, you will need to make these adjustments:

1. Warm the water to between 110°F and 115°F (43°C and 46°C).

2. Warm the eggs and egg whites (see the Techniques Glossary, page 238).

3. Follow the recipe instructions, but select the **Gluten-Free Cycle** rather than the Dough Cycle and Bake Cycle.

4. At the end of the Gluten-Free Cycle, take the temperature of the loaf using an instant-read thermometer. It is baked at 200°F (100°C). If it's between 180°F (85°C) and 200°F (100°C), leave machine on the **Keep Warm Cycle** until baked. If it's below 180°F (85°C), turn on the **Bake Cycle** and check the internal temperature every 10 minutes. (Some bread machines are automatically set for 60 minutes; others need to be set by 10-minute intervals.)

Country Harvest Bread

MAKES 15 SLICES
(1 per serving)

*This sandwich bread
with a crunch is one of
our favorites.*

Tips

To ensure success, see
page 15 for information on
using your bread machine
and page 18 for general tips
on bread machine baking.

To prevent seeds from
becoming rancid, store them
in an airtight container in
the refrigerator.

For information on
cracking flaxseed, see
the Techniques Glossary,
page 238.

1 cup	sorghum flour	250 mL
½ cup	whole bean flour	125 mL
¼ cup	flax flour	60 mL
½ cup	tapioca starch	125 mL
¼ cup	packed brown sugar	60 mL
1 tbsp	xanthan gum	15 mL
2 tsp	bread machine or instant yeast	10 mL
1¼ tsp	salt	6 mL
½ cup	cracked flaxseed	125 mL
⅓ cup	unsalted raw sunflower seeds	75 mL
2 tbsp	sesame seeds	30 mL
1¼ cups	water	300 mL
2 tbsp	vegetable oil	30 mL
1 tsp	cider vinegar	5 mL
2	eggs, lightly beaten	2
2	egg whites, lightly beaten	2

1. In a large bowl or plastic bag, combine sorghum flour,
   whole bean flour, flax flour, tapioca starch, brown sugar,
   xanthan gum, yeast, salt, flaxseed, sunflower seeds and
   sesame seeds; mix well and set aside.

2. Pour water, oil and vinegar into the bread machine baking
   pan. Add eggs and egg whites.

3. Select the **Dough Cycle**. As the bread machine is mixing,
   gradually add the dry ingredients, scraping bottom and
   sides of pan with a rubber spatula. Try to incorporate
   all the dry ingredients within 1 to 2 minutes. When the
   mixing and kneading are complete, remove the kneading
   blade, leaving the bread pan in the bread machine. Quickly
   smooth the top of the loaf. Allow the cycle to finish. Turn
   off the bread machine.

NUTRITIONAL VALUES per serving	
Calories	153
Fat, total	8 g
Fat, saturated	1 g
Cholesterol	25 mg
Sodium	214 mg
Carbohydrate	19 g
Fiber	4 g
Protein	5 g
Calcium	50 mg
Iron	2 mg

Variation
Try different types of seeds, such as poppy seeds or unsalted green pumpkin seeds, but keep the total amount the same.

4. Select the **Bake Cycle**. Set time to 60 minutes and temperature to 350°F (180°C). Allow the cycle to finish. Do not turn machine off before taking the internal temperature of the loaf with an instant-read thermometer. It should be 200°F (100°C). If it's between 180°F (85°C) and 200°F (100°C), leave machine on the **Keep Warm Cycle** until baked. If it's below 180°F (85°C), turn on the **Bake Cycle** and check the internal temperature every 10 minutes. (Some bread machines are automatically set for 60 minutes; others need to be set by 10-minute intervals.)

5. Once the loaf has reached 200°F (100°C), remove it from the pan immediately and let cool completely on a rack.

Gluten-Free Cycle

If your bread machine has a Gluten-Free Cycle, you will need to make these adjustments:

1. Warm the water to between 110°F and 115°F (43°C and 46°C).

2. Warm the eggs and egg whites (see the Techniques Glossary, page 238).

3. Follow the recipe instructions, but select the **Gluten-Free Cycle** rather than the Dough Cycle and Bake Cycle.

4. At the end of the Gluten-Free Cycle, take the temperature of the loaf using an instant-read thermometer. It is baked at 200°F (100°C). If it's between 180°F (85°C) and 200°F (100°C), leave machine on the **Keep Warm Cycle** until baked. If it's below 180°F (85°C), turn on the **Bake Cycle** and check the internal temperature every 10 minutes. (Some bread machines are automatically set for 60 minutes; others need to be set by 10-minute intervals.)

Banana Seed Bread

The combination of sorghum and bean flour really enhances the banana flavor of this loaf. Serve it for dessert or with a slice of sharp (old) Cheddar for lunch.

Tips

To ensure success, see page 15 for information on using your bread machine and page 18 for general tips on bread machine baking.

For a nuttier flavor, toast the sunflower seeds (see the Techniques Glossary, page 240, for instructions).

1 cup	sorghum flour	250 mL
1 cup	whole bean flour	250 mL
¼ cup	tapioca starch	60 mL
¼ cup	packed brown sugar	60 mL
2½ tsp	xanthan gum	12 mL
1½ tsp	bread machine or instant yeast	7 mL
1¼ tsp	salt	6 mL
½ cup	unsalted raw sunflower seeds	125 mL
¾ cup	water	175 mL
1 cup	mashed banana	250 mL
¼ cup	vegetable oil	60 mL
1 tsp	cider vinegar	5 mL
2	eggs, lightly beaten	2

1. In a large bowl or plastic bag, combine sorghum flour, whole bean flour, tapioca starch, brown sugar, xanthan gum, yeast, salt and sunflower seeds; mix well and set aside.
2. Pour water, banana, oil and vinegar into the bread machine baking pan. Add eggs.
3. Select the **Dough Cycle**. As the bread machine is mixing, gradually add the dry ingredients, scraping bottom and sides of pan with a rubber spatula. Try to incorporate all the dry ingredients within 1 to 2 minutes. When the mixing and kneading are complete, remove the kneading blade, leaving the bread pan in the bread machine. Quickly smooth the top of the loaf. Allow the cycle to finish. Turn off the bread machine.
4. Select the **Bake Cycle**. Set time to 60 minutes and temperature to 350°F (180°C). Allow the cycle to finish. Do not turn machine off before taking the internal temperature of the loaf with an instant-read thermometer. It should be 200°F (100°C). If it's between 180°F (85°C) and 200°F (100°C), leave machine on the **Keep Warm Cycle** until baked. If it's below 180°F (85°C), turn on the **Bake Cycle** and check the internal temperature every 10 minutes. (Some bread machines are automatically set for 60 minutes; others need to be set by 10-minute intervals.)
5. Once the loaf has reached 200°F (100°C), remove it from the pan immediately and let cool completely on a rack.

NUTRITIONAL VALUES per serving	
Calories	147
Fat, total	7 g
Fat, saturated	1 g
Cholesterol	25 mg
Sodium	205 mg
Carbohydrate	19 g
Fiber	2 g
Protein	4 g
Calcium	20 mg
Iron	1 mg

Variation

Unsalted green pumpkin seeds or chopped pecans can replace the sunflower seeds.

Gluten-Free Cycle

If your bread machine has a Gluten-Free Cycle, you will need to make these adjustments:

1. Warm the water to between 110°F and 115°F (43°C and 46°C).

2. Warm the eggs (see the Techniques Glossary, page 238).

3. Follow the recipe instructions, but select the **Gluten-Free Cycle** rather than the Dough Cycle and Bake Cycle.

4. At the end of the Gluten-Free Cycle, take the temperature of the loaf using an instant-read thermometer. It is baked at 200°F (100°C). If it's between 180°F (85°C) and 200°F (100°C), leave machine on the **Keep Warm Cycle** until baked. If it's below 180°F (85°C), turn on the **Bake Cycle** and check the internal temperature every 10 minutes. (Some bread machines are automatically set for 60 minutes; others need to be set by 10-minute intervals.)

Flaxseed Banana Bread

Toasting a slice brings out the banana flavor. No need to butter this bread.

Tip

To ensure success, see page 15 for information on using your bread machine and page 18 for general tips on bread machine baking.

1½ cups	brown rice flour	375 mL
⅔ cup	potato starch	150 mL
⅓ cup	tapioca starch	75 mL
1 tbsp	xanthan gum	15 mL
1½ tsp	bread machine or instant yeast	7 mL
1½ tsp	salt	7 mL
⅓ cup	cracked flaxseed	75 mL
¾ cup	water	175 mL
1 cup	mashed banana	250 mL
¼ cup	pure maple syrup	60 mL
¼ cup	vegetable oil	60 mL
2 tsp	cider vinegar	10 mL
2	eggs, lightly beaten	2
2	egg whites, lightly beaten	2

1. In a large bowl or plastic bag, combine brown rice flour, potato starch, tapioca starch, xanthan gum, yeast, salt and flaxseed; mix well and set aside.

2. Pour water, banana, maple syrup, oil and vinegar into the bread machine baking pan. Add eggs and egg whites.

3. Select the **Dough Cycle**. As the bread machine is mixing, gradually add the dry ingredients, scraping bottom and sides of pan with a rubber spatula. Try to incorporate all the dry ingredients within 1 to 2 minutes. When the mixing and kneading are complete, remove the kneading blade, leaving the bread pan in the bread machine. Quickly smooth the top of the loaf. Allow the cycle to finish. Turn off the bread machine.

4. Select the **Bake Cycle**. Set time to 60 minutes and temperature to 350°F (180°C). Allow the cycle to finish. Do not turn machine off before taking the internal temperature of the loaf with an instant-read thermometer. It should be 200°F (100°C). If it's between 180°F (85°C) and 200°F (100°C), leave machine on the **Keep Warm Cycle** until baked. If it's below 180°F (85°C), turn on the **Bake Cycle** and check the internal temperature every 10 minutes. (Some bread machines are automatically set for 60 minutes; others need to be set by 10-minute intervals.)

5. Once the loaf has reached 200°F (100°C), remove it from the pan immediately and let cool completely on a rack.

NUTRITIONAL VALUES
per serving

Calories	176
Fat, total	6 g
Fat, saturated	1 g
Cholesterol	25 mg
Sodium	251 mg
Carbohydrate	28 g
Fiber	3 g
Protein	3 g
Calcium	19 mg
Iron	1 mg

Variation
Pancake syrup (light or regular) or packed brown sugar can be substituted for the maple syrup.

Gluten-Free Cycle

If your bread machine has a Gluten-Free Cycle, you will need to make these adjustments:

1. Warm the water to between 110°F and 115°F (43°C and 46°C).
2. Warm the eggs and egg whites (see the Techniques Glossary, page 238).
3. Follow the recipe instructions, but select the **Gluten-Free Cycle** rather than the Dough Cycle and Bake Cycle.
4. At the end of the Gluten-Free Cycle, take the temperature of the loaf using an instant-read thermometer. It is baked at 200°F (100°C). If it's between 180°F (85°C) and 200°F (100°C), leave machine on the **Keep Warm Cycle** until baked. If it's below 180°F (85°C), turn on the **Bake Cycle** and check the internal temperature every 10 minutes. (Some bread machines are automatically set for 60 minutes; others need to be set by 10-minute intervals.)

Buckwheat Walnut Bread

This is the bread for those who love to combine strong, robust flavors — buckwheat, whole bean flour and cardamom.

Tips

To ensure success, see page 15 for information on using your bread machine and page 18 for general tips on bread machine baking.

Make sure buckwheat is on your list of allowable foods before you try this recipe.

1¼ cups	whole bean flour	300 mL
½ cup	buckwheat flour	125 mL
½ cup	potato starch	125 mL
¼ cup	tapioca starch	60 mL
⅓ cup	packed brown sugar	75 mL
1 tbsp	xanthan gum	15 mL
1½ tsp	bread machine or instant yeast	7 mL
1¼ tsp	salt	6 mL
1 tsp	ground cardamom	5 mL
1 cup	chopped walnuts	250 mL
1¾ cups	water	425 mL
¼ cup	vegetable oil	60 mL
1 tsp	cider vinegar	5 mL
2	eggs, lightly beaten	2

1. In a large bowl or plastic bag, combine whole bean flour, buckwheat flour, potato starch, tapioca starch, brown sugar, xanthan gum, yeast, salt, cardamom and walnuts; mix well and set aside.

2. Pour water, oil and vinegar into the bread machine baking pan. Add eggs.

3. Select the **Dough Cycle**. As the bread machine is mixing, gradually add the dry ingredients, scraping bottom and sides of pan with a rubber spatula. Try to incorporate all the dry ingredients within 1 to 2 minutes. When the mixing and kneading are complete, remove the kneading blade, leaving the bread pan in the bread machine. Quickly smooth the top of the loaf. Allow the cycle to finish. Turn off the bread machine.

4. Select the **Bake Cycle**. Set time to 60 minutes and temperature to 350°F (180°C). Allow the cycle to finish. Do not turn machine off before taking the internal temperature of the loaf with an instant-read thermometer. It should be 200°F (100°C). If it's between 180°F (85°C) and 200°F (100°C), leave machine on the **Keep Warm Cycle** until baked. If it's below 180°F (85°C), turn on the **Bake Cycle** and check the internal temperature every 10 minutes. (Some bread machines are automatically set for 60 minutes; others need to be set by 10-minute intervals.)

NUTRITIONAL VALUES
per serving

Calories	165
Fat, total	10 g
Fat, saturated	1 g
Cholesterol	25 mg
Sodium	204 mg
Carbohydrate	18 g
Fiber	2 g
Protein	4 g
Calcium	23 mg
Iron	1 mg

Variations

Substitute brown rice flour for the buckwheat flour.

Substitute fresh, dried or frozen blueberries for the walnuts. Fold in the fruit at the end of the kneading cycle.

Substitute an equal amount of ground nutmeg for the cardamom.

5. Once the loaf has reached 200°F (100°C), remove it from the pan immediately and let cool completely on a rack.

Gluten-Free Cycle

If your bread machine has a Gluten-Free Cycle, you will need to make these adjustments:

1. Warm the water to between 110°F and 115°F (43°C and 46°C).

2. Warm the eggs (see the Techniques Glossary, page 238).

3. Follow the recipe instructions, but select the **Gluten-Free Cycle** rather than the Dough Cycle and Bake Cycle.

4. At the end of the Gluten-Free Cycle, take the temperature of the loaf using an instant-read thermometer. It is baked at 200°F (100°C). If it's between 180°F (85°C) and 200°F (100°C), leave machine on the **Keep Warm Cycle** until baked. If it's below 180°F (85°C), turn on the **Bake Cycle** and check the internal temperature every 10 minutes. (Some bread machines are automatically set for 60 minutes; others need to be set by 10-minute intervals.)

Multigrain Bread

A celiac friend suggested this variation of our Whole-Grain Amaranth Bread (page 50). This soft-textured, creamy, honey-colored bread is so delicious you won't even suspect how nutritious it is.

Tips

To ensure success, see page 15 for information on using your bread machine and page 18 for general tips on bread machine baking.

See the Techniques Glossary for information on making your own oat flour (page 240) and grinding flaxseed (page 238).

¾ cup	amaranth flour	175 mL
¾ cup	brown rice flour	175 mL
½ cup	GF oat flour	125 mL
½ cup	potato starch	125 mL
¼ cup	amaranth grain	60 mL
2 tbsp	ground flaxseed	30 mL
1 tbsp	xanthan gum	15 mL
2 tsp	bread machine or instant yeast	10 mL
1½ tsp	salt	7 mL
1 cup	water	250 mL
¼ cup	vegetable oil	60 mL
¼ cup	liquid honey	60 mL
2 tsp	cider vinegar	10 mL
2	eggs, lightly beaten	2
2	egg whites, lightly beaten	2

1. In a large bowl or plastic bag, combine amaranth flour, brown rice flour, oat flour, potato starch, amaranth grain, flaxseed, xanthan gum, yeast and salt; mix well and set aside.

2. Pour water, oil, honey and vinegar into the bread machine baking pan. Add eggs and egg whites.

3. Select the **Dough Cycle**. As the bread machine is mixing, gradually add the dry ingredients, scraping bottom and sides of pan with a rubber spatula. Try to incorporate all the dry ingredients within 1 to 2 minutes. When the mixing and kneading are complete, remove the kneading blade, leaving the bread pan in the bread machine. Quickly smooth the top of the loaf. Allow the cycle to finish. Turn off the bread machine.

4. Select the **Bake Cycle**. Set time to 60 minutes and temperature to 350°F (180°C). Allow the cycle to finish. Do not turn machine off before taking the internal temperature of the loaf with an instant-read thermometer. It should be 200°F (100°C). If it's between 180°F (85°C) and 200°F (100°C), leave machine on the **Keep Warm Cycle** until baked. If it's below 180°F (85°C), turn on the **Bake Cycle** and check the internal temperature every 10 minutes. (Some bread machines are automatically set for 60 minutes; others need to be set by 10-minute intervals.)

NUTRITIONAL VALUES
per serving

Calories	165
Fat, total	7 g
Fat, saturated	1 g
Cholesterol	25 mg
Sodium	252 mg
Carbohydrate	23 g
Fiber	3 g
Protein	4 g
Calcium	31 mg
Iron	2 mg

Tips

Amaranth is high in fiber, iron and calcium and lower in sodium than most grains. Store amaranth grain in an airtight container in the refrigerator for up to 6 months.

You can use 1/2 cup (125 mL) liquid whole eggs and 1/4 cup (60 mL) liquid egg whites, if you prefer.

Variations

Substitute millet seeds or poppy seeds for the amaranth grain.

Add 2/3 cup (150 mL) dried cranberries and 2 tbsp (30 mL) grated orange zest with the dry ingredients.

5. Once the loaf has reached 200°F (100°C), remove it from the pan immediately and let cool completely on a rack.

Gluten-Free Cycle

If your bread machine has a Gluten-Free Cycle, you will need to make these adjustments:

1. Warm the water to between 110°F and 115°F (43°C and 46°C).

2. Warm the eggs and egg whites (see the Techniques Glossary, page 238).

3. Follow the recipe instructions, but select the **Gluten-Free Cycle** rather than the Dough Cycle and Bake Cycle.

4. At the end of the Gluten-Free Cycle, take the temperature of the loaf using an instant-read thermometer. It is baked at 200°F (100°C). If it's between 180°F (85°C) and 200°F (100°C), leave machine on the **Keep Warm Cycle** until baked. If it's below 180°F (85°C), turn on the **Bake Cycle** and check the internal temperature every 10 minutes. (Some bread machines are automatically set for 60 minutes; others need to be set by 10-minute intervals.)

Crunchy Multigrain Batard

The attractive, grainy slices from this loaf are a perfect accompaniment to your favorite soup or salad.

Tips

To ensure success, see page 15 for information on using your bread machine and page 18 for general tips on bread machine baking.

See the Equipment Glossary, page 230, for information about baguette pans.

Store this bread loosely covered in a paper bag to maintain the crisp crust.

Use an electric or serrated knife to thickly slice these loaves on the diagonal.

NUTRITIONAL VALUES per serving	
Calories	74
Fat, total	2 g
Fat, saturated	0 g
Cholesterol	0 mg
Sodium	152 mg
Carbohydrate	14 g
Fiber	2 g
Protein	2 g
Calcium	9 mg
Iron	1 mg

◆ **Baking sheet or baguette pan, lightly greased, then lined with parchment paper**

1½ cups	brown rice flour	375 mL
½ cup	quinoa flour	125 mL
⅔ cup	potato starch	150 mL
2 tsp	granulated sugar	10 mL
2 tsp	xanthan gum	10 mL
2 tsp	bread machine or instant yeast	10 mL
1½ tsp	salt	7 mL
⅓ cup	millet seed	75 mL
⅓ cup	cracked flaxseed	75 mL
¼ cup	GF oats	60 mL
1½ cups	water	375 mL
2 tsp	cider vinegar	10 mL
2	egg whites, lightly beaten	2

1. In a large bowl or plastic bag, combine brown rice flour, quinoa flour, potato starch, sugar, xanthan gum, yeast, salt, millet, flaxseed and oats; mix well and set aside.

2. Pour water and vinegar into the bread machine baking pan. Add egg whites.

3. Select the **Dough Cycle**. As the bread machine is mixing, gradually add the dry ingredients, scraping bottom and sides of pan with a rubber spatula. Try to incorporate all the dry ingredients within 1 to 2 minutes. Stop bread machine as soon as the kneading portion of the cycle is complete. Do not let bread machine finish the cycle.

4. Divide dough in half and form each half into the shape of a batard (wide baguette). Place parallel to each other in prepared pan, at least 3 inches (7.5 cm) apart. Using the edge of a moistened rubber spatula or a sharp knife, draw 3 or 4 diagonal lines, ¼ inch (0.5 cm) deep, across the top of each loaf. Let rise, uncovered, in a warm, draft-free place for 75 minutes. Meanwhile, preheat oven to 425°F (220°C).

5. Bake for 18 to 22 minutes or until internal temperature of loaf registers 200°F (100°C) on an instant-read thermometer. Remove from the pan immediately and let cool completely on a rack.

Luncheon and Dinner Breads

Honeyed Walnut Bread

Enhance the nutty walnut flavor of this basic brown sandwich or breakfast bread by toasting individual slices.

Tips

To ensure success, see page 15 for information on using your bread machine and page 18 for general tips on bread machine baking.

It's worth the time to toast the walnuts (for instructions, see the Techniques Glossary, page 240). No need to let them cool; just add to the dry ingredients. Toast more walnuts than you need for this recipe. Cool and store the extra in a resealable plastic bag in the refrigerator.

1½ cups	sorghum flour	375 mL
¾ cup	brown rice flour	175 mL
½ cup	cornstarch	125 mL
½ cup	rice bran	125 mL
1 tbsp	xanthan gum	15 mL
1½ tsp	bread machine or instant yeast	7 mL
1½ tsp	salt	7 mL
1 cup	coarsely chopped walnuts, toasted (see tip, at left)	250 mL
1¼ cups	water	300 mL
⅓ cup	liquid honey	75 mL
2 tbsp	walnut oil or vegetable oil	30 mL
1 tsp	cider vinegar	5 mL
2	eggs, lightly beaten	2
2	egg whites, lightly beaten	2

1. In a large bowl or plastic bag, combine sorghum flour, brown rice flour, cornstarch, rice bran, xanthan gum, yeast, salt and walnuts; mix well and set aside.

2. Pour water, honey, walnut oil and vinegar into the bread machine baking pan. Add eggs and egg whites.

3. Select the **Dough Cycle**. As the bread machine is mixing, gradually add the dry ingredients, scraping bottom and sides of pan with a rubber spatula. Try to incorporate all the dry ingredients within 1 to 2 minutes. When the mixing and kneading are complete, remove the kneading blade, leaving the bread pan in the bread machine. Quickly smooth the top of the loaf. Allow the cycle to finish. Turn off the bread machine.

4. Select the **Bake Cycle**. Set time to 60 minutes and temperature to 350°F (180°C). Allow the cycle to finish. Do not turn machine off before taking the internal temperature of the loaf with an instant-read thermometer. It should be 200°F (100°C). If it's between 180°F (85°C) and 200°F (100°C), leave machine on the **Keep Warm Cycle** until baked. If it's below 180°F (85°C), turn on the **Bake Cycle** and check the internal temperature every 10 minutes. (Some bread machines are automatically set for 60 minutes; others need to be set by 10-minute intervals.)

NUTRITIONAL VALUES
per serving

Calories	210
Fat, total	9 g
Fat, saturated	1 g
Cholesterol	25 mg
Sodium	250 mg
Carbohydrate	29 g
Fiber	2 g
Protein	5 g
Calcium	17 mg
Iron	2 mg

Tips

Store brown rice flour and rice bran in the refrigerator.

You can use ½ cup (125 mL) liquid whole eggs and ¼ cup (60 mL) liquid egg whites, if you prefer.

5. Once the loaf has reached 200°F (100°C), remove it from the pan immediately and let cool completely on a rack.

To make this recipe egg-free: Omit eggs and egg whites from recipe. Combine ⅓ cup (75 mL) flax flour or ground flaxseed with an additional ½ cup (125 mL) warm water. Set aside for 5 minutes. Add with the liquids.

Gluten-Free Cycle

If your bread machine has a Gluten-Free Cycle, you will need to make these adjustments:

1. Warm the water to between 110°F and 115°F (43°C and 46°C).

2. Warm the eggs and egg whites (see the Techniques Glossary, page 238).

3. Follow the recipe instructions, but select the **Gluten-Free Cycle** rather than the Dough Cycle and Bake Cycle.

4. At the end of the Gluten-Free Cycle, take the temperature of the loaf using an instant-read thermometer. It is baked at 200°F (100°C). If it's between 180°F (85°C) and 200°F (100°C), leave machine on the **Keep Warm Cycle** until baked. If it's below 180°F (85°C), turn on the **Bake Cycle** and check the internal temperature every 10 minutes. (Some bread machines are automatically set for 60 minutes; others need to be set by 10-minute intervals.)

Mock Swedish Limpa

**MAKES 15 SLICES
(1 per serving)**

*The traditional
Scandinavian trio of
anise, caraway and
fennel seeds gives this
orange-scented loaf a
unique flavor.*

Tips

To ensure success, see
page 15 for information on
using your bread machine
and page 18 for general tips
on bread machine baking.

For a smoother texture, use
a food mill or a clean coffee
or spice grinder to grind
the seeds.

1¾ cups	sorghum flour	425 mL
½ cup	quinoa flour	125 mL
½ cup	tapioca starch	125 mL
1 tbsp	xanthan gum	15 mL
1¼ tsp	bread machine or instant yeast	6 mL
1¼ tsp	salt	6 mL
1 tbsp	anise seeds	15 mL
1 tbsp	caraway seeds	15 mL
1 tbsp	fennel seeds	15 mL
2 tbsp	grated orange zest	30 mL
1¼ cups	water	300 mL
¼ cup	light (fancy) molasses	60 mL
2 tbsp	vegetable oil	30 mL
1 tsp	cider vinegar	5 mL
2	eggs, lightly beaten	2
2	egg whites, lightly beaten	2

1. In a large bowl or plastic bag, combine sorghum flour, quinoa flour, tapioca starch, xanthan gum, yeast, salt, anise seeds, caraway seeds, fennel seeds and orange zest; mix well and set aside.

2. Pour water, molasses, oil and vinegar into the bread machine baking pan. Add eggs and egg whites.

3. Select the **Dough Cycle**. As the bread machine is mixing, gradually add the dry ingredients, scraping bottom and sides of pan with a rubber spatula. Try to incorporate all the dry ingredients within 1 to 2 minutes. When the mixing and kneading are complete, remove the kneading blade, leaving the bread pan in the bread machine. Quickly smooth the top of the loaf. Allow the cycle to finish. Turn off the bread machine.

NUTRITIONAL VALUES per serving	
Calories	136
Fat, total	3 g
Fat, saturated	0 g
Cholesterol	25 mg
Sodium	213 mg
Carbohydrate	24 g
Fiber	2 g
Protein	4 g
Calcium	34 mg
Iron	2 mg

Variation

Substitute 3 tbsp (45 mL) flaxseed or poppy seeds for the anise, caraway and fennel seeds.

4. Select the **Bake Cycle**. Set time to 60 minutes and temperature to 350°F (180°C). Allow the cycle to finish. Do not turn machine off before taking the internal temperature of the loaf with an instant-read thermometer. It should be 200°F (100°C). If it's between 180°F (85°C) and 200°F (100°C), leave machine on the **Keep Warm Cycle** until baked. If it's below 180°F (85°C), turn on the **Bake Cycle** and check the internal temperature every 10 minutes. (Some bread machines are automatically set for 60 minutes; others need to be set by 10-minute intervals.)

5. Once the loaf has reached 200°F (100°C), remove it from the pan immediately and let cool completely on a rack.

Gluten-Free Cycle

If your bread machine has a Gluten-Free Cycle, you will need to make these adjustments:

1. Warm the water to between 110°F and 115°F (43°C and 46°C).

2. Warm the eggs and egg whites (see the Techniques Glossary, page 238).

3. Follow the recipe instructions, but select the **Gluten-Free Cycle** rather than the Dough Cycle and Bake Cycle.

4. At the end of the Gluten-Free Cycle, take the temperature of the loaf using an instant-read thermometer. It is baked at 200°F (100°C). If it's between 180°F (85°C) and 200°F (100°C), leave machine on the **Keep Warm Cycle** until baked. If it's below 180°F (85°C), turn on the **Bake Cycle** and check the internal temperature every 10 minutes. (Some bread machines are automatically set for 60 minutes; others need to be set by 10-minute intervals.)

Fruited Mock Pumpernickel Loaf

This moist, rich, dark bread is a favorite of our 93-year-old German-born neighbor. With the sweetness of apricots and dates, it's perfect with fresh fruit for lunch.

Tips

To ensure success, see page 15 for information on using your bread machine and page 18 for general tips on bread machine baking.

Pea flour, like soy flour, has a distinctive odor when wet that disappears with baking.

Be sure to sift the cocoa powder, as it tends to lump easily when stored.

Snip dates and apricots with kitchen shears. Dip shears in warm water when they become sticky.

NUTRITIONAL VALUES per serving	
Calories	180
Fat, total	3 g
Fat, saturated	0 g
Cholesterol	37 mg
Sodium	249 mg
Carbohydrate	34 g
Fiber	3 g
Protein	5 g
Calcium	29 mg
Iron	2 mg

1¼ cups	sorghum flour	300 mL
1 cup	pea flour	250 mL
½ cup	cornstarch	125 mL
⅓ cup	tapioca starch	75 mL
3 tbsp	packed brown sugar	45 mL
1 tbsp	xanthan gum	15 mL
1 tsp	bread machine or instant yeast	5 mL
1½ tsp	salt	7 mL
2 tsp	instant coffee granules	10 mL
2 tsp	unsweetened cocoa powder, sifted	10 mL
½ cup	snipped dried apricots	125 mL
½ cup	coarsely snipped pitted dates	125 mL
1⅔ cups	water	400 mL
2 tbsp	vegetable oil	30 mL
3 tbsp	light (fancy) molasses	45 mL
1 tsp	cider vinegar	5 mL
3	eggs, lightly beaten	3

1. In a large bowl or plastic bag, combine sorghum flour, pea flour, cornstarch, tapioca starch, brown sugar, xanthan gum, yeast, salt, coffee granules, cocoa, apricots and dates; mix well and set aside.
2. Pour water, oil, molasses and vinegar into the bread machine baking pan. Add eggs.
3. Select the **Dough Cycle**. As the bread machine is mixing, gradually add the dry ingredients, scraping bottom and sides of pan with a rubber spatula. Try to incorporate all the dry ingredients within 1 to 2 minutes. When the mixing and kneading are complete, remove the kneading blade, leaving the bread pan in the bread machine. Quickly smooth the top of the loaf. Allow the cycle to finish. Turn off the bread machine.

Variations

Substitute chopped prunes or figs for the dates and dried apples for the apricots.

Any type of bean flour can be substituted for the pea flour.

4. Select the **Bake Cycle**. Set time to 60 minutes and temperature to 350°F (180°C). Allow the cycle to finish. Do not turn machine off before taking the internal temperature of the loaf with an instant-read thermometer. It should be 200°F (100°C). If it's between 180°F (85°C) and 200°F (100°C), leave machine on the **Keep Warm Cycle** until baked. If it's below 180°F (85°C), turn on the **Bake Cycle** and check the internal temperature every 10 minutes. (Some bread machines are automatically set for 60 minutes; others need to be set by 10-minute intervals.)

5. Once the loaf has reached 200°F (100°C), remove it from the pan immediately and let cool completely on a rack.

To make this recipe egg-free: Omit eggs from the recipe. Combine ½ cup (125 mL) flax flour or ground flaxseed with an additional ½ cup (125 mL) warm water. Set aside for 5 minutes. Add with the liquids.

Gluten-Free Cycle

If your bread machine has a Gluten-Free Cycle, you will need to make these adjustments:

1. Warm the water to between 110°F and 115°F (43°C and 46°C).

2. Warm the eggs (see the Techniques Glossary, page 238).

3. Follow the recipe instructions, but select the **Gluten-Free Cycle** rather than the Dough Cycle and Bake Cycle.

4. At the end of the Gluten-Free Cycle, take the temperature of the loaf using an instant-read thermometer. It is baked at 200°F (100°C). If it's between 180°F (85°C) and 200°F (100°C), leave machine on the **Keep Warm Cycle** until baked. If it's below 180°F (85°C), turn on the **Bake Cycle** and check the internal temperature every 10 minutes. (Some bread machines are automatically set for 60 minutes; others need to be set by 10-minute intervals.)

Cranberry Pumpkin Seed Bread

This attractive loaf is sure to bring compliments from guests. Pumpkin flavor, flecks of red cranberries and green pumpkin seeds make it the perfect accompaniment for turkey.

Tips

To ensure success, see page 15 for information on using your bread machine and page 18 for general tips on bread machine baking.

See the Techniques Glossary for information on grinding flaxseed to make flax flour (page 238) and toasting seeds (page 240).

1½ cups	sorghum flour	375 mL
⅓ cup	flax flour	75 mL
¼ cup	quinoa flour	60 mL
½ cup	tapioca starch	125 mL
¼ cup	granulated sugar	60 mL
2½ tsp	xanthan gum	12 mL
2 tsp	bread machine or instant yeast	10 mL
1½ tsp	salt	7 mL
¾ cup	dried cranberries	175 mL
½ cup	unsalted green pumpkin seeds, toasted	125 mL
1¼ cups	pumpkin purée (not pie filling)	300 mL
¼ cup	water	60 mL
¼ cup	vegetable oil	60 mL
2 tsp	cider vinegar	10 mL
2	eggs, lightly beaten	2
2	egg whites, lightly beaten	2

1. In a large bowl or plastic bag, combine sorghum flour, flax flour, quinoa flour, tapioca starch, sugar, xanthan gum, yeast, salt, cranberries and pumpkin seeds; mix well and set aside.

2. Pour pumpkin purée, water, oil and vinegar into the bread machine baking pan. Add eggs and egg whites.

3. Select the **Dough Cycle**. As the bread machine is mixing, gradually add the dry ingredients, scraping bottom and sides of pan with a rubber spatula. Try to incorporate all the dry ingredients within 1 to 2 minutes. When the mixing and kneading are complete, remove the kneading blade, leaving the bread pan in the bread machine. Quickly smooth the top of the loaf. Allow the cycle to finish. Turn off the bread machine.

NUTRITIONAL VALUES per serving	
Calories	208
Fat, total	9 g
Fat, saturated	1 g
Cholesterol	25 mg
Sodium	252 mg
Carbohydrate	27 g
Fiber	4 g
Protein	7 g
Calcium	25 mg
Iron	3 mg

Tips

We tried this bread with sprouted flax powder, flax meal and ground flaxseed in place of the flax flour. All yielded acceptable loaves.

Be sure to use pumpkin purée; pumpkin pie filling is too sweet.

Variations

Substitute halved dried cherries for the cranberries.

Substitute chopped pecans or unsalted sunflower seeds for the pumpkin seeds.

4. Select the **Bake Cycle**. Set time to 60 minutes and temperature to 350°F (180°C). Allow the cycle to finish. Do not turn machine off before taking the internal temperature of the loaf with an instant-read thermometer. It should be 200°F (100°C). If it's between 180°F (85°C) and 200°F (100°C), leave machine on the **Keep Warm Cycle** until baked. If it's below 180°F (85°C), turn on the **Bake Cycle** and check the internal temperature every 10 minutes. (Some bread machines are automatically set for 60 minutes; others need to be set by 10-minute intervals.)

5. Once the loaf has reached 200°F (100°C), remove it from the pan immediately and let cool completely on a rack.

Gluten-Free Cycle

If your bread machine has a Gluten-Free Cycle, you will need to make these adjustments:

1. Warm the water to between 110°F and 115°F (43°C and 46°C).

2. Warm the eggs and egg whites (see the Techniques Glossary, page 238).

3. Follow the recipe instructions, but select the **Gluten-Free Cycle** rather than the Dough Cycle and Bake Cycle.

4. At the end of the Gluten-Free Cycle, take the temperature of the loaf using an instant-read thermometer. It is baked at 200°F (100°C). If it's between 180°F (85°C) and 200°F (100°C), leave machine on the **Keep Warm Cycle** until baked. If it's below 180°F (85°C), turn on the **Bake Cycle** and check the internal temperature every 10 minutes. (Some bread machines are automatically set for 60 minutes; others need to be set by 10-minute intervals.)

Cranberry Wild Rice Loaf

This attractive loaf is sure to bring compliments from guests. The nutty taste, with a hint of orange, makes this a perfect accompaniment to duck or turkey.

1¾ cups	brown rice flour	425 mL
⅔ cup	tapioca starch	150 mL
⅓ cup	potato starch	75 mL
¼ cup	granulated sugar	60 mL
2½ tsp	xanthan gum	12 mL
1½ tsp	bread machine or instant yeast	7 mL
1½ tsp	salt	7 mL
2 tsp	grated orange zest	10 mL
¾ tsp	celery seeds	3 mL
⅛ tsp	freshly ground black pepper	0.5 mL
1 cup	cooked wild rice	250 mL
¾ cup	dried cranberries	175 mL
1 cup	water	250 mL
¼ cup	frozen orange juice concentrate, thawed	60 mL
¼ cup	vegetable oil	60 mL
2	eggs, lightly beaten	2
2	egg whites, lightly beaten	2

1. In a large bowl or plastic bag, combine brown rice flour, tapioca starch, potato starch, sugar, xanthan gum, yeast, salt, orange zest, celery seeds, pepper, wild rice and cranberries; mix well and set aside.

2. Pour water, orange juice concentrate and oil into the bread machine baking pan. Add eggs and egg whites.

3. Select the **Dough Cycle**. As the bread machine is mixing, gradually add the dry ingredients, scraping bottom and sides of pan with a rubber spatula. Try to incorporate all the dry ingredients within 1 to 2 minutes. When the mixing and kneading are complete, remove the kneading blade, leaving the bread pan in the bread machine. Quickly smooth the top of the loaf. Allow the cycle to finish. Turn off the bread machine.

NUTRITIONAL VALUES
per serving

Calories	192
Fat, total	5 g
Fat, saturated	1 g
Cholesterol	25 mg
Sodium	250 mg
Carbohydrate	34 g
Fiber	2 g
Protein	3 g
Calcium	11 mg
Iron	1 mg

To ensure success, see page 15 for information on using your bread machine and page 18 for general tips on bread machine baking.

Try using raspberry- or orange-flavored dried cranberries.

4. Select the **Bake Cycle**. Set time to 60 minutes and temperature to 350°F (180°C). Allow the cycle to finish. Do not turn machine off before taking the internal temperature of the loaf with an instant-read thermometer. It should be 200°F (100°C). If it's between 180°F (85°C) and 200°F (100°C), leave machine on the **Keep Warm Cycle** until baked. If it's below 180°F (85°C), turn on the **Bake Cycle** and check the internal temperature every 10 minutes. (Some bread machines are automatically set for 60 minutes; others need to be set by 10-minute intervals.)

5. Once the loaf has reached 200°F (100°C), remove it from the pan immediately and let cool completely on a rack.

Gluten-Free Cycle

If your bread machine has a Gluten-Free Cycle, you will need to make these adjustments:

1. Warm the water to between 110°F and 115°F (43°C and 46°C).

2. Warm the eggs and egg whites (see the Techniques Glossary, page 238).

3. Follow the recipe instructions, but select the **Gluten-Free Cycle** rather than the Dough Cycle and Bake Cycle.

4. At the end of the Gluten-Free Cycle, take the temperature of the loaf using an instant-read thermometer. It is baked at 200°F (100°C). If it's between 180°F (85°C) and 200°F (100°C), leave machine on the **Keep Warm Cycle** until baked. If it's below 180°F (85°C), turn on the **Bake Cycle** and check the internal temperature every 10 minutes. (Some bread machines are automatically set for 60 minutes; others need to be set by 10-minute intervals.)

Sun-Dried Tomato Rice Loaf

Here's a savory version of the Cranberry Wild Rice Loaf (page 90), suggested by Larry, a member of our focus group.

Tips

To ensure success, see page 15 for information on using your bread machine and page 18 for general tips on bread machine baking.

Use dry, not oil-packed, sun-dried tomatoes. Snip them with kitchen shears.

See the Techniques Glossary, page 240, for instructions on cooking wild rice.

1¾ cups	brown rice flour	425 mL
⅔ cup	tapioca starch	150 mL
⅓ cup	potato starch	75 mL
¼ cup	granulated sugar	60 mL
2½ tsp	xanthan gum	12 mL
1½ tsp	bread machine or instant yeast	7 mL
½ tsp	salt	2 mL
¾ tsp	celery seeds	3 mL
¼ tsp	freshly ground black pepper	1 mL
1 cup	cooked wild rice	250 mL
⅔ cup	snipped sun-dried tomatoes	150 mL
1¼ cups	water	300 mL
¼ cup	vegetable oil	60 mL
2	eggs, lightly beaten	2
2	egg whites, lightly beaten	2

1. In a large bowl or plastic bag, combine brown rice flour, tapioca starch, potato starch, sugar, xanthan gum, yeast, salt, celery seeds, pepper, wild rice and sun-dried tomatoes; mix well and set aside.

2. Pour water and oil into the bread machine baking pan. Add eggs and egg whites.

3. Select the **Dough Cycle**. As the bread machine is mixing, gradually add the dry ingredients, scraping bottom and sides of pan with a rubber spatula. Try to incorporate all the dry ingredients within 1 to 2 minutes. When the mixing and kneading are complete, remove the kneading blade, leaving the bread pan in the bread machine. Quickly smooth the top of the loaf. Allow the cycle to finish. Turn off the bread machine.

4. Select the **Bake Cycle**. Set time to 60 minutes and temperature to 350°F (180°C). Allow the cycle to finish. Do not turn machine off before taking the internal temperature of the loaf with an instant-read thermometer. It should be 200°F (100°C). If it's between 180°F (85°C) and 200°F (100°C), leave machine on the **Keep Warm Cycle** until baked. If it's below 180°F (85°C), turn on the **Bake Cycle** and check the internal temperature every 10 minutes. (Some bread machines are automatically set for 60 minutes; others need to be set by 10-minute intervals.)

NUTRITIONAL VALUES	
per serving	
Calories	172
Fat, total	5 g
Fat, saturated	1 g
Cholesterol	25 mg
Sodium	145 mg
Carbohydrate	29 g
Fiber	1 g
Protein	4 g
Calcium	12 mg
Iron	1 mg

5. Once the loaf has reached 200°F (100°C), remove it from the pan immediately and let cool completely on a rack.

Gluten-Free Cycle

If your bread machine has a Gluten-Free Cycle, you will need to make these adjustments:

1. Warm the water to between 110°F and 115°F (43°C and 46°C).

2. Warm the eggs and egg whites (see the Techniques Glossary, page 238).

3. Follow the recipe instructions, but select the **Gluten-Free Cycle** rather than the Dough Cycle and Bake Cycle.

4. At the end of the Gluten-Free Cycle, take the temperature of the loaf using an instant-read thermometer. It is baked at 200°F (100°C). If it's between 180°F (85°C) and 200°F (100°C), leave machine on the **Keep Warm Cycle** until baked. If it's below 180°F (85°C), turn on the **Bake Cycle** and check the internal temperature every 10 minutes. (Some bread machines are automatically set for 60 minutes; others need to be set by 10-minute intervals.)

Tomato Rosemary Bread

This pretty loaf is packed full of flavor.

Tips

To ensure success, see page 15 for information on using your bread machine and page 18 for general tips on bread machine baking.

The tomato vegetable juice should be at room temperature. If using it cold from the refrigerator, warm it on High in the microwave for 1 minute.

1 cup	sorghum flour	250 mL
½ cup	whole bean flour	125 mL
½ cup	cornstarch	125 mL
¼ cup	granulated sugar	60 mL
1 tbsp	xanthan gum	15 mL
2 tsp	bread machine or instant yeast	10 mL
½ tsp	salt	2 mL
2 tsp	dried rosemary	10 mL
½ cup	snipped sun-dried tomatoes	125 mL
1⅓ cups	tomato vegetable juice	300 mL
¼ cup	vegetable oil	60 mL
2	eggs, lightly beaten	2

1. In a large bowl or plastic bag, combine sorghum flour, whole bean flour, cornstarch, sugar, xanthan gum, yeast, salt, rosemary and sun-dried tomatoes; mix well and set aside.

2. Pour vegetable juice and oil into the bread machine baking pan. Add eggs.

3. Select the **Dough Cycle**. As the bread machine is mixing, gradually add the dry ingredients, scraping bottom and sides of pan with a rubber spatula. Try to incorporate all the dry ingredients within 1 to 2 minutes. When the mixing and kneading are complete, remove the kneading blade, leaving the bread pan in the bread machine. Quickly smooth the top of the loaf. Allow the cycle to finish. Turn off the bread machine.

4. Select the **Bake Cycle**. Set time to 60 minutes and temperature to 350°F (180°C). Allow the cycle to finish. Do not turn machine off before taking the internal temperature of the loaf with an instant-read thermometer. It should be 200°F (100°C). If it's between 180°F (85°C) and 200°F (100°C), leave machine on the **Keep Warm Cycle** until baked. If it's below 180°F (85°C), turn on the **Bake Cycle** and check the internal temperature every 10 minutes. (Some bread machines are automatically set for 60 minutes; others need to be set by 10-minute intervals.)

5. Once the loaf has reached 200°F (100°C), remove it from the pan immediately and let cool completely on a rack.

NUTRITIONAL VALUES
per serving

Calories	117
Fat, total	5 g
Fat, saturated	0 g
Cholesterol	25 mg
Sodium	124 mg
Carbohydrate	17 g
Fiber	1 g
Protein	3 g
Calcium	12 mg
Iron	1 mg

Gluten-Free Cycle

If your bread machine has a Gluten-Free Cycle, you will need to make these adjustments:

1. Warm the tomato vegetable juice to between 110°F and 115°F (43°C and 46°C).
2. Warm the eggs (see the Techniques Glossary, page 238).
3. Follow the recipe instructions, but select the **Gluten-Free Cycle** rather than the Dough Cycle and Bake Cycle.
4. At the end of the Gluten-Free Cycle, take the temperature of the loaf using an instant-read thermometer. It is baked at 200°F (100°C). If it's between 180°F (85°C) and 200°F (100°C), leave machine on the **Keep Warm Cycle** until baked. If it's below 180°F (85°C), turn on the **Bake Cycle** and check the internal temperature every 10 minutes. (Some bread machines are automatically set for 60 minutes; others need to be set by 10-minute intervals.)

Cheese Onion Loaf

This bread is a perfect accompaniment to homemade chili or beef stew. It slices well and stays moist for a second day.

Tips

To ensure success, see page 15 for information on using your bread machine and page 18 for general tips on bread machine baking.

Do not substitute fresh onion for the dried onion. The extra moisture will lead to a weak-flavored, shorter loaf.

For the amount of cheese to purchase, see the weight/ volume equivalents in the Ingredient Glossary, page 233.

1²⁄₃ cups	brown rice flour	400 mL
²⁄₃ cup	sorghum flour	150 mL
¹⁄₃ cup	arrowroot starch	75 mL
¹⁄₄ cup	nonfat dry milk or skim milk powder	60 mL
2 tbsp	granulated sugar	30 mL
1 tbsp	xanthan gum	15 mL
1¹⁄₂ tsp	bread machine or instant yeast	7 mL
1¹⁄₄ tsp	salt	6 mL
1 cup	shredded sharp (old) Cheddar cheese	250 mL
¹⁄₄ cup	freshly grated Parmesan cheese	60 mL
2 tbsp	minced dried onion	30 mL
¹⁄₄ tsp	dry mustard	1 mL
1¹⁄₄ cups	water	300 mL
2 tsp	cider vinegar	10 mL
2	eggs, lightly beaten	2
2	egg whites, lightly beaten	2

1. In a large bowl or plastic bag, combine brown rice flour, sorghum flour, arrowroot starch, dry milk, sugar, xanthan gum, yeast, salt, Cheddar, Parmesan, onion and mustard; mix well and set aside.

2. Pour water and vinegar into the bread machine baking pan. Add eggs and egg whites.

3. Select the **Dough Cycle**. As the bread machine is mixing, gradually add the dry ingredients, scraping bottom and sides of pan with a rubber spatula. Try to incorporate all the dry ingredients within 1 to 2 minutes. When the mixing and kneading are complete, remove the kneading blade, leaving the bread pan in the bread machine. Quickly smooth the top of the loaf. Allow the cycle to finish. Turn off the bread machine.

NUTRITIONAL VALUES per serving	
Calories	157
Fat, total	4 g
Fat, saturated	2 g
Cholesterol	33 mg
Sodium	266 mg
Carbohydrate	26 g
Fiber	1 g
Protein	6 g
Calcium	79 mg
Iron	1 mg

Variation

You can replace the Cheddar cheese with Monterey Jack or Swiss cheese. Or try a combination, but do not exceed the total volume in the recipe or the loaf will be short and heavy.

4. Select the **Bake Cycle**. Set time to 60 minutes and temperature to 350°F (180°C). Allow the cycle to finish. Do not turn machine off before taking the internal temperature of the loaf with an instant-read thermometer. It should be 200°F (100°C). If it's between 180°F (85°C) and 200°F (100°C), leave machine on the **Keep Warm Cycle** until baked. If it's below 180°F (85°C), turn on the **Bake Cycle** and check the internal temperature every 10 minutes. (Some bread machines are automatically set for 60 minutes; others need to be set by 10-minute intervals.)

5. Once the loaf has reached 200°F (100°C), remove it from the pan immediately and let cool completely on a rack.

Gluten-Free Cycle

If your bread machine has a Gluten-Free Cycle, you will need to make these adjustments:

1. Warm the water to between 110°F and 115°F (43°C and 46°C).

2. Warm the eggs and egg whites (see the Techniques Glossary, page 238).

3. Follow the recipe instructions, but select the **Gluten-Free Cycle** rather than the Dough Cycle and Bake Cycle.

4. At the end of the Gluten-Free Cycle, take the temperature of the loaf using an instant-read thermometer. It is baked at 200°F (100°C). If it's between 180°F (85°C) and 200°F (100°C), leave machine on the **Keep Warm Cycle** until baked. If it's below 180°F (85°C), turn on the **Bake Cycle** and check the internal temperature every 10 minutes. (Some bread machines are automatically set for 60 minutes; others need to be set by 10-minute intervals.)

Cottage Cheese Dill Loaf

MAKES 15 SLICES
(1 per serving)

Serve this twist on traditional white bread with salmon or your favorite seafood entrée.

Tips

To ensure success, see page 15 for information on using your bread machine and page 18 for general tips on bread machine baking.

Any type of cottage cheese — large- or small-curd, high- or low-fat — works well in this recipe.

2 cups	brown rice flour	500 mL
2/3 cup	potato starch	150 mL
1/3 cup	tapioca starch	75 mL
2 1/2 tsp	xanthan gum	12 mL
1 3/4 tsp	bread machine or instant yeast	8 mL
1 1/2 tsp	salt	7 mL
1 1/2 tsp	dried dillweed	7 mL
1 cup	water	250 mL
1/2 cup	cottage cheese (see tip, at left)	125 mL
1/4 cup	vegetable oil	60 mL
1/4 cup	liquid honey	60 mL
1 tsp	cider vinegar	5 mL
4	eggs, lightly beaten	4

1. In a large bowl or plastic bag, combine brown rice flour, potato starch, tapioca starch, xanthan gum, yeast, salt and dill; mix well and set aside.

2. Pour water, cottage cheese, oil, honey, and vinegar into the bread machine baking pan. Add eggs.

3. Select the **Dough Cycle**. As the bread machine is mixing, gradually add the dry ingredients, scraping bottom and sides of pan with a rubber spatula. Try to incorporate all the dry ingredients within 1 to 2 minutes. When the mixing and kneading are complete, remove the kneading blade, leaving the bread pan in the bread machine. Quickly smooth the top of the loaf. Allow the cycle to finish. Turn off the bread machine.

4. Select the **Bake Cycle**. Set time to 60 minutes and temperature to 350°F (180°C). Allow the cycle to finish. Do not turn machine off before taking the internal temperature of the loaf with an instant-read thermometer. It should be 200°F (100°C). If it's between 180°F (85°C) and 200°F (100°C), leave machine on the **Keep Warm Cycle** until baked. If it's below 180°F (85°C), turn on the **Bake Cycle** and check the internal temperature every 10 minutes. (Some bread machines are automatically set for 60 minutes; others need to be set by 10-minute intervals.)

5. Once the loaf has reached 200°F (100°C), remove it from the pan immediately and let cool completely on a rack.

NUTRITIONAL VALUES
per serving

Calories	179
Fat, total	5 g
Fat, saturated	1 g
Cholesterol	51 mg
Sodium	277 mg
Carbohydrate	30 g
Fiber	1 g
Protein	4 g
Calcium	18 mg
Iron	1 mg

Variation

Substitute rosemary, marjoram or savory for the dill.

Gluten-Free Cycle

If your bread machine has a Gluten-Free Cycle, you will need to make these adjustments:

1. Warm the water to between 110°F and 115°F (43°C and 46°C).

2. Warm the eggs (see the Techniques Glossary, page 238).

3. Follow the recipe instructions, but select the **Gluten-Free Cycle** rather than the Dough Cycle and Bake Cycle.

4. At the end of the Gluten-Free Cycle, take the temperature of the loaf using an instant-read thermometer. It is baked at 200°F (100°C). If it's between 180°F (85°C) and 200°F (100°C), leave machine on the **Keep Warm Cycle** until baked. If it's below 180°F (85°C), turn on the **Bake Cycle** and check the internal temperature every 10 minutes. (Some bread machines are automatically set for 60 minutes; others need to be set by 10-minute intervals.)

Roasted Garlic Potato Bread

This flavorful loaf with a warm, creamy color is a perfect accompaniment to soup on a cold winter's night.

Tips

To ensure success, see page 15 for information on using your bread machine and page 18 for general tips on bread machine baking.

For information on roasting garlic, see the Techniques Glossary, page 240.

Normally, garlic and yeast are enemies; however, they get along well after garlic is roasted. Still, even roasted garlic inhibits the action of the yeast, so avoid the temptation to use more than 3 cloves. Too much garlic, and the loaf will be short and heavy.

NUTRITIONAL VALUES per serving	
Calories	154
Fat, total	7 g
Fat, saturated	1 g
Cholesterol	25 mg
Sodium	253 mg
Carbohydrate	20 g
Fiber	2 g
Protein	4 g
Calcium	32 mg
Iron	2 mg

1 cup	brown rice flour	250 mL
1 cup	almond flour	250 mL
½ cup	amaranth flour	125 mL
⅓ cup	potato starch	75 mL
1 tbsp	xanthan gum	15 mL
1¾ tsp	bread machine or instant yeast	8 mL
1½ tsp	salt	7 mL
½ cup	instant potato flakes	125 mL
1⅓ cups	water	325 mL
2 tbsp	extra virgin olive oil	30 mL
3 tbsp	liquid honey	45 mL
1 tsp	cider vinegar	5 mL
3	cloves roasted garlic (see tips, at left)	3
2	eggs, lightly beaten	2
2	egg whites, lightly beaten	2

1. In a large bowl or plastic bag, combine brown rice flour, almond flour, amaranth flour, potato starch, xanthan gum, yeast, salt and potato flakes; mix well and set aside.

2. Pour water, oil, honey, vinegar and garlic into the bread machine baking pan. Add eggs and egg whites.

3. Select the **Dough Cycle**. As the bread machine is mixing, gradually add the dry ingredients, scraping bottom and sides of pan with a rubber spatula. Try to incorporate all the dry ingredients within 1 to 2 minutes. When the mixing and kneading are complete, remove the kneading blade, leaving the bread pan in the bread machine. Quickly smooth the top of the loaf. Allow the cycle to finish. Turn off the bread machine.

4. Select the **Bake Cycle**. Set time to 60 minutes and temperature to 350°F (180°C). Allow the cycle to finish. Do not turn machine off before taking the internal temperature of the loaf with an instant-read thermometer. It should be 200°F (100°C). If it's between 180°F (85°C) and 200°F (100°C), leave machine on the **Keep Warm Cycle** until baked. If it's below 180°F (85°C), turn on the **Bake Cycle** and check the internal temperature every 10 minutes. (Some bread machines are automatically set for 60 minutes; others need to be set by 10-minute intervals.)

Variations

Substitute ⅓ cup (75 mL) mashed potato for the instant potato flakes. Add with the liquids.

For a stronger, more prominent garlic flavor, serve toasted or warmed with either a garlic butter or a garlic-flavored spread.

Potato Chive Bread: Omit the roasted garlic and add ¼ cup (60 mL) snipped fresh parsley and ⅓ cup (75 mL) snipped fresh chives with the liquids.

Potato Dill Bread: Omit the roasted garlic and add ¼ cup (60 mL) snipped fresh dill with the liquids.

5. Once the loaf has reached 200°F (100°C), remove it from the pan immediately and let cool completely on a rack.

Gluten-Free Cycle

If your bread machine has a Gluten-Free Cycle, you will need to make these adjustments:

1. Warm the water to between 110°F and 115°F (43°C and 46°C).
2. Warm the eggs and egg whites (see the Techniques Glossary, page 238).
3. Follow the recipe instructions, but select the **Gluten-Free Cycle** rather than the Dough Cycle and Bake Cycle.
4. At the end of the Gluten-Free Cycle, take the temperature of the loaf using an instant-read thermometer. It is baked at 200°F (100°C). If it's between 180°F (85°C) and 200°F (100°C), leave machine on the **Keep Warm Cycle** until baked. If it's below 180°F (85°C), turn on the **Bake Cycle** and check the internal temperature every 10 minutes. (Some bread machines are automatically set for 60 minutes; others need to be set by 10-minute intervals.)

Cornbread

MAKES 15 SLICES
(1 per serving)

Tiny bits of moist corn kernels dot this warm yellow loaf.

Tips

To ensure success, see page 15 for information on using your bread machine and page 18 for general tips on bread machine baking.

Drain canned corn before measuring. If using frozen corn, thaw and drain before measuring.

1¼ cups	brown rice flour	300 mL
1 cup	cornmeal	250 mL
½ cup	potato starch	125 mL
¼ cup	tapioca starch	60 mL
3 tbsp	granulated sugar	45 mL
1 tbsp	xanthan gum	15 mL
2 tsp	bread machine or instant yeast	10 mL
1½ tsp	salt	7 mL
1¼ cups	water	300 mL
¼ cup	vegetable oil	60 mL
1 tsp	cider vinegar	5 mL
1 cup	well-drained corn kernels	250 mL
3	eggs, lightly beaten	3
2	egg whites, lightly beaten	2

1. In a large bowl or plastic bag, combine brown rice flour, cornmeal, potato starch, tapioca starch, sugar, xanthan gum, yeast and salt; mix well and set aside.

2. Pour water, oil, vinegar and corn into bread machine baking pan. Add eggs and egg whites.

3. Select the **Dough Cycle**. As the bread machine is mixing, gradually add the dry ingredients, scraping bottom and sides of pan with a rubber spatula. Try to incorporate all the dry ingredients within 1 to 2 minutes. When the mixing and kneading are complete, remove the kneading blade, leaving the bread pan in the bread machine. Quickly smooth the top of the loaf. Allow the cycle to finish. Turn off the bread machine.

4. Select the **Bake Cycle**. Set time to 60 minutes and temperature to 350°F (180°C). Allow the cycle to finish. Do not turn machine off before taking the internal temperature of the loaf with an instant-read thermometer. It should be 200°F (100°C). If it's between 180°F (85°C) and 200°F (100°C), leave machine on the **Keep Warm Cycle** until baked. If it's below 180°F (85°C), turn on the **Bake Cycle** and check the internal temperature every 10 minutes. (Some bread machines are automatically set for 60 minutes; others need to be set by 10-minute intervals.)

5. Once the loaf has reached 200°F (100°C), remove it from the pan immediately and let cool completely on a rack.

NUTRITIONAL VALUES
per serving

Calories	175
Fat, total	5 g
Fat, saturated	1 g
Cholesterol	37 mg
Sodium	255 mg
Carbohydrate	29 g
Fiber	2 g
Protein	4 g
Calcium	9 mg
Iron	1 mg

Variations

Add ¼ cup (60 mL) freshly grated Parmesan cheese or 2 or 3 strips of crumbled crisp bacon with the dry ingredients.

Add ½ cup (125 mL) finely chopped red and/or green bell peppers with the corn.

Gluten-Free Cycle

If your bread machine has a Gluten-Free Cycle, you will need to make these adjustments:

1. Warm the water to between 110°F and 115°F (43°C and 46°C).

2. Warm the eggs and egg whites (see the Techniques Glossary, page 238).

3. Follow the recipe instructions, but select the **Gluten-Free Cycle** rather than the Dough Cycle and Bake Cycle.

4. At the end of the Gluten-Free Cycle, take the temperature of the loaf using an instant-read thermometer. It is baked at 200°F (100°C). If it's between 180°F (85°C) and 200°F (100°C), leave machine on the **Keep Warm Cycle** until baked. If it's below 180°F (85°C), turn on the **Bake Cycle** and check the internal temperature every 10 minutes. (Some bread machines are automatically set for 60 minutes; others need to be set by 10-minute intervals.)

Sun-Dried Tomato Cornbread

MAKES 15 SLICES
(1 per serving)

Serve this moist savory cornbread, flavored with salty bursts of sun-dried tomatoes, with salad for lunch.

Tips

To ensure success, see page 15 for information on using your bread machine and page 18 for general tips on bread machine baking.

Use dry, not oil-packed, sun-dried tomatoes in this recipe. Snip them with kitchen shears.

1½ cups	amaranth flour	375 mL
1 cup	cornmeal	250 mL
½ cup	tapioca starch	125 mL
3 tbsp	granulated sugar	45 mL
1 tbsp	xanthan gum	15 mL
2 tsp	bread machine or instant yeast	10 mL
1¼ tsp	salt	6 mL
⅔ cup	snipped sun-dried tomatoes	150 mL
1¼ cups	water	300 mL
¼ cup	vegetable oil	60 mL
1 tsp	cider vinegar	5 mL
3	eggs, lightly beaten	3
2	egg whites, lightly beaten	2

1. In a large bowl or plastic bag, combine amaranth flour, cornmeal, tapioca starch, sugar, xanthan gum, yeast, salt and sun-dried tomatoes; mix well and set aside.

2. Pour water, oil and vinegar into the bread machine baking pan. Add eggs and egg whites.

3. Select the **Dough Cycle**. As the bread machine is mixing, gradually add the dry ingredients, scraping bottom and sides of pan with a rubber spatula. Try to incorporate all the dry ingredients within 1 to 2 minutes. When the mixing and kneading are complete, remove the kneading blade, leaving the bread pan in the bread machine. Quickly smooth the top of the loaf. Allow the cycle to finish. Turn off the bread machine.

4. Select the **Bake Cycle**. Set time to 60 minutes and temperature to 350°F (180°C). Allow the cycle to finish. Do not turn machine off before taking the internal temperature of the loaf with an instant-read thermometer. It should be 200°F (100°C). If it's between 180°F (85°C) and 200°F (100°C), leave machine on the **Keep Warm Cycle** until baked. If it's below 180°F (85°C), turn on the **Bake Cycle** and check the internal temperature every 10 minutes. (Some bread machines are automatically set for 60 minutes; others need to be set by 10-minute intervals.)

5. Once the loaf has reached 200°F (100°C), remove it from the pan immediately and let cool completely on a rack.

NUTRITIONAL VALUES	
per serving	
Calories	159
Fat, total	5 g
Fat, saturated	1 g
Cholesterol	37 mg
Sodium	263 mg
Carbohydrate	23 g
Fiber	2 g
Protein	5 g
Calcium	25 mg
Iron	3 mg

Variation

Add ½ cup (125 mL) thinly sliced green onions with the sun-dried tomatoes.

Gluten-Free Cycle

If your bread machine has a Gluten-Free Cycle, you will need to make these adjustments:

1. Warm the water to between 110°F and 115°F (43°C and 46°C).

2. Warm the eggs and egg whites (see the Techniques Glossary, page 238).

3. Follow the recipe instructions, but select the **Gluten-Free Cycle** rather than the Dough Cycle and Bake Cycle.

4. At the end of the Gluten-Free Cycle, take the temperature of the loaf using an instant-read thermometer. It is baked at 200°F (100°C). If it's between 180°F (85°C) and 200°F (100°C), leave machine on the **Keep Warm Cycle** until baked. If it's below 180°F (85°C), turn on the **Bake Cycle** and check the internal temperature every 10 minutes. (Some bread machines are automatically set for 60 minutes; others need to be set by 10-minute intervals.)

Oatmeal Casserole Bread

Casserole breads are so easy to make. Cut this soft, sweet loaf into slices for a breakfast or brunch buffet.

Tips

To ensure success, see page 15 for information on using your bread machine and page 18 for general tips on bread machine baking.

If desired, you can sprinkle the top of the risen loaf with 2 tbsp (30 mL) GF oats before baking.

Variation

Add 1 cup (250 mL) raisins or chopped dates with the dry ingredients.

◆ **10-cup (2.5 L) casserole dish, lightly greased**

¾ cup	brown rice flour	175 mL
½ cup	GF oat flour	125 mL
½ cup	sorghum flour	125 mL
⅓ cup	tapioca starch	75 mL
1 cup	GF oats	250 mL
2½ tsp	xanthan gum	12 mL
1 tbsp	bread machine yeast	15 mL
1½ tsp	salt	7 mL
¼ cup	nonfat dry milk or skim milk powder	60 mL
1¼ cups	water	300 mL
⅓ cup	liquid honey	75 mL
2 tbsp	vegetable oil	30 mL
1 tsp	cider vinegar	5 mL
2	eggs, lightly beaten	2

1. In a large bowl or plastic bag, combine brown rice flour, oat flour, sorghum flour, tapioca starch, oats, xanthan gum, yeast, salt and dry milk; mix well and set aside.

2. Pour water, honey, oil and vinegar into the bread machine baking pan. Add eggs.

3. Select the **Dough Cycle**. As the bread machine is mixing, gradually add the dry ingredients, scraping bottom and sides of pan with a rubber spatula. Try to incorporate all the dry ingredients within 1 to 2 minutes. Stop bread machine as soon as the kneading portion of the cycle is complete. Do not let bread machine finish the cycle.

4. Using a rubber spatula, pour dough into prepared dish, making sure not to fill it more than half-full. Let rise, uncovered, in a warm, draft-free place for 60 minutes. Meanwhile, preheat oven to 350°F (180°C).

5. Bake for 25 minutes. Tent loaf with foil and bake for 15 to 20 minutes or until deep golden brown. Serve warm.

NUTRITIONAL VALUES per serving	
Calories	143
Fat, total	3 g
Fat, saturated	1 g
Cholesterol	24 mg
Sodium	232 mg
Carbohydrate	25 g
Fiber	2 g
Protein	4 g
Calcium	27 mg
Iron	1 mg

Mixes and Sourdoughs

Single-Loaf White Bread Mix

**MAKES ABOUT
3½ CUPS (875 ML),
ENOUGH FOR
1 LOAF**

*You asked us for a white
bread mix you could
use to make a variety
of nutritious loaves and
rolls. We've done you
one better and given
you the recipe in three
different batch sizes.
Here's a single-loaf mix
you can try before making
the larger batches on
pages 109 and 110. You
can use this mix to make
Dinner Rolls (page 111),
Sandwich Bread
(page 112), Cheese Rolls
(page 114), Rosemary
Breadsticks (page 115) or
Orange Chocolate Chip
Loaf (page 116). This
is sure to become your
favorite nutritious white
bread mix.*

1¼ cups	brown rice flour	300 mL
½ cup	almond flour	125 mL
½ cup	amaranth flour	125 mL
½ cup	quinoa flour	125 mL
⅓ cup	potato starch	75 mL
¼ cup	tapioca starch	60 mL
1 tbsp	xanthan gum	15 mL
1¼ tsp	bread machine or instant yeast	6 mL
1¼ tsp	salt	6 mL

1. In a large bowl, combine brown rice flour, almond flour, amaranth flour, quinoa flour, potato starch, tapioca starch, xanthan gum, yeast and salt; mix well.

2. Use right away or seal tightly in a plastic bag, removing as much air as possible. Store at room temperature for up to 3 days or in the freezer for up to 6 months.

Working with Bread Mix

- Label and date the package if not using bread mix immediately. We add the page number of the recipe to the label as a quick reference.
- Let bread mix warm to room temperature, and mix well before using.

NUTRITIONAL VALUES per serving	
Calories	113
Fat, total	3 g
Fat, saturated	0 g
Cholesterol	0 mg
Sodium	198 mg
Carbohydrate	20 g
Fiber	2 g
Protein	3 g
Calcium	19 mg
Iron	2 mg

Four-Loaf White Bread Mix

*Here's the four-loaf
version of our bread
machine white bread
mix. Use it to make the
recipes on pages 112–116.*

Tips

For accuracy, use a 1-cup
(250 mL) dry measure
several times to measure
each type of flour and
starch. If you use a 4-cup
(1 L) liquid measure, it's
difficult to get an accurate
volume and you'll end up
with extra flour in the mix.

We used a large roasting
pan to combine all the
ingredients.

5 cups	brown rice flour	1.25 L
2 cups	almond flour	500 mL
2 cups	amaranth flour	500 mL
2 cups	quinoa flour	500 mL
$1\frac{1}{3}$ cups	potato starch	325 mL
1 cup	tapioca starch	250 mL
$\frac{1}{4}$ cup	xanthan gum	60 mL
2 tbsp	bread machine or instant yeast	30 mL
2 tbsp	salt	30 mL

1. In a very large container, combine brown rice flour, almond flour, amaranth flour, quinoa flour, potato starch, tapioca starch, xanthan gum, yeast and salt; mix well.

2. Divide into 4 equal portions of about $3\frac{1}{2}$ cups (875 mL) each. Seal tightly in plastic bags, removing as much air as possible. Store at room temperature for up to 3 days or in the freezer for up to 6 weeks.

Working with Bread Mix

- In step 2, stir the mix before spooning it very lightly into the dry measures. Do not pack.

- Be sure to divide the mix into equal portions. Depending on how much air you incorporate into the mix, and the texture of the individual gluten-free flours, the total volume of the mix can vary slightly. The important thing is to make the number of portions specified in the recipe.

- Label and date the packages before storing. We add the page number of the recipe to the labels as a quick reference.

- Let bread mix warm to room temperature, and mix well before using.

NUTRITIONAL VALUES per serving	
Calories	118
Fat, total	3 g
Fat, saturated	0 g
Cholesterol	0 mg
Sodium	236 mg
Carbohydrate	21 g
Fiber	2 g
Protein	3 g
Calcium	20 mg
Iron	2 mg

Six-Loaf White Bread Mix

*When you want to make
a really big batch of
white bread mix, this is
the recipe for you. Use it
to make the recipes on
pages 112–116.*

Tips

For accuracy, use a 1-cup
(250 mL) dry measure
several times to measure
each type of flour and
starch. If you use a 4-cup
(1 L) liquid measure, it's
difficult to get an accurate
volume and you'll end up
with extra flour in the mix.

We used a large roasting
pan to combine all the
ingredients.

7½ cups	brown rice flour	1.875 L
3 cups	almond flour	750 mL
3 cups	amaranth flour	750 mL
3 cups	quinoa flour	750 mL
2 cups	potato starch	500 mL
1½ cups	tapioca starch	375 mL
⅓ cup	xanthan gum	75 mL
2½ tbsp	bread machine or instant yeast	37 mL
3 tbsp	salt	45 mL

1. In a very large container, combine brown rice flour, almond flour, amaranth flour, quinoa flour, potato starch, tapioca starch, xanthan gum, yeast and salt; mix well. (When working with this large volume of ingredients, it is especially important to mix them very well before portioning.)

2. Divide into 6 equal portions of about 3½ cups (875 mL) each. Seal tightly in plastic bags, removing as much air as possible. Store at room temperature for up to 3 days or freeze for up to 6 weeks.

Working with Bread Mix

- In step 2, stir the mix before spooning it very lightly into the dry measures. Do not pack.
- Be sure to divide the mix into equal portions. Depending on how much air you incorporate into the mix, and the texture of the individual gluten-free flours, the total volume of the mix can vary slightly. The important thing is to make the number of portions specified in the recipe.
- Label and date the packages before storing. We add the page number of the recipe to the labels as a quick reference.
- Let bread mix warm to room temperature, and mix well before using.

NUTRITIONAL VALUES	
per serving	
Calories	105
Fat, total	3 g
Fat, saturated	0 g
Cholesterol	0 mg
Sodium	198 mg
Carbohydrate	18 g
Fiber	2 g
Protein	3 g
Calcium	14 mg
Iron	1 mg

Dinner Rolls

MAKES 12 ROLLS
(1 per serving)

Everyone loves a golden brown dinner roll, and they're so easy to make from our mix.

Tips

To ensure success, see page 15 for information on using your bread machine and page 18 for general tips on bread machine baking.

For a softer crust, brush the rolls with melted butter as soon as you remove them from the oven.

You can use ½ cup (125 mL) liquid whole eggs and 2 tbsp (30 mL) liquid egg white, if you prefer.

◆ **12-cup muffin tin, lightly greased**

1¼ cups	water	300 mL
¼ cup	liquid honey	60 mL
2 tbsp	vegetable oil	30 mL
1 tsp	cider vinegar	5 mL
2	eggs, lightly beaten	2
1	egg white, lightly beaten	1
3½ cups	White Bread Mix (pages 108–110)	875 mL

1. Pour water, honey, oil and vinegar into the bread machine baking pan. Add eggs and egg white.

2. Select the **Dough Cycle**. As the bread machine is mixing, gradually add the bread mix, scraping bottom and sides of pan with a rubber spatula. Try to incorporate all the bread mix within 1 to 2 minutes. Stop bread machine as soon as the kneading portion of the cycle is complete. Do not let bread machine finish the cycle.

3. Using a ¼-cup (60 mL) scoop, divide dough into 12 equal amounts and place in cups of prepared muffin tin. Let rise, uncovered, in a warm, draft-free place for 60 to 75 minutes or until dough has risen to the top of the cups. Meanwhile, preheat oven to 350°F (180°C).

4. Bake for 18 to 20 minutes or until internal temperature of rolls registers 200°F (100°C) on an instant-read thermometer. Remove from the tin immediately and let cool completely on a rack.

NUTRITIONAL VALUES
per serving

Calories	185
Fat, total	6 g
Fat, saturated	1 g
Cholesterol	25 mg
Sodium	262 mg
Carbohydrate	29 g
Fiber	3 g
Protein	4 g
Calcium	22 mg
Iron	1 mg

Sandwich Bread

*This is sure to become
your favorite nutritious
white sandwich bread.
It won't crumble in your
packed lunch.*

Tip

To ensure success, see
page 15 for information on
using your bread machine
and page 18 for general tips
on bread machine baking.

1¼ cups	water	300 mL
2 tbsp	vegetable oil	30 mL
2 tbsp	liquid honey	30 mL
1 tsp	cider vinegar	5 mL
2	eggs, lightly beaten	2
2	egg whites, lightly beaten	2
3½ cups	White Bread Mix (pages 108–110)	875 mL

1. Pour water, oil, honey and vinegar into the bread machine baking pan. Add eggs and egg whites.
2. Select the **Dough Cycle**. As the bread machine is mixing, gradually add the bread mix, scraping bottom and sides of pan with a rubber spatula. Try to incorporate all the bread mix within 1 to 2 minutes. When the mixing and kneading are complete, remove the kneading blade, leaving the bread pan in the bread machine. Quickly smooth the top of the loaf. Allow the cycle to finish. Turn off the bread machine.
3. Select the **Bake Cycle**. Set time to 60 minutes and temperature to 350°F (180°C). Allow the cycle to finish. Do not turn machine off before taking the internal temperature of the loaf with an instant-read thermometer. It should be 200°F (100°C). If it's between 180°F (85°C) and 200°F (100°C), leave machine on the **Keep Warm Cycle** until baked. If it's below 180°F (85°C), turn on the **Bake Cycle** and check the internal temperature every 10 minutes. (Some bread machines are automatically set for 60 minutes; others need to be set by 10-minute intervals.)
4. Once the loaf has reached 200°F (100°C), remove it from the pan immediately and let cool completely on a rack.

NUTRITIONAL VALUES per serving	
Calories	148
Fat, total	5 g
Fat, saturated	1 g
Cholesterol	25 mg
Sodium	212 mg
Carbohydrate	23 g
Fiber	2 g
Protein	4 g
Calcium	23 mg
Iron	2 mg

Variation

To turn this into a raisin loaf, add $\frac{1}{2}$ cup (125 mL) raisins and 1 tsp (5 mL) ground cinnamon with the bread mix.

Gluten-Free Cycle

If your bread machine has a Gluten-Free Cycle, you will need to make these adjustments:

1. Increase the water in the recipe to $1\frac{1}{2}$ cups (375 mL).
2. Warm the water to between 110°F and 115°F (43°C and 46°C).
3. Warm the eggs and egg whites (see the Techniques Glossary, page 238).
4. Follow the recipe instructions, but select the **Gluten-Free Cycle** rather than the Dough Cycle and Bake Cycle.
5. At the end of the Gluten-Free Cycle, take the temperature of the loaf using an instant-read thermometer. It is baked at 200°F (100°C). If it's between 180°F (85°C) and 200°F (100°C), leave machine on the **Keep Warm Cycle** until baked. If it's below 180°F (85°C), turn on the **Bake Cycle** and check the internal temperature every 10 minutes. (Some bread machines are automatically set for 60 minutes; others need to be set by 10-minute intervals.)

Cheese Rolls

So delicious, and so easy to make from our mix.

Tips

To ensure success, see page 15 for information on using your bread machine and page 18 for general tips on bread machine baking.

For a sharper flavor, double the amount of cayenne pepper.

For a softer crust, brush the rolls with melted butter as soon as you remove them from the oven.

Variation

Make 10 larger buns for hamburgers. Spoon batter onto a baking sheet lined with parchment paper and flatten the tops slightly. Let rise, uncovered, for 1 hour. Bake for 15 to 20 minutes.

NUTRITIONAL VALUES
per serving

Calories	213
Fat, total	7 g
Fat, saturated	2 g
Cholesterol	40 mg
Sodium	344 mg
Carbohydrate	31 g
Fiber	3 g
Protein	7 g
Calcium	108 mg
Iron	2 mg

◆ **12-cup muffin tin, lightly greased**

3½ cups	White Bread Mix (pages 108–110)	875 mL
¾ cup	shredded sharp (old) Cheddar cheese	175 mL
¼ cup	freshly grated Parmesan cheese	60 mL
½ tsp	bread machine or instant yeast	2 mL
⅛ tsp	dry mustard	0.5 mL
⅛ tsp	cayenne pepper	0.5 mL
1¼ cups	water	300 mL
¼ cup	liquid honey	60 mL
1 tsp	cider vinegar	5 mL
2	eggs, lightly beaten	2
1	egg white, lightly beaten	1

1. In a large bowl or plastic bag, combine bread mix, Cheddar, Parmesan, yeast, mustard and cayenne; mix well and set aside.

2. Pour water, honey and vinegar into the bread machine baking pan. Add eggs and egg white.

3. Select the **Dough Cycle**. As the bread machine is mixing, gradually add the bread mix, scraping bottom and sides of pan with a rubber spatula. Try to incorporate all the bread mix within 1 to 2 minutes. Stop bread machine as soon as the kneading portion of the cycle is complete. Do not let bread machine finish the cycle.

4. Using a ¼ cup (60 mL) scoop, divide dough into 12 equal amounts and place in cups of prepared muffin tin. Let rise, uncovered, in a warm, draft-free place for 60 to 75 minutes or until dough has risen to the top of the cups. Meanwhile, preheat oven to 350°F (180°C).

5. Bake for 18 to 20 minutes or until internal temperature of rolls registers 200°F (100°C) on an instant-read thermometer. Remove from the tin immediately and let cool completely on a rack.

Rosemary Breadsticks

**MAKES
24 BREADSTICKS
(1 per serving)**

Longing for a crunchy breadstick with a warm, golden brown, crisp crust? Try this twice-baked version.

Tips

To ensure success, see page 15 for information on using your bread machine and page 18 for general tips on bread machine baking.

For uniform breadsticks, cut bread in half, then lengthwise into quarters. Finally, cut each quarter lengthwise into 3 strips.

If breadsticks become soft during storage, crisp them in a toaster oven or conventional oven at 350°F (180°C) for a few minutes.

**NUTRITIONAL VALUES
per serving**

Calories	87
Fat, total	3 g
Fat, saturated	1 g
Cholesterol	2 mg
Sodium	163 mg
Carbohydrate	12 g
Fiber	1 g
Protein	2 g
Calcium	39 mg
Iron	1 mg

◆ **Two 9-inch (23 cm) square baking pans, lightly greased**
◆ **Baking sheets, ungreased**

2 cups	water	500 mL
2 tbsp	extra virgin olive oil	30 mL
1 tsp	cider vinegar	5 mL
3½ cups	White Bread Mix (pages 108–110)	875 mL
¼ cup	snipped fresh rosemary	60 mL
1 tsp	granulated sugar	5 mL
½ tsp	freshly ground black pepper	2 mL
½ cup	freshly grated Parmesan cheese, divided	125 mL

1. Pour water, oil and vinegar into the bread machine baking pan.

2. Select the **Dough Cycle**. As the bread machine is mixing, gradually add the bread mix, rosemary, sugar and pepper, scraping bottom and sides of pan with a rubber spatula. Try to incorporate all the dry ingredients within 1 to 2 minutes. Stop bread machine as soon as the kneading portion of the cycle is complete. Do not let bread machine finish the cycle.

3. Sprinkle 2 tbsp (30 mL) of the Parmesan in the bottom of each prepared pan. Drop dough by spoonfuls over the Parmesan. Using a moistened rubber spatula, spread dough evenly to the edges of the pan. Sprinkle each with 2 tbsp (30 mL) Parmesan. Let rise, uncovered, in a warm, draft-free place for 30 minutes or until dough has risen to the top of the pans. Meanwhile, preheat oven to 400°F (200°C).

4. Bake for 12 to 15 minutes or until light brown. Remove from pan and transfer immediately to a cutting board. Reduce oven temperature to 350°F (180°C). Using a pizza wheel or a sharp knife, cut bread into 12 equal strips.

5. Arrange breadsticks, cut side up, at least ½ inch (1 cm) apart on baking sheets. Bake for 20 to 25 minutes or until dry, crisp and golden brown. Turn off oven and let breadsticks cool completely in oven.

6. Store in an airtight container at room temperature for up to 1 week.

Orange Chocolate Chip Loaf

This dessert bread is delightful when served warm. Enjoy for a quick snack.

Tip

To ensure success, see page 15 for information on using your bread machine and page 18 for general tips on bread machine baking.

¾ cup	water	175 mL
1 tbsp	grated orange zest	15 mL
¾ cup	freshly squeezed orange juice	175 mL
¼ cup	liquid honey	60 mL
2 tbsp	vegetable oil	30 mL
1 tsp	cider vinegar	5 mL
2	eggs, lightly beaten	2
1	egg white, lightly beaten	1
3½ cups	White Bread Mix (pages 108–110)	875 mL
1 cup	jumbo or mini semisweet chocolate chips	250 mL

1. Pour water, orange zest, orange juice, honey, oil and vinegar into the bread machine baking pan. Add eggs and egg white.

2. Select the **Dough Cycle**. As the bread machine is mixing, gradually add the bread mix and chocolate chips, scraping bottom and sides of pan with a rubber spatula. Try to incorporate all the dry ingredients within 1 to 2 minutes. When the mixing and kneading are complete, remove the kneading blade, leaving the bread pan in the bread machine. Quickly smooth the top of the loaf. Allow the cycle to finish. Turn off the bread machine.

3. Select the **Bake Cycle**. Set time to 60 minutes and temperature to 350°F (180°C). Allow the cycle to finish. Do not turn machine off before taking the internal temperature of the loaf with an instant-read thermometer. It should be 200°F (100°C). If it's between 180°F (85°C) and 200°F (100°C), leave machine on the **Keep Warm Cycle** until baked. If it's below 180°F (85°C), turn on the **Bake Cycle** and check the internal temperature every 10 minutes. (Some bread machines are automatically set for 60 minutes; others need to be set by 10-minute intervals.)

4. Once the loaf has reached 200°F (100°C), remove it from the pan immediately and let cool completely on a rack.

NUTRITIONAL VALUES per serving	
Calories	219
Fat, total	9 g
Fat, saturated	3 g
Cholesterol	27 mg
Sodium	218 mg
Carbohydrate	33 g
Fiber	3 g
Protein	5 g
Calcium	46 mg
Iron	1 mg

Tips

When oranges are in season, freeze extra zest and juice to have ready for recipes like this one.

Chocolate chips partially melt in most bread machines, giving a marbled effect to the bread.

Gluten-Free Cycle

If your bread machine has a Gluten-Free Cycle, you will need to make these adjustments:

1. Increase the water in the recipe to 1 cup (250 mL).

2. Warm the water to between 110°F and 115°F (43°C and 46°C).

3. Warm the eggs and egg white (see the Techniques Glossary, page 238).

4. Follow the recipe instructions, but select the **Gluten-Free Cycle** rather than the Dough Cycle and Bake Cycle.

5. At the end of the Gluten-Free Cycle, take the temperature of the loaf using an instant-read thermometer. It is baked at 200°F (100°C). If it's between 180°F (85°C) and 200°F (100°C), leave machine on the **Keep Warm Cycle** until baked. If it's below 180°F (85°C), turn on the **Bake Cycle** and check the internal temperature every 10 minutes. (Some bread machines are automatically set for 60 minutes; others need to be set by 10-minute intervals.)

Single-Loaf Brown Bread Mix

**MAKES ABOUT
3½ CUPS (875 ML),
ENOUGH FOR
1 LOAF**

You asked us for a brown bread mix you could use to make a variety of nutritious loaves and rolls. We've done you one better and given you the recipe in two different batch sizes. Here's a single-loaf mix you can try before making the larger batch on page 119. You can use this nutritious mix to make Maritime (Boston) Brown Bread (page 120), Mock Bran Bread (page 122), Quick and Easy Pumpernickel Bread (page 124) or Pizza Crust (page 126).

1¼ cups	sorghum flour	300 mL
⅔ cup	whole bean flour	150 mL
½ cup	brown rice flour	125 mL
2 tbsp	quinoa flour	30 mL
⅓ cup	potato starch	75 mL
3 tbsp	tapioca starch	45 mL
2 tbsp	packed brown sugar	30 mL
1 tbsp	xanthan gum	15 mL
1½ tsp	bread machine or instant yeast	7 mL
1½ tsp	salt	7 mL

1. In a large bowl, combine sorghum flour, whole bean flour, brown rice flour, quinoa flour, potato starch, tapioca starch, brown sugar, xanthan gum, yeast and salt; mix well.

2. Use right away or seal tightly in a plastic bag, removing as much air as possible. Store at room temperature for up to 3 days or in the freezer for up to 6 weeks.

Working with Bread Mix

- Be sure the brown sugar is well distributed and any lumps are broken up; it clumps easily when mixed with other dry ingredients.
- Label and date the package if not using bread mix immediately. We add the page number of the recipe to the label as a quick reference.
- Let bread mix warm to room temperature, and mix well before using.

NUTRITIONAL VALUES per serving	
Calories	94
Fat, total	1 g
Fat, saturated	0 g
Cholesterol	0 mg
Sodium	235 mg
Carbohydrate	20 g
Fiber	2 g
Protein	3 g
Calcium	10 mg
Iron	1 mg

Four-Loaf Brown Bread Mix

**MAKES ABOUT
14 CUPS (3.5 L),
ENOUGH FOR
4 LOAVES**

*Here's the four-loaf
version of our bread
machine brown bread
mix, a nutritious mix
that makes great
whole-grain breads. Use
it to make the recipes on
pages 120–126.*

Tips

For accuracy, use a 1-cup
(250 mL) dry measure
several times to measure
each type of flour and
starch. If you use a 4-cup
(1 L) liquid measure, it's
difficult to get an accurate
volume and you'll end up
with extra flour in the mix.

We used a large roasting
pan to combine all the
ingredients.

	NUTRITIONAL VALUES per serving	
Calories	94
Fat, total	1 g
Fat, saturated	0 g
Cholesterol	0 mg
Sodium	234 mg
Carbohydrate	20 g
Fiber	1 g
Protein	3 g
Calcium	10 mg
Iron	1 mg

5 cups	sorghum flour	1.25 L
2⅔ cups	whole bean flour	650 mL
2 cups	brown rice flour	500 mL
½ cup	quinoa flour	125 mL
1¼ cups	potato starch	300 mL
¾ cup	tapioca starch	175 mL
½ cup	packed brown sugar	125 mL
¼ cup	xanthan gum	60 mL
2 tbsp	bread machine or instant yeast	30 mL
2 tbsp	salt	30 mL

1. In a very large container, combine sorghum flour, whole bean flour, brown rice flour, quinoa flour, potato starch, tapioca starch, brown sugar, xanthan gum, yeast and salt; mix well.

2. Divide into 4 equal portions of about 3½ cups (875 mL) each. Seal tightly in plastic bags, removing as much air as possible. Store at room temperature for up to 3 days or in the freezer for up to 6 weeks.

Working with Bread Mix

- Be sure the brown sugar is well distributed and any lumps are broken up; it clumps easily when mixed with other dry ingredients.

- In step 2, stir the mix before spooning it very lightly into the dry measures. Do not pack.

- Be sure to divide the mix into equal portions. Depending on how much air you incorporate into the mix, and the texture of the individual gluten-free flours, the total volume of the mix can vary slightly. The important thing is to make the number of portions specified in the recipe.

- Label and date the packages before storing. We add the page number of the recipe to the labels as a quick reference.

- Let bread mix warm to room temperature, and mix well before using.

Maritime (Boston) Brown Bread

MAKES 15 SLICES
(1 per serving)

*Here's a good basic brown
bread for sandwiches
and everyday use. It's
especially good with
homemade baked beans.*

Tips

To ensure success, see
page 15 for information on
using your bread machine
and page 18 for general tips
on bread machine baking.

Measuring the oil before
the molasses ensures that
the molasses slides out
of the measure. We enjoy
using the Oxo sloped ¼-cup
(60 mL) measure for this. If
the molasses is really thick
or is straight out of the
refrigerator, warm it slightly
in the microwave before
measuring.

1¼ cups	water	300 mL
3 tbsp	vegetable oil	45 mL
2 tbsp	light (fancy) molasses	30 mL
1 tsp	cider vinegar	5 mL
2	eggs, lightly beaten	2
2	egg whites, lightly beaten	2
3½ cups	Brown Bread Mix (pages 118–119)	875 mL

1. Pour water, oil, molasses and vinegar into the bread machine baking pan. Add eggs and egg whites.

2. Select the **Dough Cycle**. As the bread machine is mixing, gradually add the bread mix, scraping bottom and sides of pan with a rubber spatula. Try to incorporate all the bread mix within 1 to 2 minutes. When the mixing and kneading are complete, remove the kneading blade, leaving the bread pan in the bread machine. Quickly smooth the top of the loaf. Allow the cycle to finish. Turn off the bread machine.

3. Select the **Bake Cycle**. Set time to 60 minutes and temperature to 350°F (180°C). Allow the cycle to finish. Do not turn machine off before taking the internal temperature of the loaf with an instant-read thermometer. It should be 200°F (100°C). If it's between 180°F (85°C) and 200°F (100°C), leave machine on the **Keep Warm Cycle** until baked. If it's below 180°F (85°C), turn on the **Bake Cycle** and check the internal temperature every 10 minutes. (Some bread machines are automatically set for 60 minutes; others need to be set by 10-minute intervals.)

4. Once the loaf has reached 200°F (100°C), remove it from the pan immediately and let cool completely on a rack.

NUTRITIONAL VALUES
per serving

Calories	136
Fat, total	4 g
Fat, saturated	0 g
Cholesterol	25 mg
Sodium	251 mg
Carbohydrate	22 g
Fiber	2 g
Protein	4 g
Calcium	18 mg
Iron	1 mg

Variation

Add ½ cup (125 mL) raisins or chopped walnuts with the bread mix.

Gluten-Free Cycle

If your bread machine has a Gluten-Free Cycle, you will need to make these adjustments:

1. Increase the water in the recipe to 1½ cups (375 mL).
2. Warm the water to between 110°F and 115°F (43°C and 46°C).
3. Warm the eggs and egg whites (see the Techniques Glossary, page 238).
4. Follow the recipe instructions, but select the **Gluten-Free Cycle** rather than the Dough Cycle and Bake Cycle.
5. At the end of the Gluten-Free Cycle, take the temperature of the loaf using an instant-read thermometer. It is baked at 200°F (100°C). If it's between 180°F (85°C) and 200°F (100°C), leave machine on the **Keep Warm Cycle** until baked. If it's below 180°F (85°C), turn on the **Bake Cycle** and check the internal temperature every 10 minutes. (Some bread machines are automatically set for 60 minutes; others need to be set by 10-minute intervals.)

Mock Bran Bread

This is a sweeter, higher-fiber version of our basic Brown Sandwich Bread (page 32). You'll love using this bread for all of your sandwiches.

Tips

To ensure success, see page 15 for information on using your bread machine and page 18 for general tips on bread machine baking.

Warm rice bran that has been stored in the refrigerator or freezer to room temperature.

2 tbsp	rice bran	30 mL
3½ cups	Brown Bread Mix (pages 118–119)	875 mL
1½ cups	water	375 mL
3 tbsp	vegetable oil	45 mL
1 tbsp	liquid honey	15 mL
1 tbsp	light (fancy) molasses	15 mL
1 tsp	cider vinegar	5 mL
2	eggs, lightly beaten	2
2	egg whites, lightly beaten	2

1. Add rice bran to the bread mix; mix well and set aside.
2. Pour water, oil, honey, molasses and vinegar into the bread machine baking pan. Add eggs and egg whites.
3. Select the **Dough Cycle**. As the bread machine is mixing, gradually add the bread mix, scraping bottom and sides of pan with a rubber spatula. Try to incorporate all the bread mix within 1 to 2 minutes. When the mixing and kneading are complete, remove the kneading blade, leaving the bread pan in the bread machine. Quickly smooth the top of the loaf. Allow the cycle to finish. Turn off the bread machine.
4. Select the **Bake Cycle**. Set time to 60 minutes and temperature to 350°F (180°C). Allow the cycle to finish. Do not turn machine off before taking the internal temperature of the loaf with an instant-read thermometer. It should be 200°F (100°C). If it's between 180°F (85°C) and 200°F (100°C), leave machine on the **Keep Warm Cycle** until baked. If it's below 180°F (85°C), turn on the **Bake Cycle** and check the internal temperature every 10 minutes. (Some bread machines are automatically set for 60 minutes; others need to be set by 10-minute intervals.)
5. Once the loaf has reached 200°F (100°C), remove it from the pan immediately and let cool completely on a rack.

NUTRITIONAL VALUES
per serving

Calories	140
Fat, total	4 g
Fat, saturated	0 g
Cholesterol	25 mg
Sodium	250 mg
Carbohydrate	23 g
Fiber	2 g
Protein	4 g
Calcium	16 mg
Iron	1 mg

Variations

Add ½ cup (125 mL) raisins, chopped dates or chopped walnuts with the bread mix.

Substitute GF oat bran for the rice bran.

Gluten-Free Cycle

If your bread machine has a Gluten-Free Cycle, you will need to make these adjustments:

1. Increase the water in the recipe to 1¾ cups (425 mL).

2. Warm the water to between 110°F and 115°F (43°C and 46°C).

3. Warm the eggs and egg whites (see the Techniques Glossary, page 238).

4. Follow the recipe instructions, but select the **Gluten Free Cycle** rather than the Dough Cycle and Bake Cycle.

5. At the end of the Gluten-Free Cycle, take the temperature of the loaf using an instant-read thermometer. It is baked at 200°F (100°C). If it's between 180°F (85°C) and 200°F (100°C), leave machine on the **Keep Warm Cycle** until baked. If it's below 180°F (85°C), turn on the **Bake Cycle** and check the internal temperature every 10 minutes. (Some bread machines are automatically set for 60 minutes; others need to be set by 10-minute intervals.)

Quick and Easy Pumpernickel Bread

MAKES 15 SLICES
(1 per serving)

It is so handy to have the mix ready when you're in the mood for pumpernickel.

Tips

To ensure success, see page 15 for information on using your bread machine and page 18 for general tips on bread machine baking.

Sift cocoa just before using, as it lumps easily.

1 tbsp	instant coffee granules	15 mL
1 tbsp	unsweetened cocoa powder, sifted	15 mL
½ tsp	ground ginger	2 mL
3½ cups	Brown Bread Mix (pages 118–119)	875 mL
1½ cups	water	375 mL
3 tbsp	vegetable oil	45 mL
2 tbsp	light (fancy) molasses	30 mL
1 tsp	cider vinegar	5 mL
2	eggs, lightly beaten	2
2	egg whites, lightly beaten	2

1. Add coffee granules, cocoa and ginger to the bread mix; mix well and set aside.

2. Pour water, oil, molasses and vinegar into the bread machine baking pan. Add eggs and egg whites.

3. Select the **Dough Cycle**. As the bread machine is mixing, gradually add the bread mix, scraping bottom and sides of pan with a rubber spatula. Try to incorporate all the bread mix within 1 to 2 minutes. When the mixing and kneading are complete, remove the kneading blade, leaving the bread pan in the bread machine. Quickly smooth the top of the loaf. Allow the cycle to finish. Turn off the bread machine.

4. Select the **Bake Cycle**. Set time to 60 minutes and temperature to 350°F (180°C). Allow the cycle to finish. Do not turn machine off before taking the internal temperature of the loaf with an instant-read thermometer. It should be 200°F (100°C). If it's between 180°F (85°C) and 200°F (100°C), leave machine on the **Keep Warm Cycle** until baked. If it's below 180°F (85°C), turn on the **Bake Cycle** and check the internal temperature every 10 minutes. (Some bread machines are automatically set for 60 minutes; others need to be set by 10-minute intervals.)

5. Once the loaf has reached 200°F (100°C), remove it from the pan immediately and let cool completely on a rack.

NUTRITIONAL VALUES
per serving

Calories	139
Fat, total	4 g
Fat, saturated	0 g
Cholesterol	25 mg
Sodium	251 mg
Carbohydrate	23 g
Fiber	2 g
Protein	4 g
Calcium	20 mg
Iron	1 mg

Variations

Add 2 tbsp (30 mL) caraway, fennel or anise seeds with the bread mix.

Substitute an equal quantity of strong brewed room-temperature coffee for the water.

Gluten-Free Cycle

If your bread machine has a Gluten-Free Cycle, you will need to make these adjustments:

1. Increase the water in the recipe to 1¾ cups (425 mL).

2. Warm the water to between 110°F and 115°F (43°C and 46°C).

3. Warm the eggs and egg whites (see the Techniques Glossary, page 238).

4. Follow the recipe instructions, but select the **Gluten-Free Cycle** rather than the Dough Cycle and Bake Cycle.

5. At the end of the Gluten-Free Cycle, take the temperature of the loaf using an instant-read thermometer. It is baked at 200°F (100°C). If it's between 180°F (85°C) and 200°F (100°C), leave machine on the **Keep Warm Cycle** until baked. If it's below 180°F (85°C), turn on the **Bake Cycle** and check the internal temperature every 10 minutes. (Some bread machines are automatically set for 60 minutes; others need to be set by 10-minute intervals.)

Pizza Crust

You requested a whole-grain pizza crust recipe — here it is.

Tips

To ensure success, see page 15 for information on using your bread machine and page 18 for general tips on bread machine baking.

To make pizza, add your favorite topping ingredients and bake until crust is brown and crisp and top is bubbly.

Pizza dough can be prepared through Step 3, wrapped airtight and stored in the freezer for up to 1 month. Thaw in the refrigerator before using.

If you like a thicker crust, leave the dough in one piece, spread it in the pan and let rise for 30 minutes before baking.

NUTRITIONAL VALUES per serving	
Calories	121
Fat, total	4 g
Fat, saturated	1 g
Cholesterol	0 mg
Sodium	221 mg
Carbohydrate	19 g
Fiber	2 g
Protein	3 g
Calcium	9 mg
Iron	1 mg

◆ **Two 15- by 10-inch (40 by 25 cm) rimmed baking sheets, lightly greased**

2 tsp	bread machine or instant yeast	10 mL
3½ cups	Brown Bread Mix (pages 118–119)	875 mL
2¼ cups	water	550 mL
¼ cup	extra virgin olive oil	60 mL
1 tsp	cider vinegar	5 mL

1. Add yeast to the bread mix; mix well and set aside.
2. Pour water, oil and vinegar into the bread machine baking pan.
3. Select the **Dough Cycle**. As the bread machine is mixing, gradually add the dry ingredients, scraping bottom and sides of pan with a rubber spatula. Try to incorporate all the dry ingredients within 1 to 2 minutes. Stop bread machine as soon as the kneading portion of the cycle is complete. Do not let bread machine finish the cycle.
4. Meanwhile, preheat oven to 400°F (200°C).
5. Divide dough in half. Place half the dough in each prepared pan and , using a moistened rubber spatula spread evenly to the edges. Do not smooth tops.
6. Bake for 12 minutes or until bottom is golden and crust is partially baked.
7. Use right away to make pizza with your favorite toppings, or wrap airtight and store in the freezer for up to 1 month. Thaw in the refrigerator overnight before using.

Sourdough Starter

MAKES 3½ CUPS (875 ML)
(1 cup/250 mL per serving)

You've been asking us for a sourdough bread with a tangy taste. Begin by making this starter, and you'll be on your way to enjoying gluten-free sourdough breads.

Tips

If the starter liquid turns green, pink or orange — or develops mold — throw it out and start again.

During hot weather, use a triple layer of cheesecloth to cover the sourdough starter when it is at room temperature. A loose-fitting lid on a large casserole dish works well too.

3 cups	warm water	750 mL
2 tbsp	granulated sugar	30 mL
2 tbsp	instant or bread machine yeast	30 mL
3 cups	sorghum flour	750 mL

1. In a very large glass bowl, combine water and sugar. Sprinkle with yeast, gently stir to moisten and let stand for 10 minutes.
2. Add sorghum flour and whisk until smooth.
3. Cover with a double layer of cheesecloth or a loose-fitting lid. Secure so that it is not touching the starter. Let stand at room temperature for 2 to 4 days, stirring 2 to 3 times a day. When ready to use, starter has a sour smell, with small bubbles rising to the surface.
4. Store, loosely covered, in the refrigerator until needed. If not used regularly, stir in 1 tsp (5 mL) granulated sugar every 10 days.

NUTRITIONAL VALUES
per serving

Calories	536
Fat, total	4 g
Fat, saturated	0 g
Cholesterol	0 mg
Sodium	9 mg
Carbohydrate	111 g
Fiber	14 g
Protein	19 g
Calcium	46 mg
Iron	7 mg

Sourdough Loaf

MAKES 15 SLICES
(1 per serving)

Try this warm, creamy loaf the next time you feel like a sandwich.

Tip

To ensure success, see page 15 for information on using your bread machine, page 18 for general tips on bread machine baking and page 136 for tips on using and feeding the starter.

1 cup	brown rice flour	250 mL
1 cup	amaranth flour	250 mL
½ cup	potato starch	125 mL
2 tbsp	granulated sugar	30 mL
1 tbsp	xanthan gum	15 mL
1 tbsp	bread machine or instant yeast	15 mL
1½ tsp	salt	7 mL
1 cup	Sourdough Starter (page 127), at room temperature	250 mL
¼ cup	water	60 mL
¼ cup	vegetable oil	60 mL
2	eggs, lightly beaten	2
2	egg whites, lightly beaten	2

1. In a large bowl or plastic bag, combine brown rice flour, amaranth flour, potato starch, sugar, xanthan gum, yeast and salt; mix well and set aside.

2. Pour sourdough starter, water and oil into the bread machine baking pan. Add eggs and egg whites.

3. Select the **Dough Cycle**. As the bread machine is mixing, gradually add the dry ingredients, scraping bottom and sides of pan with a rubber spatula. Try to incorporate all the dry ingredients within 1 to 2 minutes. When the mixing and kneading are complete, remove the kneading blade, leaving the bread pan in the bread machine. Quickly smooth the top of the loaf. Allow the cycle to finish. Turn off the bread machine.

4. Select the **Bake Cycle**. Set time to 60 minutes and temperature to 350°F (180°C). Allow the cycle to finish. Do not turn machine off before taking the internal temperature of the loaf with an instant-read thermometer. It should be 200°F (100°C). If it's between 180°F (85°C) and 200°F (100°C), leave machine on the **Keep Warm Cycle** until baked. If it's below 180°F (85°C), turn on the **Bake Cycle** and check the internal temperature every 10 minutes. (Some bread machines are automatically set for 60 minutes; others need to be set by 10-minute intervals.)

5. Once the loaf has reached 200°F (100°C), remove it from the pan immediately and let cool completely on a rack.

NUTRITIONAL VALUES per serving	
Calories	171
Fat, total	5 g
Fat, saturated	1 g
Cholesterol	25 mg
Sodium	250 mg
Carbohydrate	27 g
Fiber	3 g
Protein	5 g
Calcium	19 mg
Iron	3 mg

Variation

For an even tangier taste, add 1 tsp (5 mL) cider vinegar with the liquids.

To make this recipe egg-free: Omit eggs from the recipe. Combine ¾ cup (175 mL) flax flour or ground flaxseed with an additional ¾ cup (175 mL) warm water. Set aside for 5 minutes. Add with the liquids.

Gluten-Free Cycle

If your bread machine has a Gluten-Free Cycle, you will need to make these adjustments:

1. Warm the water to between 110°F and 115°F (43°C and 46°C).
2. Warm the eggs and egg whites (see the Techniques Glossary, page 238).
3. Follow the recipe instructions, but select the **Gluten-Free Cycle** rather than the Dough Cycle and Bake Cycle.
4. At the end of the Gluten-Free Cycle, take the temperature of the loaf using an instant-read thermometer. It is baked at 200°F (100°C). If it's between 180°F (85°C) and 200°F (100°C), leave machine on the **Keep Warm Cycle** until baked. If it's below 180°F (85°C), turn on the **Bake Cycle** and check the internal temperature every 10 minutes. (Some bread machines are automatically set for 60 minutes; others need to be set by 10-minute intervals.)

Sourdough Brown Bread

This dense, moist, tangy bread makes wonderful sandwich bread or breakfast toast.

Tips

To ensure success, see page 15 for information on using your bread machine, page 18 for general tips on bread machine baking and page 136 for tips on using and feeding the starter.

Don't forget about the sourdough starter sitting in your refrigerator. If you haven't used it to make a loaf in the last 10 days, see page 136 for information on feeding it.

1 cup	sorghum flour	250 mL
⅔ cup	whole bean flour	150 mL
⅓ cup	tapioca starch	75 mL
1 tbsp	xanthan gum	15 mL
1 tbsp	bread machine or instant yeast	15 mL
1¼ tsp	salt	6 mL
1 cup	Sourdough Starter (page 127), at room temperature	250 mL
¾ cup	water	175 mL
2 tbsp	vegetable oil	30 mL
2 tbsp	liquid honey	30 mL
2 tbsp	light (fancy) molasses	30 mL
2	eggs, lightly beaten	2

1. In a large bowl or plastic bag, combine sorghum flour, whole bean flour, tapioca starch, xanthan gum, yeast and salt; mix well and set aside.

2. Pour sourdough starter, water, oil, honey and molasses into the bread machine baking pan. Add eggs.

3. Select the **Dough Cycle**. As the bread machine is mixing, gradually add the dry ingredients, scraping bottom and sides of pan with a rubber spatula. Try to incorporate all the dry ingredients within 1 to 2 minutes. When the mixing and kneading are complete, remove the kneading blade, leaving the bread pan in the bread machine. Quickly smooth the top of the loaf. Allow the cycle to finish. Turn off the bread machine.

4. Select the **Bake Cycle**. Set time to 60 minutes and temperature to 350°F (180°C). Allow the cycle to finish. Do not turn machine off before taking the internal temperature of the loaf with an instant-read thermometer. It should be 200°F (100°C). If it's between 180°F (85°C) and 200°F (100°C), leave machine on the **Keep Warm Cycle** until baked. If it's below 180°F (85°C), turn on the **Bake Cycle** and check the internal temperature every 10 minutes. (Some bread machines are automatically set for 60 minutes; others need to be set by 10-minute intervals.)

5. Once the loaf has reached 200°F (100°C), remove it from the pan immediately and let cool completely on a rack.

NUTRITIONAL VALUES per serving	
Calories	131
Fat, total	3 g
Fat, saturated	0 g
Cholesterol	25 mg
Sodium	204 mg
Carbohydrate	23 g
Fiber	2 g
Protein	4 g
Calcium	19 mg
Iron	1 mg

Tip

It is easier to measure honey and molasses if they are warmed in the microwave for a few seconds, or set in a pan of hot water for a few minutes. Measure the oil first, then measure the honey and molasses; they will slide off the measuring spoon more easily that way.

Variations

Substitute ¼ cup (60 mL) packed brown sugar for the honey and the molasses.

For an even tangier taste, add 1 tsp (5 mL) cider vinegar with the liquids.

To make this recipe egg-free: Omit eggs from the recipe. Combine ⅓ cup (75 mL) flax flour or ground flaxseed with an additional ⅓ cup (75 mL) warm water. Set aside for 5 minutes. Add with the liquids.

Gluten-Free Cycle

If your bread machine has a Gluten-Free Cycle, you will need to make these adjustments:

1. Warm the water to between 110°F and 115°F (43°C and 46°C).
2. Warm the eggs (see the Techniques Glossary, page 238).
3. Follow the recipe instructions, but select the **Gluten-Free Cycle** rather than the Dough Cycle and Bake Cycle.
4. At the end of the Gluten-Free Cycle, take the temperature of the loaf using an instant-read thermometer. It is baked at 200°F (100°C). If it's between 180°F (85°C) and 200°F (100°C), leave machine on the **Keep Warm Cycle** until baked. If it's below 180°F (85°C), turn on the **Bake Cycle** and check the internal temperature every 10 minutes. (Some bread machines are automatically set for 60 minutes; others need to be set by 10-minute intervals.)

Sourdough Walnut Bread

We have adapted this loaf from a traditional French Canadian sourdough hearth bread.

Tip

To ensure success, see page 15 for information on using your bread machine, page 18 for general tips on bread machine baking and page 136 for tips on using and feeding the starter.

1¼ cups	amaranth flour	300 mL
½ cup	quinoa flour	125 mL
½ cup	tapioca starch	125 mL
¼ cup	packed brown sugar	60 mL
1 tbsp	xanthan gum	15 mL
1½ tsp	bread machine or instant yeast	7 mL
1¼ tsp	salt	6 mL
1 cup	chopped walnuts	250 mL
1 cup	Sourdough Starter (page 127), at room temperature	250 mL
⅔ cup	water	150 mL
2 tbsp	vegetable oil	30 mL
2	eggs, lightly beaten	2

1. In a large bowl or plastic bag, combine amaranth flour, quinoa flour, tapioca starch, brown sugar, xanthan gum, yeast, salt and walnuts; mix well and set aside.

2. Pour sourdough starter, water and oil into the bread machine baking pan. Add eggs.

3. Select the **Dough Cycle**. As the bread machine is mixing, gradually add the dry ingredients, scraping bottom and sides of pan with a rubber spatula. Try to incorporate all the dry ingredients within 1 to 2 minutes. When the mixing and kneading are complete, remove the kneading blade, leaving the bread pan in the bread machine. Quickly smooth the top of the loaf. Allow the cycle to finish. Turn off the bread machine.

4. Select the **Bake Cycle**. Set time to 60 minutes and temperature to 350°F (180°C). Allow the cycle to finish. Do not turn machine off before taking the internal temperature of the loaf with an instant-read thermometer. It should be 200°F (100°C). If it's between 180°F (85°C) and 200°F (100°C), leave machine on the **Keep Warm Cycle** until baked. If it's below 180°F (85°C), turn on the **Bake Cycle** and check the internal temperature every 10 minutes. (Some bread machines are automatically set for 60 minutes; others need to be set by 10-minute intervals.)

5. Once the loaf has reached 200°F (100°C), remove it from the pan immediately and let cool completely on a rack.

NUTRITIONAL VALUES
per serving

Calories	197
Fat, total	9 g
Fat, saturated	1 g
Cholesterol	25 mg
Sodium	206 mg
Carbohydrate	26 g
Fiber	3 g
Protein	5 g
Calcium	34 mg
Iron	4 mg

For an even tangier taste, add 1 tsp (5 mL) cider vinegar with the liquids.

To make this recipe egg-free: Omit eggs from the recipe. Increase yeast to 1 tbsp (15 mL). Combine ⅓ cup (75 mL) flax flour or ground flaxseed with an additional ⅓ cup (75 mL) warm water. Set aside for 5 minutes. Add with the liquids.

Gluten-Free Cycle

If your bread machine has a Gluten-Free Cycle, you will need to make these adjustments:

1. Warm the water to between 110°F and 115°F (43°C and 46°C).

2. Warm the eggs (see the Techniques Glossary, page 238).

3. Follow the recipe instructions, but select the **Gluten-Free Cycle** rather than the Dough Cycle and Bake Cycle.

4. At the end of the Gluten-Free Cycle, take the temperature of the loaf using an instant-read thermometer. It is baked at 200°F (100°C). If it's between 180°F (85°C) and 200°F (100°C), leave machine on the **Keep Warm Cycle** until baked. If it's below 180°F (85°C), turn on the **Bake Cycle** and check the internal temperature every 10 minutes. (Some bread machines are automatically set for 60 minutes; others need to be set by 10-minute intervals.)

Sourdough Savory Ciabatta

The name "ciabatta" refers to the traditional slipper shape. We've adapted the shape to accommodate the batter-like gluten-free dough. This version has a designer twist for those who like their yeast breads tangy and sour.

Tips

To ensure success, see page 15 for information on using your bread machine, page 18 for general tips on bread machine baking and page 136 for tips on using and feeding the starter.

We like this ciabatta best served hot out of the oven.

Break this bread into pieces to serve with soups or salads.

A silicone baking pan works well for this recipe.

NUTRITIONAL VALUES
per serving

Calories	198
Fat, total	6 g
Fat, saturated	1 g
Cholesterol	47 mg
Sodium	164 mg
Carbohydrate	31 g
Fiber	5 g
Protein	7 g
Calcium	73 mg
Iron	5 mg

◆ **8-inch (20 cm) round baking pan, lightly greased and floured with sweet rice flour**

1/2 cup	amaranth flour	125 mL
1/3 cup	sorghum flour	75 mL
1/4 cup	tapioca starch	60 mL
1 tbsp	granulated sugar	15 mL
2 tsp	xanthan gum	10 mL
2 tbsp	bread machine or instant yeast	30 mL
1/2 tsp	salt	2 mL
1/4 cup	snipped fresh savory	60 mL
1 cup	Sourdough Starter (page 127), at room temperature	250 mL
1/4 cup	water	60 mL
2 tbsp	extra virgin olive oil	30 mL
2	eggs, lightly beaten	2
2 to 3 tbsp	sweet rice flour, brown rice flour or sorghum flour	30 to 45 mL

1. In a large bowl or plastic bag, combine amaranth flour, sorghum flour, tapioca starch, sugar, xanthan gum, yeast, salt and savory; mix well and set aside.

2. Pour sourdough starter, water and oil into the bread machine baking pan. Add eggs.

3. Select the **Dough Cycle**. As the bread machine is mixing, gradually add the dry ingredients, scraping bottom and sides of pan with a rubber spatula. Try to incorporate all the dry ingredients within 1 to 2 minutes. Stop bread machine as soon as the kneading portion of the cycle is complete. Do not let bread machine finish the cycle.

Variations

If fresh savory is not available, use one-third the amount of dried savory. Or substitute an equal amount of your favorite herb — rosemary, thyme or cilantro work well, to name a few.

For a thinner ciabatta, bake in a 9-inch (23 cm) round baking pan and increase the baking time to 21 minutes.

For an even tangier taste, add 1 tsp (5 mL) cider vinegar with the liquids.

4. Gently transfer dough to prepared pan and spread evenly to the edges, leaving the top rough and uneven. Generously dust top with sweet rice flour. With well-floured fingers, make deep indents all over the dough, pressing all the way down to the pan. Let rise, uncovered, in a warm, draft-free place for 45 to 60 minutes or until almost doubled in volume. Meanwhile, preheat oven to 425°F (220°C).

5. Bake for 18 to 20 minutes or until internal temperature of loaf registers 200°F (100°C) on an instant-read thermometer. Remove from the pan immediately. Cut into 8 wedges and serve hot.

To make this recipe egg-free: Omit eggs from the recipe. Combine ⅓ cup (75 mL) flax flour or ground flaxseed with an additional ¼ cup (60 mL) warm water. Set aside for 5 minutes. Add with liquid ingredients.

Tips for Successful Starters

Using the Starter

- It is normal for a starter to separate. The grayish liquid rises to the top, while the very thick part settles to the bottom of the storage container. Stir well before each use.
- The starter should have the consistency of pancake batter. If it's too thick, add a small amount of water before measuring. If your bread machine does not have a 20-minute delay to preheat before mixing, or if you're using the mixer method, bring the starter to room temperature by placing it in a bowl of warm water for 15 minutes before measuring. Until the starter becomes established and is working well, remove only 1 cup (250 mL) at a time.
- Make sure all utensils and pans that come into contact with the starter go through the dishwasher or are rinsed with a mild solution of water and bleach.

Feeding the Starter

- To replace each cup (250 mL) of starter used in preparing a recipe, add ¾ cup (175 mL) water, ¾ cup (175 mL) sorghum flour and 1 tsp (5 mL) granulated sugar to the remaining starter. Stir well, cover with a double layer of cheesecloth or a loose-fitting lid and let stand at room temperature for at least 24 hours or until bubbly and sour-smelling. Refrigerate, loosely covered.
- If not used regularly, stir in 1 tsp (5 mL) granulated sugar every 10 days.

Rolls by the Basketful

Rich Dinner Rolls

*This is the answer
to a special request for
a recipe to make
just a half-dozen
everyday dinner rolls.*

Tips

To ensure success, see
page 15 for information on
using your bread machine
and page 18 for general tips
on bread machine baking.

If only a 12-cup muffin tin is
available, fill the empty cups
one-quarter full with water
before baking.

For instructions on making
your own almond flour,
see under Nut flour in
the Techniques Glossary,
page 242.

◆ 6-cup muffin tin, lightly greased

½ cup	almond flour	125 mL
½ cup	brown rice flour	125 mL
¼ cup	amaranth flour	60 mL
¼ cup	potato starch	60 mL
2 tsp	xanthan gum	10 mL
1¾ tsp	bread machine or instant yeast	8 mL
¾ tsp	salt	3 mL
¾ cup	plain yogurt	175 mL
2 tbsp	vegetable oil	30 mL
2 tbsp	liquid honey	30 mL
1	egg, lightly beaten	1
1	egg white, lightly beaten	1

1. In a large bowl or plastic bag, combine almond flour, brown rice flour, amaranth flour, potato starch, xanthan gum, yeast and salt; mix well and set aside.

2. Pour yogurt, oil and honey into the bread machine baking pan. Add egg and egg white.

3. Select the **Dough Cycle**. As the bread machine is mixing, gradually add the dry ingredients, scraping bottom and sides of pan with a rubber spatula. Try to incorporate all the dry ingredients within 1 to 2 minutes. Stop bread machine as soon as the kneading portion of the cycle is complete. Do not let bread machine finish the cycle.

4. Using a ¼-cup (60 mL) scoop, divide dough into 6 equal amounts and place in cups of prepared muffin tin. Let rise, uncovered, in a warm, draft-free place for 60 to 75 minutes or until dough has risen to the top of the cups. Meanwhile, preheat oven to 400°F (200°C).

5. Bake for 18 to 20 minutes or until internal temperature of rolls registers 200°F (100°C) on an instant-read thermometer. Remove from the pan immediately and let cool completely on a rack.

To make this recipe egg-free: Omit egg and egg white from the recipe. Add 1 tbsp (15 mL) powdered egg replacer with the dry ingredients and add ¼ cup (60 mL) of water with the yogurt.

NUTRITIONAL VALUES
per serving

Calories	234
Fat, total	11 g
Fat, saturated	1 g
Cholesterol	31 mg
Sodium	319 mg
Carbohydrate	29 g
Fiber	3 g
Protein	6 g
Calcium	81 mg
Iron	2 mg

Egg-Free, Corn-Free, Dairy-Free, Soy-Free White Dinner Rolls

MAKES 10 ROLLS
(1 per serving)

These rolls are perfect for those who must eliminate eggs, corn, dairy and/or soy from their diet but enjoy a roll with dinner.

Tips

To ensure success, see page 15 for information on using your bread machine and page 18 for general tips on bread machine baking.

For information about egg replacer, see the Ingredient Glossary, page 232.

Variation

Add ½ cup (125 mL) unsalted raw sunflower seeds or green pumpkin seeds with the dry ingredients.

NUTRITIONAL VALUES
per serving

Calories	172
Fat, total	4 g
Fat, saturated	1 g
Cholesterol	9 mg
Sodium	305 mg
Carbohydrate	32 g
Fiber	2 g
Protein	3 g
Calcium	15 mg
Iron	1 mg

◆ **Baking sheet, lightly greased**

1¾ cups	brown rice flour	425 mL
⅓ cup	amaranth flour	75 mL
⅓ cup	potato starch	75 mL
¼ cup	tapioca starch	60 mL
1 tbsp	powdered egg replacer	15 mL
2 tbsp	granulated sugar	30 mL
2½ tsp	xanthan gum	12 mL
1 tbsp	bread machine or instant yeast	15 mL
1¼ tsp	salt	6 mL
1⅓ cups	water	325 mL
2 tbsp	vegetable oil	30 mL
2 tsp	cider vinegar	10 mL

1. In a large bowl or plastic bag, combine brown rice flour, amaranth flour, potato starch, tapioca starch, egg replacer, sugar, xanthan gum, yeast and salt; mix well and set aside.

2. Pour water, oil, and vinegar into the bread machine baking pan.

3. Select the **Dough Cycle**. As the bread machine is mixing, gradually add the dry ingredients, scraping bottom and sides of pan with a rubber spatula. Try to incorporate all the dry ingredients within 1 to 2 minutes. Stop bread machine as soon as the kneading portion of the cycle is complete. Do not let bread machine finish the cycle.

4. Using a ¼-cup (60 mL) scoop, drop 10 scoops of dough at least 2 inches (5 cm) apart onto prepared baking sheet. Let rise, uncovered, in a warm, draft-free place for 75 minutes. Meanwhile, preheat oven to 350°F (180°C).

5. Bake for 20 to 22 minutes or until internal temperature of rolls registers 200°F (100°C) on an instant-read thermometer. Remove from the pan immediately and let cool completely on a rack.

Oatmeal Dinner Rolls

MAKES 12 ROLLS
(1 per serving)

Everyone loves these easy-to-make, golden brown dinner rolls.

Tips

To ensure success, see page 15 for information on using your bread machine and page 18 for general tips on bread machine baking.

The batter will appear thinner than most as you are incorporating the dry ingredients, but it will thicken; don't adjust any of the ingredient amounts.

For a softer crust, brush the rolls with melted butter as soon as you remove them from the oven.

See the Techniques Glossary, page 240, for information on toasting seeds.

NUTRITIONAL VALUES	
per serving	
Calories	207
Fat, total	8 g
Fat, saturated	1 g
Cholesterol	32 mg
Sodium	271 mg
Carbohydrate	28 g
Fiber	3 g
Protein	7 g
Calcium	58 mg
Iron	3 mg

◆ **12-cup muffin tin, lightly greased**

1½ cups	sorghum flour	375 mL
⅓ cup	GF oats	75 mL
⅓ cup	GF oat flour	75 mL
⅓ cup	tapioca starch	75 mL
3 tbsp	packed brown sugar	45 mL
1 tbsp	xanthan gum	15 mL
1 tbsp	bread machine or instant yeast	15 mL
1¼ tsp	salt	6 mL
1½ tsp	ground ginger	7 mL
¾ cup	unsalted green pumpkin seeds, toasted	175 mL
1½ cups	milk, warmed to room temperature	375 mL
2 tbsp	vegetable oil	30 mL
1 tsp	cider vinegar	5 mL
2	eggs, lightly beaten	2

1. In a large bowl or plastic bag, combine sorghum flour, oats, oat flour, tapioca starch, brown sugar, xanthan gum, yeast, salt, ginger and pumpkin seeds; mix well and set aside.

2. Pour milk, oil and vinegar into the bread machine baking pan. Add eggs.

3. Select the **Dough Cycle**. As the bread machine is mixing, gradually add the dry ingredients, scraping bottom and sides of pan with a rubber spatula. Try to incorporate all the dry ingredients within 1 to 2 minutes. Stop bread machine as soon as the kneading portion of the cycle is complete. Do not let bread machine finish the cycle.

4. Using a ¼-cup (60 mL) scoop, divide dough into 12 equal amounts and place in cups of prepared muffin tin. Let rise, uncovered, in a warm, draft-free place for 60 to 75 minutes or until dough has risen to the top of the cups. Meanwhile, preheat oven to 350°F (180°C).

5. Bake for 18 to 20 minutes or until internal temperature of rolls registers 200°F (100°C) on an instant-read thermometer. Remove from the pan immediately and let cool completely on a rack.

Brown Seed Dinner Rolls

Longing for a rich, dark dinner roll? We've added three kinds of seeds for extra crunch.

Tips

To ensure success, see page 15 for information on using your bread machine and page 18 for general tips on bread machine baking.

If you don't have a scoop, use a large serving spoon and drop into muffin cups by large rounded spoonfuls.

If you don't have a muffin tin, drop 12 scoops of dough at least 2 inches (5 cm) apart onto a lightly greased baking sheet.

Variation

Before letting dough rise, sprinkle tops with ¼ cup (60 mL) sesame seeds.

NUTRITIONAL VALUES
per serving

Calories	192
Fat, total	11 g
Fat, saturated	1 g
Cholesterol	31 mg
Sodium	256 mg
Carbohydrate	20 g
Fiber	3 g
Protein	6 g
Calcium	56 mg
Iron	3 mg

◆ **12-cup muffin tin, lightly greased**

¾ cup	sorghum flour	175 mL
¾ cup	whole bean flour	175 mL
¼ cup	potato starch	60 mL
¼ cup	rice bran	60 mL
2½ tsp	xanthan gum	12 mL
1 tbsp	bread machine or instant yeast	15 mL
1¼ tsp	salt	6 mL
⅓ cup	unsalted green pumpkin seeds	75 mL
⅓ cup	unsalted raw sunflower seeds	75 mL
¼ cup	sesame seeds	60 mL
1¼ cups	water	300 mL
¼ cup	vegetable oil	60 mL
2 tbsp	liquid honey	30 mL
2 tbsp	light (fancy) molasses	30 mL
1 tsp	cider vinegar	5 mL
2	eggs, lightly beaten	2

1. In a large bowl or plastic bag, combine sorghum flour, whole bean flour, potato starch, rice bran, xanthan gum, yeast, salt, pumpkin seeds, sunflower seeds and sesame seeds; mix well and set aside.

2. Pour water, oil, honey, molasses and vinegar into the bread machine baking pan. Add eggs.

3. Select the **Dough Cycle**. As the bread machine is mixing, gradually add the dry ingredients, scraping bottom and sides of pan with a rubber spatula. Try to incorporate all the dry ingredients within 1 to 2 minutes. Stop bread machine as soon as the kneading portion of the cycle is complete. Do not let bread machine finish the cycle.

4. Using a ¼-cup (60 mL) scoop, divide dough into 12 equal amounts and place in cups of prepared muffin tin. Let rise, uncovered, in a warm, draft-free place for 60 to 75 minutes or until dough has risen to the top of the cups. Meanwhile, preheat oven to 350°F (180°C).

5. Bake for 18 to 20 minutes or until internal temperature of rolls registers 200°F (100°C) on an instant-read thermometer. Remove from the pan immediately and let cool completely on a rack.

French Onion Rolls

White as snow, these crispy, crusty rolls have a fantastic flavor.

Tips

To ensure success, see page 15 for information on using your bread machine and page 18 for general tips on bread machine baking.

Store these rolls loosely covered in a paper bag to maintain the crisp crust.

Do not add onion salt; the flavor is strong enough, and it will inhibit the action of the yeast.

Do not substitute fresh onion; there is too much water in it for this recipe.

Variation

For a plain crusty white roll, omit the onion.

NUTRITIONAL VALUES
per serving

Calories	150
Fat, total	1 g
Fat, saturated	0 g
Cholesterol	0 mg
Sodium	306 mg
Carbohydrate	33 g
Fiber	2 g
Protein	3 g
Calcium	9 mg
Iron	0 mg

◆ **Baking sheet, sprinkled with cornmeal**

2 cups	brown rice flour	500 mL
2/3 cup	potato starch	150 mL
2 tsp	granulated sugar	10 mL
2 tsp	xanthan gum	10 mL
2 tsp	bread machine or instant yeast	10 mL
1 1/4 tsp	salt	6 mL
1/4 cup	minced dried onion	60 mL
1 1/2 cups	water	375 mL
2 tsp	cider vinegar	10 mL
2	egg whites, lightly beaten	2

1. In a large bowl or plastic bag, combine brown rice flour, potato starch, sugar, xanthan gum, yeast, salt and onion; mix well and set aside.

2. Pour water and vinegar into the bread machine baking pan. Add egg whites.

3. Select the **Dough Cycle**. As the bread machine is mixing, gradually add the dry ingredients, scraping bottom and sides of pan with a rubber spatula. Try to incorporate all the dry ingredients within 1 to 2 minutes. Stop bread machine as soon as the kneading portion of the cycle is complete. Do not let bread machine finish the cycle.

4. Using a 1/4-cup (60 mL) scoop, drop 10 scoops of dough at least 2 inches (5 cm) apart onto prepared baking sheet. Let rise, uncovered, in a warm, draft-free place for 75 minutes. Meanwhile, preheat oven to 350°F (180°C).

5. Bake for 20 to 22 minutes or until internal temperature of rolls registers 200°F (100°C) on an instant-read thermometer. Remove from the pan immediately and let cool completely on a rack.

Zucchini Dinner Gems

MAKES 12 ROLLS
(1 per serving)

There's an old piece of gardening wisdom that says, "Before you plant zucchini, make sure you have lots of friends." Here's the perfect recipe to help you use up some of that zucchini crop.

Tips

To ensure success, see page 15 for information on using your bread machine and page 18 for general tips on bread machine baking.

For a softer crust, brush the rolls with melted butter as soon as you remove them from the oven.

Variation

Substitute 1 cup (250 mL) grated carrot for the zucchini.

NUTRITIONAL VALUES per serving	
Calories	171
Fat, total	5 g
Fat, saturated	1 g
Cholesterol	33 mg
Sodium	294 mg
Carbohydrate	28 g
Fiber	2 g
Protein	5 g
Calcium	53 mg
Iron	3 mg

◆ **12-cup muffin tin, lightly greased**

1¼ cups	brown rice flour	300 mL
¾ cup	amaranth flour	175 mL
½ cup	quinoa flour	125 mL
¼ cup	tapioca starch	60 mL
1 tbsp	xanthan gum	15 mL
1¼ tsp	bread machine or instant yeast	6 mL
1¼ tsp	salt	6 mL
¼ cup	freshly grated Parmesan cheese	60 mL
¼ cup	snipped fresh tarragon	60 mL
1 cup	water	250 mL
1 cup	shredded zucchini	250 mL
2 tbsp	vegetable oil	30 mL
3 tbsp	liquid honey	45 mL
1 tsp	cider vinegar	5 mL
2	eggs, lightly beaten	2

1. In a large bowl or plastic bag, combine brown rice flour, amaranth flour, quinoa flour, tapioca starch, xanthan gum, yeast, salt, cheese and tarragon; mix well and set aside.

2. Pour water, zucchini, oil, honey and vinegar into the bread machine baking pan. Add eggs.

3. Select the **Dough Cycle**. As the bread machine is mixing, gradually add the dry ingredients, scraping bottom and sides of pan with a rubber spatula. Try to incorporate all the dry ingredients within 1 to 2 minutes. Stop bread machine as soon as the kneading portion of the cycle is complete. Do not let bread machine finish the cycle.

4. Using a ¼-cup (60 mL) scoop, divide dough into 12 equal amounts and place in cups of prepared muffin tin. Let rise, uncovered, in a warm, draft-free place for 60 to 75 minutes or until dough has risen to the top of the cups. Meanwhile, preheat oven to 350°F (180°C).

5. Bake for 18 to 20 minutes or until internal temperature of rolls registers 200°F (100°C) on an instant-read thermometer. Remove from the pan immediately and let cool completely on a rack.

Grainy Mustard Mock Rye Buns

MAKES 12 ROLLS
(1 per serving)

Heather takes these to her daughter-in-law's for Easter dinner, to serve with the ham.

Tips

To ensure success, see page 15 for information on using your bread machine and page 18 for general tips on bread machine baking.

Do not substitute Dijonnaise for the Dijon mustard — it is too high in fat. You can, however, substitute a green peppercorn Dijon, if you like.

If desired, make extra glaze to brush over rolls again after 10 minutes of baking.

◆ 12-cup muffin tin, lightly greased

1¼ cups	sorghum flour	300 mL
1 cup	whole bean flour	250 mL
½ cup	tapioca starch	125 mL
¼ cup	packed brown sugar	60 mL
1 tbsp	xanthan gum	15 mL
1¼ tsp	bread machine or instant yeast	6 mL
1¼ tsp	salt	6 mL
1¼ cups	water	300 mL
3 tbsp	grainy Dijon mustard	45 mL
2 tbsp	vegetable oil	30 mL
1 tsp	cider vinegar	5 mL
2	eggs, lightly beaten	2
2	egg whites, lightly beaten	2

Grainy Dijon Mustard Glaze

1	egg yolk	1
1 tbsp	grainy Dijon mustard	15 mL

1. In a large bowl or plastic bag, combine sorghum flour, whole bean flour, tapioca starch, brown sugar, xanthan gum, yeast and salt; mix well and set aside.

2. Pour water, mustard, oil and vinegar into the bread machine baking pan. Add eggs and egg whites.

3. Select the **Dough Cycle**. As the bread machine is mixing, gradually add the dry ingredients, scraping bottom and sides of pan with a rubber spatula. Try to incorporate all the dry ingredients within 1 to 2 minutes. Stop bread machine as soon as the kneading portion of the cycle is complete. Do not let bread machine finish the cycle.

4. Using a ¼-cup (60 mL) scoop, divide dough into 12 equal amounts and place in cups of prepared muffin tin. Let rise, uncovered, in a warm, draft-free place for 60 to 75 minutes or until dough has risen to the top of the cups. Meanwhile, preheat oven to 350°F (180°C).

5. *Prepare the glaze:* Combine egg and mustard. Brush over risen rolls.

6. Bake for 18 to 20 minutes or until internal temperature of buns registers 200°F (100°C) on an instant-read thermometer. Remove from the pan immediately and let cool completely on a rack.

NUTRITIONAL VALUES per serving	
Calories	143
Fat, total	4 g
Fat, saturated	0 g
Cholesterol	31 mg
Sodium	358 mg
Carbohydrate	24 g
Fiber	2 g
Protein	5 g
Calcium	24 mg
Iron	1 mg

Historic Grains Bread (page 64)

Sunflower Flax Bread (page 54)

Sun-Dried Tomato Rice Loaf (page 92),
Cranberry Wild Rice Loaf (page 90)
and Teff Bread (page 60)

Olive Ciabatta (page 158)

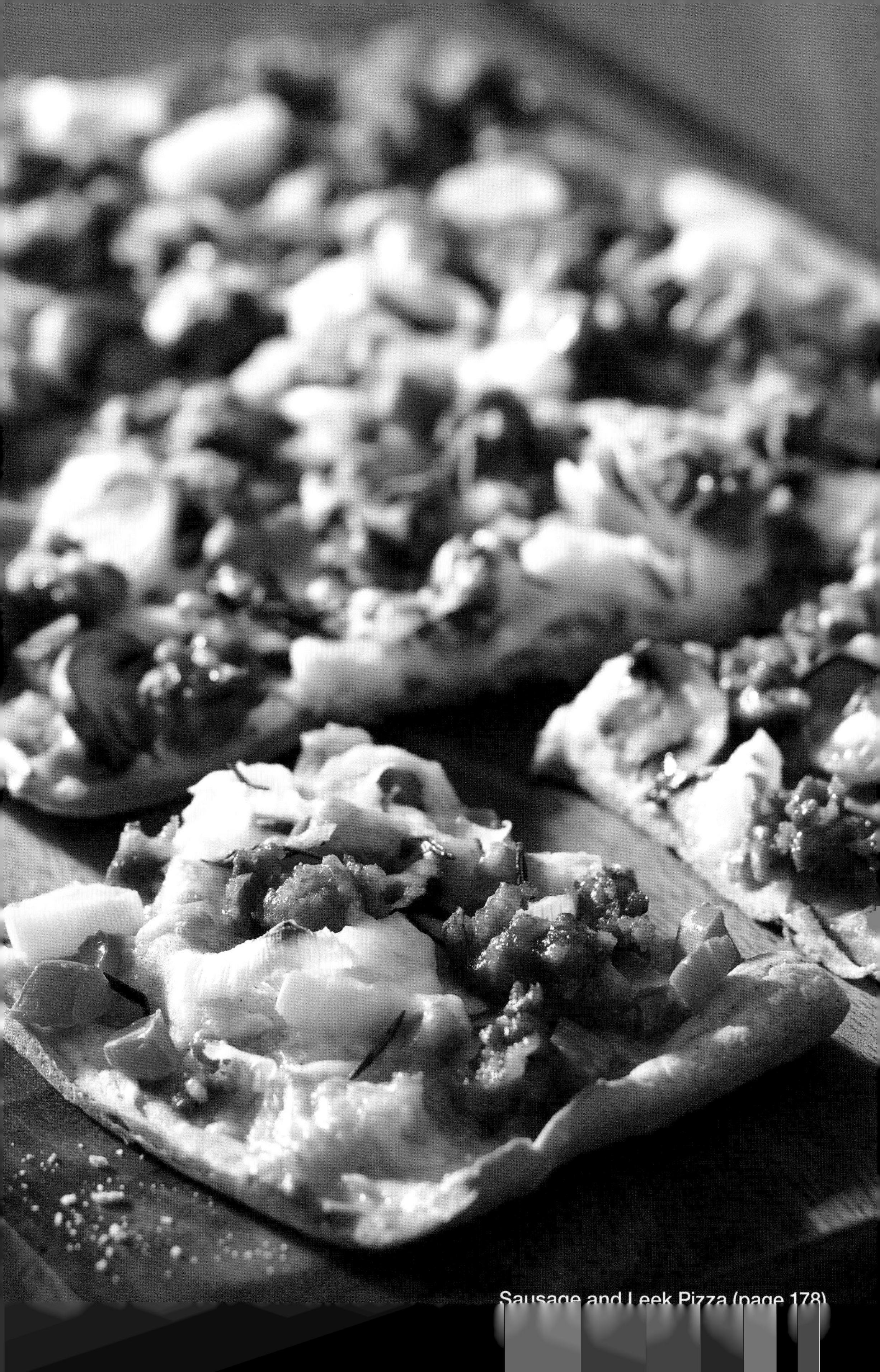

Sausage and Leek Pizza (page 178)

Cinnamon Buns (page 210)

Banana Raisin Sticky Buns (page 212)

Breadsticks (page 146)

Hamburger Buns

**MAKES 6
HAMBURGER BUNS
(1 per serving)**

Though formed into the traditional shape for hamburger buns, these white bread rolls are also great both for sandwiches and as a dinner accompaniment.

Tips

To ensure success, see page 15 for information on using your bread machine and page 18 for general tips on bread machine baking.

If you don't have a hamburger bun pan, try a cast-iron corncob-shaped bread pan or English muffin rings, or make free-form buns on a lightly greased baking sheet. Decrease the water by 2 tbsp (30 mL) for free-form buns.

NUTRITIONAL VALUES per serving	
Calories	375
Fat, total	12 g
Fat, saturated	2 g
Cholesterol	63 mg
Sodium	639 mg
Carbohydrate	62 g
Fiber	3 g
Protein	7 g
Calcium	54 mg
Iron	1 mg

◆ **Hamburger bun baking pan, lightly greased**

1¾ cups	brown rice flour	425 mL
⅔ cup	potato starch	150 mL
⅓ cup	tapioca starch	75 mL
¼ cup	nonfat dry milk or skim milk powder	60 mL
¼ cup	granulated sugar	60 mL
2½ tsp	xanthan gum	12 mL
1 tbsp	bread machine or instant yeast	15 mL
1½ tsp	salt	7 mL
1¼ cups	water	300 mL
¼ cup	vegetable oil	60 mL
1 tsp	cider vinegar	5 mL
2	eggs, lightly beaten	2
2	egg whites, lightly beaten	2

1. In a large bowl or plastic bag, combine brown rice flour, potato starch, tapioca starch, dry milk, sugar, xanthan gum, yeast and salt; mix well and set aside.

2. Pour water, oil and vinegar into the bread machine baking pan. Add eggs and egg whites.

3. Select the **Dough Cycle**. As the bread machine is mixing, gradually add the dry ingredients, scraping bottom and sides of pan with a rubber spatula. Try to incorporate all the dry ingredients within 1 to 2 minutes. Stop bread machine as soon as the kneading portion of the cycle is complete. Do not let bread machine finish the cycle.

4. Spoon ⅔ cup (150 mL) dough into each cup of prepared pan, mounding toward the center of each bun. Smooth the tops with a moistened rubber spatula. Let rise in a warm, draft-free place for 30 to 45 minutes or until dough has almost doubled in volume. Meanwhile, preheat oven to 350°F (180°C).

5. Bake for 15 to 20 minutes or until internal temperature of buns registers 200°F (100°C) on an instant-read thermometer. Remove from the pan immediately and let cool completely on a rack.

Breadsticks

**MAKES
12 BREADSTICKS
(1 per serving)**

*Serve these breadsticks
as Italian restaurants
do — with a dish of
flavored olive oil for
dipping.*

Tips

To ensure success, see
page 15 for information on
using your bread machine
and page 18 for general tips
on bread machine baking.

Thoroughly mix the dry
ingredients before adding
them to the liquids — they
are powder-fine and can
clump together.

Don't worry when seeds
move as you spread the
dough to the edges of the
pan — they will still coat
the breadsticks.

NUTRITIONAL VALUES
per serving

Calories	124
Fat, total	4 g
Fat, saturated	0 g
Cholesterol	21 mg
Sodium	170 mg
Carbohydrate	20 g
Fiber	1 g
Protein	3 g
Calcium	8 mg
Iron	1 mg

◆ **9-inch (23 cm) square baking pan, lightly greased**

⅔ cup	brown rice flour	150 mL
2 tbsp	almond flour	30 mL
¼ cup	potato starch	60 mL
2 tbsp	tapioca starch	30 mL
1 tbsp	granulated sugar	15 mL
1¼ tsp	xanthan gum	6 mL
2 tsp	bread machine or instant yeast	10 mL
¾ tsp	salt	3 mL
¾ cup	water	175 mL
1 tbsp	vegetable oil	15 mL
1 tsp	cider vinegar	5 mL
3 tbsp	sesame seeds	45 mL

1. In a large bowl or plastic bag, combine brown rice flour, almond flour, potato starch, tapioca starch, sugar, xanthan gum, yeast and salt; mix well and set aside.

2. Pour water, oil and vinegar into the bread machine baking pan.

3. Select the **Dough Cycle**. As the bread machine is mixing, gradually add the dry ingredients, scraping bottom and sides of pan with a rubber spatula. Try to incorporate all the dry ingredients within 1 to 2 minutes. Stop bread machine as soon as the kneading portion of the cycle is complete. Do not let bread machine finish the cycle.

4. Sprinkle 2 tbsp (30 mL) of the sesame seeds in bottom of prepared pan. Drop dough by spoonfuls over the sesame seeds. Using a moistened rubber spatula, spread dough evenly to the edges of the pan. Sprinkle with the remaining sesame seeds. Using moistened rubber spatula, press seeds into dough. Let rise, uncovered, in a warm, draft-free place for 30 minutes. Meanwhile, preheat oven to 400°F (200°C).

Tips

For uniform breadsticks, cut bread in half, then lengthwise into quarters. Finally, cut each quarter lengthwise into 3 strips.

If breadsticks become soft, crisp in a toaster oven or conventional oven at 350°F (180°C) for a few minutes.

Use any leftover breadsticks to make dry bread crumbs (see the Techniques Glossary, page 237).

Variations

Substitute poppy seeds for the sesame seeds.

For an Italian herb flavor, add 2 to 3 tsp (10 to 15 mL) of your favorite dried herb with the dry ingredients and use extra virgin olive oil instead of vegetable oil.

5. Bake for 10 to 12 minutes or until light brown. Remove from the pan and transfer immediately to a cutting board. Reduce oven temperature to 350°F (180°C). Using a pizza wheel or a sharp knife, cut bread into 12 equal strips. Roll strips in loose sesame seeds in pan, pressing seeds into cut sides.

6. Arrange slices, with cut sides exposed, at least $1/2$ inch (1 cm) apart on a baking sheet. Bake for 20 to 25 minutes or until dry, crisp and golden brown. Remove from the pan immediately and let cool completely on a rack.

English Muffins

A popular breakfast or brunch treat! Just split with a fork and toast. Your butter and jam will ooze into the crevices.

Tips

To ensure success, see page 15 for information on using your bread machine and page 18 for general tips on bread machine baking.

To serve, use a fork to split each English muffin horizontally in half. Toast until golden and serve warm.

Variation

Cinnamon Raisin English Muffins: Add ⅔ cup (150 mL) raisins and 1 tsp (5 mL) ground cinnamon with the dry ingredients.

NUTRITIONAL VALUES per serving	
Calories	124
Fat, total	4 g
Fat, saturated	0 g
Cholesterol	21 mg
Sodium	170 mg
Carbohydrate	20 g
Fiber	1 g
Protein	3 g
Calcium	8 mg
Iron	1 mg

◆ **Baking sheets, lined with parchment and generously sprinkled with cornmeal**

1 cup	sorghum flour	250 mL
1 cup	brown rice flour	250 mL
½ cup	tapioca starch	125 mL
2 tbsp	potato flour (not potato starch)	30 mL
2 tbsp	granulated sugar	30 mL
2 tsp	xanthan gum	10 mL
2 tbsp	bread machine or instant yeast	30 mL
1¼ tsp	salt	6 mL
1¼ cups	milk, warmed to room temperature	300 mL
¼ cup	vegetable oil	60 mL
2	eggs, lightly beaten	2
⅓ to ½ cup	cornmeal	75 to 125 mL

1. In a large bowl or plastic bag, combine sorghum flour, brown rice flour, tapioca starch, potato flour, sugar, xanthan gum, yeast and salt; mix well and set aside.

2. Pour milk and oil into the bread machine baking pan. Add eggs.

3. Select the **Dough Cycle**. As the bread machine is mixing, gradually add the dry ingredients, scraping bottom and sides of pan with a rubber spatula. Try to incorporate all the dry ingredients within 1 to 2 minutes. Stop bread machine as soon as the kneading portion of the cycle is complete. Do not let bread machine finish the cycle.

4. Using a ¼-cup (60 mL) scoop, drop 18 scoops of dough at least 2 inches (5 cm) apart onto prepared baking sheets. Sprinkle each with cornmeal. Top with a sheet of parchment paper. Gently pat each into a ½-inch (1 cm) thick circle. Remove parchment. Let rise, uncovered, in a warm, draft-free place for 30 minutes. Meanwhile, preheat oven to 400°F (200°C).

5. Bake for 13 to 15 minutes or until internal temperature of muffins registers 200°F (100°C) on an instant-read thermometer. Remove from the pan immediately and let cool completely on a rack.

Savory Flatbreads

Scandinavian Sesame Wafers

Enjoy these rich, savory sesame wafers with a salad or soup!

Tips

To ensure success, see page 15 for information on using your bread machine and page 18 for general tips on bread machine baking.

Watch these carefully during baking — 1 minute too long can cause the bottoms to burn.

Store in an airtight container at room temperature for up to 3 weeks.

Variation

For a mild-flavored wafer, substitute 2 tbsp (30 mL) flaxseed or poppy seeds for the anise, caraway and fennel seeds.

NUTRITIONAL VALUES
per serving

Calories	50
Fat, total	4 g
Fat, saturated	0 g
Cholesterol	0 mg
Sodium	1 mg
Carbohydrate	3 g
Fiber	1 g
Protein	1 g
Calcium	52 mg
Iron	1 mg

◆ **Preheat oven to 325°F (160°C), with oven rack placed in the top position**
◆ **Baking sheets, lined with parchment paper**

²⁄₃ cup	low-fat soy flour	150 mL
1 tsp	bread machine or instant yeast	5 mL
½ cup	granulated sugar	125 mL
2 cups	sesame seeds, toasted	500 mL
1 tbsp	anise seeds	15 mL
1 tbsp	caraway seeds	15 mL
1 tbsp	fennel seeds	15 mL
½ cup	water	125 mL
⅓ cup	vegetable oil	75 mL

1. In a large bowl or plastic bag, combine soy flour, yeast, sugar, sesame seeds, anise seeds, caraway seeds and fennel seeds; mix well and set aside.

2. Pour water and oil into the bread machine pan.

3. Select the **Dough Cycle**. As the bread machine is mixing, gradually add the dry ingredients, scraping bottom and sides of pan with a rubber spatula. Try to incorporate all the dry ingredients within 1 to 2 minutes. Stop bread machine as soon as the kneading portion of the cycle is complete. Do not let bread machine finish the cycle.

4. Drop by small spoonfuls at least 2 inches (5 cm) apart onto prepared baking sheets. Using a small square of parchment paper, cover each mound, then flatten with a flat-bottomed drinking glass. Remove parchment.

5. Bake, one sheet at a time, on top rack of preheated oven for 8 to 11 minutes or until lightly browned. Let cool on baking sheet for 2 to 3 minutes. Transfer to a rack and let cool completely.

Lavosh

*Keep this thin, low-fat,
crisp Armenian flatbread
on hand to serve as
a snack with fresh
vegetables, for dipping
in salsa or with soups
or salads.*

Tips

To ensure success, see
page 15 for information on
using your bread machine
and page 18 for general tips
on bread machine baking.

Store in an airtight
container at room
temperature for up to
3 months. If necessary,
crisp the lavosh in a 300°F
(150°C) oven for 5 minutes
before serving.

NUTRITIONAL VALUES
per serving

Calories	29
Fat, total	1 g
Fat, saturated	0 g
Cholesterol	0 mg
Sodium	37 mg
Carbohydrate	5 g
Fiber	0 g
Protein	1 g
Calcium	12 mg
Iron	0 mg

◆ **Preheat oven to 375°F (190°C)**
◆ **Large baking sheet, lightly greased**

¾ cup	brown rice flour	175 mL
⅓ cup	tapioca starch	75 mL
1 tsp	granulated sugar	5 mL
1½ tsp	xanthan gum	7 mL
1½ tsp	bread machine or instant yeast	7 mL
½ tsp	salt	2 mL
¾ cup	water	175 mL
1 tbsp	vegetable or sesame oil	15 mL
1 tsp	cider vinegar	5 mL
¼ cup	sesame seeds	60 mL
1 to 2 tbsp	sweet rice flour	15 to 30 mL

1. In a large bowl or plastic bag, combine brown rice flour, tapioca starch, sugar, xanthan gum, yeast and salt; mix well and set aside.

2. Pour water, oil and vinegar into the bread machine pan.

3. Select the **Dough Cycle**. As the bread machine is mixing, gradually add the dry ingredients, scraping bottom and sides of pan with a rubber spatula. Try to incorporate all the dry ingredients within 1 to 2 minutes. Stop bread machine as soon as the kneading portion of the cycle is complete. Do not let bread machine finish the cycle.

4. Sprinkle prepared baking sheet with half the sesame seeds. Remove dough to prepared sheet. Sprinkle generously with sweet rice flour. With floured fingers, gently pat out the dough to fill the pan evenly, sprinkling with sweet rice flour if dough becomes too sticky to handle. (Or, to more easily pat out the dough, place waxed paper dusted with sweet rice flour on top. Gently pat the waxed paper to spread the dough, lifting the paper frequently to check the thickness of the dough. The thinner the dough is spread, the more authentic the cracker will be.) Sprinkle with the remaining sesame seeds and press lightly into dough.

5. Bake in preheated oven for 20 to 25 minutes or until lightly browned. Turn off oven and let cool in the oven for 1 hour. Remove from oven and break into pieces.

Sun-Dried Tomato Lavosh

**MAKES ABOUT
48 CRACKERS**
(1/16 recipe per serving)

*This delicious crisp is
the perfect addition to a
basket of fresh rolls.*

Tips

To ensure success, see
page 15 for information on
using your bread machine
and page 18 for general tips
on bread machine baking.

Purchase dry, not oil-packed,
sun-dried tomatoes. Snip
them with kitchen shears.

The thinner the dough is
spread, the more authentic
the cracker will be. To more
easily spread the dough,
moisten the rubber spatula
as needed. Don't worry: you
can't use too much water.
If you create holes, that's
fine — just leave them.

NUTRITIONAL VALUES per serving	
Calories	64
Fat, total	3 g
Fat, saturated	1 g
Cholesterol	2 mg
Sodium	178 mg
Carbohydrate	8 g
Fiber	1 g
Protein	3 g
Calcium	57 mg
Iron	1 mg

♦ **Preheat oven to 375°F (190°C)**
♦ **15- by 10-inch (40 by 25 cm) jelly roll pan, lightly greased**

1/2 cup	sorghum flour	125 mL
1/3 cup	whole bean flour	75 mL
1/4 cup	tapioca starch	60 mL
1 tsp	granulated sugar	5 mL
1/2 tsp	xanthan gum	2 mL
1 1/2 tsp	bread machine or instant yeast	7 mL
1/2 tsp	salt	2 mL
2 tbsp	dried basil	30 mL
2/3 cup	snipped sun-dried tomatoes (see tip, at left)	150 mL
3/4 cup	water	175 mL
2 tbsp	extra virgin olive oil	30 mL
1 tsp	cider vinegar	5 mL
1/2 cup	freshly grated Parmesan cheese, divided	125 mL

1. In a large bowl or plastic bag, combine sorghum flour, whole bean flour, tapioca starch, sugar, xanthan gum, yeast, salt, basil and tomatoes; mix well and set aside.

2. Pour water, oil and vinegar into the bread machine baking pan.

3. Select the **Dough Cycle**. As the bread machine is mixing, gradually add the dry ingredients, scraping bottom and sides of pan with a rubber spatula. Try to incorporate all the dry ingredients within 1 to 2 minutes. Stop bread machine as soon as the kneading portion of the cycle is complete. Do not let bread machine finish the cycle.

4. Sprinkle prepared pan with half the Parmesan. Remove dough to prepared pan. Using a moistened rubber spatula, spread out the dough to fill the pan evenly, sprinkling with Parmesan if dough becomes too sticky to handle. Sprinkle with the remaining Parmesan and press lightly into dough.

5. Bake in preheated oven for 16 to 18 minutes or until golden brown. Turn off oven and let cool in the oven for 1 hour. Remove from oven and break into pieces.

6. Store in an airtight container at room temperature for up to 3 months. If necessary, crisp the lavosh in a 300°F (150°C) oven for 5 minutes before serving.

Moroccan Anise Bread

**MAKES ABOUT
30 CRACKERS**
(1/15 recipe per serving)

Making dough doesn't get much easier or faster than this. The hands-on preparation is less than 15 minutes. Dip pieces of this savory crispbread in hummus or a vegetable dip.

Tips

To ensure success, see page 15 for information on using your bread machine and page 18 for general tips on bread machine baking.

Make lots of holes with the fork, as this gives an interesting finish to the top crust.

Variation

Substitute an equal quantity of cumin seeds for the anise seeds.

NUTRITIONAL VALUES per serving	
Calories	134
Fat, total	4 g
Fat, saturated	0 g
Cholesterol	0 mg
Sodium	196 mg
Carbohydrate	22 g
Fiber	3 g
Protein	3 g
Calcium	23 mg
Iron	2 mg

◆ **Two baking sheets, sprinkled with cornmeal**

1½ cups	sorghum flour	375 mL
¾ cup	teff flour	175 mL
¼ cup	cornmeal	60 mL
½ cup	tapioca starch	125 mL
1 tsp	granulated sugar	5 mL
1 tbsp	xanthan gum	15 mL
2 tsp	bread machine or instant yeast	10 mL
1¼ tsp	salt	6 mL
2 tbsp	anise seeds	30 mL
2 cups	water	500 mL
¼ cup	vegetable oil	60 mL
2 tsp	cider vinegar	10 mL

1. In a large bowl or plastic bag, combine sorghum flour, teff flour, cornmeal, tapioca starch, sugar, xanthan gum, yeast, salt and anise seeds; mix well and set aside.

2. Pour water, oil and vinegar into the bread machine baking pan.

3. Select the **Dough Cycle**. As the bread machine is mixing, gradually add the dry ingredients, scraping bottom and sides of pan with a rubber spatula. Try to incorporate all the dry ingredients within 1 to 2 minutes. Stop bread machine as soon as the kneading portion of the cycle is complete. Do not let bread machine finish the cycle.

4. Immediately pour half the batter onto each prepared baking sheet. Using a moistened rubber spatula, spread each evenly into a 10-inch (25 cm) round, leaving the top rough. Let rise, uncovered, in a warm, draft-free place for 15 minutes. Meanwhile, preheat oven to 400°F (200°C).

5. Using a fork, pierce the dough all over, pressing all the way down to the baking sheet. Bake in preheated oven for 15 minutes, rotating pans halfway through, or until firm. Remove from pans and place directly on oven rack. Bake for 8 to 10 minutes or until crisp. Remove from the oven immediately and let cool completely on racks. Break into pieces.

Ciabatta

From the Italian for "old slipper," ciabatta are flat, chewy loaves that are fun to make. Poke them full of dimples before letting them rise. The flour-coated crust provides an interesting open texture. Our round version is easily cut into wedges.

Tips

To ensure success, see page 15 for information on using your bread machine and page 18 for general tips on bread machine baking.

When dusting with rice flour, use a flour sifter for a light, even sprinkle.

This bread freezes well. Cut into wedges and freeze individually for sandwiches.

NUTRITIONAL VALUES
per serving

Calories	144
Fat, total	5 g
Fat, saturated	1 g
Cholesterol	47 mg
Sodium	162 mg
Carbohydrate	22 g
Fiber	1 g
Protein	3 g
Calcium	13 mg
Iron	1 mg

◆ **8-inch (20 cm) round baking pan, lightly floured**

½ cup	whole bean flour	125 mL
½ cup	brown rice flour	125 mL
½ cup	tapioca starch	125 mL
2 tbsp	granulated sugar	30 mL
2 tsp	xanthan gum	10 mL
1 tbsp	bread machine or instant yeast	15 mL
½ tsp	salt	2 mL
¾ cup	water	175 mL
1 tsp	cider vinegar	5 mL
2 tbsp	extra virgin olive oil	30 mL
2	eggs, lightly beaten	2
2 to 3 tbsp	sweet rice flour	30 to 45 mL

1. In a large bowl or plastic bag, combine whole bean flour, brown rice flour, tapioca starch, sugar, xanthan gum, yeast and salt; mix well and set aside.

2. Pour water, vinegar and oil into the bread machine baking pan. Add eggs.

3. Select the **Dough Cycle**. As the bread machine is mixing, gradually add the dry ingredients, scraping bottom and sides of pan with a rubber spatula. Try to incorporate all the dry ingredients within 1 to 2 minutes. Stop bread machine as soon as the kneading portion of the cycle is complete. Do not let bread machine finish the cycle.

4. Gently transfer dough to prepared pan and spread evenly to the edges, leaving the top rough and uneven. Generously dust top with sweet rice flour. With well-floured fingers, make deep indents all over the dough, pressing all the way down to the pan. Let rise, uncovered, in a warm, draft-free place for 40 to 50 minutes or until almost doubled in volume. Meanwhile, preheat oven to 425°F (220°C).

5. Bake for 15 to 20 minutes or until top is golden. Remove from the pan immediately and let cool on a rack. Cut into 8 wedges and serve warm.

Grilled Ham and Cheese Ciabatta Sandwich

MAKES 6 WEDGES
(1 per serving)

Here's a quick lunch for six adults (or, as we learned, two teenage boys with large appetites). Try our grilled version.

Tip

You can also use an indoor contact grill or a panini grill; in that case, there's no need to turn the sandwich, as both sides cook at once.

Variations

Feel free to pile on lots of thinly sliced GF cold cuts.

If you prefer a cold sandwich to a grilled one, you can add some mixed salad greens.

◆ Preheat barbecue grill to high or preheat broiler

1	Ciabatta (page 154), left whole	1
1 to 2 tbsp	Dijon mustard	15 to 30 mL
12 oz	GF smoked ham, thinly sliced	375 g
12 oz	Swiss cheese, thinly sliced	375 g
2	large tomatoes, sliced	2
	Bean sprouts	
	Extra virgin olive oil	

1. Slice ciabatta in half horizontally. Spread Dijon mustard to taste on the bottom half. Layer with ham, cheese, tomatoes and bean sprouts. Cover with top half of ciabatta and brush both sides of the sandwich with a thin layer of oil.
2. Place on preheated barbecue or under preheated broiler. Cook, turning once, until ciabatta is browned and crisp and cheese is melted. Cut into 6 wedges and serve hot.

NUTRITIONAL VALUES per serving	
Calories	475
Fat, total	24 g
Fat, saturated	11 g
Cholesterol	140 mg
Sodium	160 mg
Carbohydrate	34 g
Fiber	2 g
Protein	31 g
Calcium	465 mg
Iron	2 mg

Sun-Dried Tomato Ciabatta

Sun-dried tomatoes, Parmesan cheese and fresh rosemary take this Italian flatbread a step above the ordinary. It's fabulous served with soup or salad.

Tips

To ensure success, see page 15 for information on using your bread machine and page 18 for general tips on bread machine baking.

We like this ciabatta best served hot out of the oven.

Variation

Substitute 2 to 3 tbsp (30 to 45 mL) dried basil or oregano for the fresh rosemary and sprinkle the risen dough with 2 tbsp (30 mL) freshly grated Parmesan cheese.

NUTRITIONAL VALUES
per serving

Calories	155
Fat, total	8 g
Fat, saturated	3 g
Cholesterol	38 mg
Sodium	278 mg
Carbohydrate	15 g
Fiber	2 g
Protein	7 g
Calcium	131 mg
Iron	1 mg

◆ **9-inch (23 cm) round baking pan, lightly floured with sweet rice flour**

½ cup	brown rice flour	125 mL
½ cup	whole bean flour	125 mL
⅓ cup	tapioca starch	75 mL
2 tbsp	granulated sugar	30 mL
2 tsp	xanthan gum	10 mL
2 tbsp	bread machine or instant yeast	30 mL
¼ tsp	salt	1 mL
1 cup	freshly grated Parmesan cheese	250 mL
½ cup	snipped fresh rosemary	125 mL
¾ cup	water	175 mL
¼ cup	extra virgin olive oil	60 mL
1 tsp	cider vinegar	5 mL
2	eggs, lightly beaten	2
2	cloves garlic, minced	2
⅔ cup	snipped sun-dried tomatoes	150 mL
	Sweet rice flour	

1. In a large bowl or plastic bag, combine brown rice flour, whole bean flour, tapioca starch, sugar, xanthan gum, yeast, salt, Parmesan and rosemary; mix well and set aside.

2. Pour water, oil and vinegar into the bread machine baking pan. Add eggs, garlic and sun-dried tomatoes.

3. Select the **Dough Cycle**. As the bread machine is mixing, gradually add the dry ingredients, scraping bottom and sides of pan with a rubber spatula. Try to incorporate all the dry ingredients within 1 to 2 minutes. Stop bread machine as soon as the kneading portion of the cycle is complete. Do not let bread machine finish the cycle.

4. Gently transfer dough to prepared pan and spread evenly to the edges, leaving the top rough and uneven. Generously dust top with sweet rice flour. With well-floured fingers, make deep indents all over the dough, pressing all the way down to the pan. Let rise, uncovered, in a warm, draft-free place for 60 minutes or until almost doubled in volume. Meanwhile, preheat oven to 425°F (220°C).

5. Bake for 18 to 25 minutes or until top is golden. Remove from the pan immediately, cut into 12 wedges and serve hot.

Blue Cheese Walnut Ciabatta

We've had many requests for ciabatta with this flavor combination. Right from the oven, this quick and easy flatbread with a tangy crunch complements soup, salad or stew.

Tips

To ensure success, see page 15 for information on using your bread machine and page 18 for general tips on bread machine baking.

This dough is thicker than most gluten-free doughs. Resist the temptation to add extra liquid.

Cut the cheese into ½-inch (1 cm) cubes.

When dusting with sweet rice flour, use a flour sifter for a light, even sprinkle.

NUTRITIONAL VALUES
per serving

Calories	224
Fat, total	13 g
Fat, saturated	3 g
Cholesterol	55 mg
Sodium	319 mg
Carbohydrate	20 g
Fiber	2 g
Protein	9 g
Calcium	95 mg
Iron	3 mg

◆ **8-inch (20 cm) round baking pan, lightly greased and floured with sweet rice flour**

¾ cup	whole bean flour	175 mL
½ cup	amaranth flour	125 mL
¼ cup	tapioca starch	60 mL
2 tbsp	granulated sugar	30 mL
2 tsp	xanthan gum	10 mL
1 tbsp	bread machine or instant yeast	15 mL
2 tbsp	snipped fresh marjoram	30 mL
½ tsp	each salt and black pepper	2 mL
½ cup	chopped walnuts	125 mL
¾ cup	water	175 mL
2 tbsp	vegetable oil	30 mL
1 tsp	cider vinegar	5 mL
2	eggs, lightly beaten	2
⅔ cup	cubed GF blue cheese or Stilton	150 mL
2 to 3 tbsp	sweet rice flour	30 to 45 mL

1. In a large bowl or plastic bag, combine whole bean flour, amaranth flour, tapioca starch, sugar, xanthan gum, yeast, marjoram, salt, pepper and walnuts; mix well and set aside.

2. Pour water, oil and vinegar into the bread machine baking pan. Add eggs.

3. Select the **Dough Cycle**. As the bread machine is mixing, gradually add the dry ingredients, scraping bottom and sides of pan with a rubber spatula. Try to incorporate all the dry ingredients within 1 to 2 minutes. Stop bread machine as soon as the kneading portion of the cycle is complete. Do not let bread machine finish the cycle. Remove baking pan from the bread machine. Fold in blue cheese.

4. Gently transfer dough to prepared pan and spread evenly to the edges, leaving the top rough and uneven. Generously dust top with sweet rice flour. With well-floured fingers, make deep indents all over the dough, pressing all the way down to the pan. Let rise, uncovered, in a warm, draft-free place for 60 to 75 minutes or until almost doubled in volume. Meanwhile, preheat oven to 400°F (200°C).

5. Bake for 20 to 25 minutes or until top is golden. Remove from the pan immediately and let cool on a rack. Cut into 8 wedges and serve warm.

Olive Ciabatta

MAKES 8 WEDGES
(1 per serving)

Black and green olives and a good-quality olive oil combine to make this strong-flavored, irresistible Italian bread. We've adapted the shape to accommodate the batter-like gluten-free dough.

Tips

To ensure success, see page 15 for information on using your bread machine and page 18 for general tips on bread machine baking.

When dusting with sweet rice flour, use a flour sifter for a light, even sprinkle.

Be sure olives are well drained and pat dry with paper towels.

◆ **8-inch (20 cm) round baking pan, lightly greased**

½ cup	hazelnut flour	125 mL
½ cup	whole bean flour	125 mL
¼ cup	quinoa flour	60 mL
¼ cup	tapioca starch	60 mL
2 tbsp	granulated sugar	30 mL
2 tsp	xanthan gum	10 mL
1 tbsp	bread machine or instant yeast	15 mL
1 tsp	salt	5 mL
1 tbsp	dried oregano	15 mL
1 tbsp	dried rosemary	15 mL
¾ cup	water	175 mL
2 tbsp	extra virgin olive oil	30 mL
1 tsp	cider vinegar	5 mL
2	eggs, lightly beaten	2
¾ cup	sliced pitted kalamata olives	175 mL
¾ cup	sliced pitted green olives	175 mL
½ cup	chopped hazelnuts	125 mL
2 to 3 tbsp	sweet rice flour, brown rice flour or whole bean flour	30 to 45 mL

1. In a large bowl or plastic bag, combine hazelnut flour, whole bean flour, quinoa flour, tapioca starch, sugar, xanthan gum, yeast, salt, oregano and rosemary; mix well and set aside.

2. Pour water, oil and vinegar into the bread machine baking pan. Add eggs.

3. Select the **Dough Cycle**. As the bread machine is mixing, gradually add the dry ingredients, scraping bottom and sides of pan with a rubber spatula. Try to incorporate all the dry ingredients within 1 to 2 minutes. Stop bread machine as soon as the kneading portion of the cycle is complete. Do not let bread machine finish the cycle. Remove baking pan from the bread machine. Fold in kalamata olives, green olives and hazelnuts.

NUTRITIONAL VALUES
per serving

Calories	237
Fat, total	16 g
Fat, saturated	2 g
Cholesterol	47 mg
Sodium	528 mg
Carbohydrate	19 g
Fiber	4 g
Protein	6 g
Calcium	66 mg
Iron	3 mg

Variations

To make 4 to 6 individual ciabatta, use English muffin rings on a floured rimmed baking sheet and fill two-thirds full.

To turn this into a Mediterranean-style ciabatta, add ½ cup (125 mL) finely chopped red onion with the kalamata olives and substitute 1 tbsp (15 mL) snipped fresh cilantro or mint for the green olives.

Substitute pecan flour for the hazelnut flour and pecans for the hazelnuts.

4. Gently transfer dough to prepared pan and spread evenly to the edges, leaving the top rough and uneven. Generously dust top with sweet rice flour. With well-floured fingers, make deep indents all over the dough, pressing all the way down to the pan. Let rise, uncovered, in a warm, draft-free place for 60 to 75 minutes or until almost doubled in volume. Meanwhile, preheat oven to 400°F (200°C).

5. Bake for 20 to 25 minutes or until top is golden. Remove from the pan immediately and let cool on a rack. Cut into 8 wedges and serve warm.

To make this recipe egg-free: Omit eggs from the recipe. Combine ½ cup (125 mL) flax flour or ground flaxseed with an additional ¼ cup (60 mL) warm water. Set aside for 5 minutes. Add with the liquids.

Focaccia

Plan to serve this chewy flatbread hot from the oven along with soup or salad lunches, or cut into smaller pieces and serve as hors d'oeuvres.

Tips

To ensure success, see page 15 for information on using your bread machine and page 18 for general tips on bread machine baking.

Can't decide which topping to make? Make a different topping for each pan.

Reheat under the broiler to enjoy crisp focaccia.

Focaccia can be reheated in just a few minutes in a toaster oven set to 375°F (190°C).

NUTRITIONAL VALUES
per serving

Calories	53
Fat, total	1 g
Fat, saturated	0 g
Cholesterol	0 mg
Sodium	98 mg
Carbohydrate	9 g
Fiber	1 g
Protein	2 g
Calcium	9 mg
Iron	1 mg

◆ **Two 9-inch (23 cm) square baking pans, lightly greased**

⅔ cup	amaranth flour	150 mL
½ cup	pea flour	125 mL
⅓ cup	potato starch	75 mL
¼ cup	tapioca starch	60 mL
1 tsp	granulated sugar	5 mL
2 tsp	xanthan gum	10 mL
1 tbsp	bread machine or instant yeast	15 mL
¾ tsp	salt	3 mL
1½ cups	water	375 mL
1 tbsp	extra virgin olive oil	15 mL
1 tsp	cider vinegar	5 mL
	Topping mixture (pages 161–163)	

1. In a large bowl or plastic bag, combine amaranth flour, pea flour, potato starch, tapioca starch, sugar, xanthan gum, yeast and salt; mix well and set aside.

2. Pour water, oil and vinegar into the bread machine baking pan.

3. Select the **Dough Cycle**. As the bread machine is mixing, gradually add the dry ingredients, scraping bottom and sides of pan with a rubber spatula. Try to incorporate all the dry ingredients within 1 to 2 minutes. Stop bread machine as soon as the kneading portion of the cycle is complete. Do not let bread machine finish the cycle.

4. Gently transfer dough to prepared pans and spread evenly to the edges, leaving the tops rough and uneven. Let rise, uncovered, in a warm draft-free place for 20 minutes. Meanwhile, preheat oven to 375°F (190°C).

5. Bake for 10 minutes or until bottoms are golden.

6. Cover with preferred topping mixture. Bake for 20 to 25 minutes or until tops are golden. Remove from the pans immediately, cut each into 9 pieces and serve hot.

Parmesan Walnut Focaccia Topping

**MAKES ENOUGH
TOPPING FOR
ONE 9-INCH
(23 CM) SQUARE
BAKING PAN**
($\frac{1}{9}$ recipe per
serving)

*Walnuts with freshly
grated Parmesan cheese is
a combination of flavors
sure to please.*

Tip
Store walnuts in the
refrigerator and taste for
freshness before using.

Variation
Substitute pine nuts for
the walnuts and Romano
or Asiago cheese for the
Parmesan.

2	cloves garlic, minced	2
2 tbsp	extra virgin olive oil	30 mL
$\frac{3}{4}$ cup	finely chopped walnuts	175 mL
3 tbsp	freshly grated Parmesan cheese	45 mL

1. In a small bowl, combine garlic and oil; let stand while focaccia rises.
2. Drizzle over the partially cooked focaccia. Sprinkle with walnuts and Parmesan.

NUTRITIONAL VALUES
per serving

Calories	102
Fat, total	10 g
Fat, saturated	1 g
Cholesterol	2 mg
Sodium	39 mg
Carbohydrate	2 g
Fiber	1 g
Protein	2 g
Calcium	40 mg
Iron	0 mg

Mediterranean Focaccia Topping

Top focaccia with sweet onions, slowly caramelized in a small amount of olive oil until golden.

Tip

No need for extra oil: if onions start to stick, add 1 tbsp (15 mL) white wine or water.

Variation

Add $\frac{1}{2}$ cup (125 mL) snipped sun-dried tomatoes with the olives.

2 tbsp	extra virgin olive oil	30 mL
4 cups	sliced Vidalia or other sweet onions	1 L
2 tbsp	snipped fresh thyme	30 mL
1 tbsp	balsamic vinegar	15 mL
12	kalamata olives, pitted and sliced	12
$\frac{1}{2}$ cup	crumbled feta cheese	125 mL

1. In a skillet, heat oil over medium-low heat. Sauté onions for 20 minutes or until tender and light golden brown. Remove from heat and stir in thyme and vinegar. Let cool slightly.

2. Spoon over the partially cooked focaccia. Sprinkle with olives and feta.

NUTRITIONAL VALUES per serving	
Calories	92
Fat, total	6 g
Fat, saturated	2 g
Cholesterol	7 mg
Sodium	177 mg
Carbohydrate	7 g
Fiber	1 g
Protein	2 g
Calcium	64 mg
Iron	0 mg

Triple-Cheese Focaccia Topping

A trio of cheeses sprinkled over focaccia dough creates the perfect bread to accompany gazpacho on a hot summer day.

Tip

Use the amount of cheese stated in the recipe: too much results in a greasy focaccia.

Variation

Substitute your favorite lower-fat varieties for the cheeses.

2	cloves garlic, minced	2
2 tbsp	extra virgin olive oil	30 mL
1 tbsp	dried basil	15 mL
²/₃ cup	shredded Asiago cheese	150 mL
²/₃ cup	shredded mozzarella cheese	150 mL
¹/₃ cup	freshly grated Parmesan cheese	75 mL
1 cup	GF salsa	250 mL

1. In a small bowl, combine garlic, oil and basil; let stand while focaccia rises.
2. In another small bowl, combine Asiago, mozzarella and Parmesan.
3. Drizzle garlic-oil mixture over the partially cooked focaccia. Top with salsa and cheese mixture.

NUTRITIONAL VALUES
per serving

Calories	103
Fat, total	8 g
Fat, saturated	3 g
Cholesterol	15 mg
Sodium	204 mg
Carbohydrate	2 g
Fiber	1 g
Protein	6 g
Calcium	204 mg
Iron	0 mg

Honey Dijon Toastie

A small amount of honey mustard added to the dough makes this open-textured bread an ideal sandwich bread (see Barbecued Tuscan Toastie, opposite) or accompaniment to a baked ham dinner. Or cut it into wedges to serve with soups or salads.

Tip

To ensure success, see page 15 for information on using your bread machine and page 18 for general tips on bread machine baking.

Variation

Add 2 to 3 tsp (10 to 15 mL) dried herbs to the dough, then sprinkle with 2 to 3 tbsp (30 to 45 mL) freshly grated Parmesan cheese before making indents.

NUTRITIONAL VALUES
per serving

Calories	146
Fat, total	6 g
Fat, saturated	1 g
Cholesterol	0 mg
Sodium	151 mg
Carbohydrate	20 g
Fiber	1 g
Protein	3 g
Calcium	18 mg
Iron	1 mg

◆ **9-inch (23 cm) round baking pan, lightly greased**

1¼ cups	whole bean flour	300 mL
¼ cup	quinoa flour	60 mL
⅓ cup	tapioca starch	75 mL
2 tsp	xanthan gum	10 mL
2 tbsp	bread machine or instant yeast	30 mL
¼ tsp	salt	1 mL
2 tsp	dried thyme	10 mL
1¾ cups	water	425 mL
¼ cup	extra virgin olive oil	60 mL
¼ cup	liquid honey	60 mL
¼ cup	honey Dijon mustard	60 mL
1 tsp	cider vinegar	5 mL
2	cloves garlic, minced	2

1. In a large bowl or plastic bag, combine whole bean flour, quinoa flour, tapioca starch, xanthan gum, yeast, salt and thyme; mix well and set aside.

2. Pour water, oil, honey, mustard, vinegar and garlic into the bread machine baking pan.

3. Select the **Dough Cycle**. As the bread machine is mixing, gradually add the dry ingredients, scraping bottom and sides of pan with a rubber spatula. Try to incorporate all the dry ingredients within 1 to 2 minutes. Stop bread machine as soon as the kneading portion of the cycle is complete. Do not let bread machine finish cycle.

4. Gently transfer dough to prepared pan and spread evenly to the edges. With wet fingers, make deep indents all over the dough, pressing all the way down to the pan. Let rise, uncovered, in a warm, draft-free place for 30 to 45 minutes or until dough has risen almost to the top of the pan. Meanwhile, preheat oven to 375°F (190°C).

5. Bake for 18 to 25 minutes or until top is golden. Remove from the pan immediately, cut into 10 wedges and serve hot, or transfer to a rack and let cool completely.

Barbecued Tuscan Toastie

**MAKES
4 SERVINGS**

Try this sandwich, and you'll understand the Tuscan attitude to food: "With love, from the heart."

Tips

Choose two to three kinds of cold cuts, such as GF prosciutto, GF smoked turkey, GF salami or mild, hot or extra-hot capicollo.

Choose a couple of kinds of cheese, such as Swiss, Cheddar, mozzarella, American or roasted garlic–flavored.

You can also use an indoor contact grill or a panini grill; in that case, there's no need to turn the toastie, as both sides cook at once.

◆ **Preheat broiler or preheat barbecue grill to high**

1	Honey Dijon Toastie (page 164), left whole	1
2 tbsp	GF mayonnaise	30 mL
1 tbsp	Dijon mustard	15 mL
10 oz	thinly sliced GF cold cuts	300 g
6 oz	sliced cheese	175 g
1 cup	mesclun	250 mL
1 tbsp	extra virgin olive oil	15 mL

1. Slice toastie in half horizontally. Spread mayonnaise and mustard on the bottom half. Layer with cold cuts, cheese and mesclun. Cover with top half of toastie and press together. Brush both sides of the sandwich with oil.

2. Place under preheated broiler or on preheated barbecue. Cook, turning once, until toastie is browned and crisp and cheese is melted. Cut into 4 wedges and serve hot.

NUTRITIONAL VALUES per serving	
Calories	480
Fat, total	21 g
Fat, saturated	1 g
Cholesterol	31 mg
Sodium	948 mg
Carbohydrate	51 g
Fiber	3 g
Protein	20 g
Calcium	40 mg
Iron	3 mg

Savory Onion Toastie

Instead of using this open-textured bread to make a sandwich, we've put an onion topping on it.

Tips

To ensure success, see page 15 for information on using your bread machine and page 18 for general tips on bread machine baking.

Before measuring honey, coat the measuring spoon with vegetable spray; the honey will flow more easily and rapidly.

Xanthan gum helps prevent baked goods from crumbling, gives them greater volume, improves their texture and extends their shelf life.

◆ **12-inch (30 cm) pizza pan, lightly greased and sprinkled with cornmeal**

Onion Topping

2 tbsp	butter	30 mL
4	onions, finely chopped	4
2 tbsp	snipped fresh thyme	30 mL
2 tbsp	liquid honey	30 mL

Toastie

1 cup	whole bean flour	250 mL
1 cup	sorghum flour	250 mL
1/3 cup	tapioca starch	75 mL
1 tsp	granulated sugar	5 mL
1 tsp	xanthan gum	5 mL
1 tbsp	bread machine or instant yeast	15 mL
1 tsp	salt	5 mL
1 1/2 cups	water	375 mL
1/4 cup	vegetable oil	60 mL
2 tsp	cider vinegar	10 mL
	Sweet rice flour	
1/2 cup	freshly grated Parmesan cheese	125 mL

1. *For the topping:* In a skillet, melt butter over medium-low heat. Sauté onions for 20 minutes or until tender and light golden brown. Remove from heat and stir in thyme and honey. Let cool.

2. *For the toastie:* In a large bowl or plastic bag, combine whole bean flour, sorghum flour, tapioca starch, sugar, xanthan gum, yeast and salt; mix well and set aside.

3. Pour water, oil and vinegar into the bread machine baking pan.

4. Select the **Dough Cycle**. As the bread machine is mixing, gradually add the dry ingredients, scraping bottom and sides of pan with a rubber spatula. Try to incorporate all the dry ingredients within 1 to 2 minutes. Stop bread machine as soon as the kneading portion of the cycle is complete. Do not let bread machine finish cycle.

NUTRITIONAL VALUES
per serving

Calories	260
Fat, total	12 g
Fat, saturated	4 g
Cholesterol	13 mg
Sodium	327 mg
Carbohydrate	32 g
Fiber	7 g
Protein	7 g
Calcium	116 mg
Iron	2 mg

5. Drop dough by large spoonfuls onto prepared pan. Using a moistened rubber spatula, spread evenly to the edges. Generously dust top with sweet rice flour. With well-floured fingers, make deep indents all over the dough, pressing all the way down to the pan. Let rise, uncovered, in a warm, draft-free place for 20 minutes. Meanwhile, preheat oven to 400°F (200°C).

6. Sprinkle dough with Parmesan. Spread onion mixture over cheese.

7. Bake for 20 to 25 minutes or until top is golden. Remove from pan immediately, cut into 8 wedges and serve warm.

Swedish Wraps

Use these to make the ever-popular wrap luncheon sandwich.

Tips

To ensure success, see page 15 for information on using your bread machine and page 18 for general tips on bread machine baking.

Roll these wraps around your favorite sandwich fillings.

Dipping the spatula repeatedly into warm water makes it easier to spread this dough thinly and evenly.

To make this recipe dairy-free, use non-dairy powdered milk substitute and water.

◆ **Preheat oven to 400°F (200°C)**
◆ **15- by 10-inch (40 by 25 cm) jelly roll pan, lightly greased and lined with parchment paper**

¼ cup	sorghum flour	60 mL
¼ cup	amaranth flour	60 mL
¼ cup	potato starch	60 mL
¼ cup	tapioca starch	60 mL
1 tsp	granulated sugar	5 mL
2 tsp	xanthan gum	10 mL
1 tbsp	bread machine or instant yeast	15 mL
¾ tsp	salt	3 mL
1 tsp	anise seeds	5 mL
1 tsp	caraway seeds	5 mL
1 tsp	fennel seeds	5 mL
¾ cup	milk, warmed to room temperature	175 mL
1 tsp	extra virgin olive oil	5 mL
1 tsp	cider vinegar	5 mL

1. In a large bowl or plastic bag, combine sorghum flour, amaranth flour, potato starch, tapioca starch, sugar, xanthan gum, yeast, salt, anise seeds, caraway seeds and fennel seeds; mix well and set aside.

2. Pour milk, oil and vinegar into the bread machine baking pan.

3. Select the **Dough Cycle**. As the bread machine is mixing, gradually add the dry ingredients, scraping bottom and sides of pan with a rubber spatula. Try to incorporate all the dry ingredients within 1 to 2 minutes. Stop bread machine as soon as the kneading portion of the cycle is complete. Do not let bread machine finish the cycle.

4. Remove dough to prepared pan. Using a moistened rubber spatula, spread evenly to the edges. Bake in preheated oven for 12 to 14 minutes or until edges are brown and top begins to brown. Let cool completely on pan on a rack. Remove from pan and cut into quarters.

NUTRITIONAL VALUES
per serving

Calories	165
Fat, total	3 g
Fat, saturated	0 g
Cholesterol	2 mg
Sodium	461 mg
Carbohydrate	31 g
Fiber	3 g
Protein	5 g
Calcium	86 mg
Iron	3 mg

Pizzas

Plain Pizza Crust

MAKES 8 WEDGES
(1 per serving)

When you're looking for a traditional pizza crust, try this recipe.

Tips

To ensure success, see page 15 for information on using your bread machine and page 18 for general tips on bread machine baking.

To make pizza, add your favorite toppings (see recipes, pages 172–174) and bake until crust is brown and crisp and top is bubbly.

This recipe can be easily doubled to make two pizza crusts. Partially bake both, top one to bake and eat. Wrap the other airtight and freeze for up to 4 weeks. Thaw in the refrigerator overnight before using to make pizza.

NUTRITIONAL VALUES	
per serving	
Calories	104
Fat, total	2 g
Fat, saturated	0 g
Cholesterol	0 mg
Sodium	148 mg
Carbohydrate	20 g
Fiber	1 g
Protein	2 g
Calcium	6 mg
Iron	1 mg

◆ **One 12-inch (30 cm) pizza pan, generously greased**

¾ cup	brown rice flour	175 mL
⅓ cup	potato starch	75 mL
1 tsp	granulated sugar	5 mL
1½ tsp	xanthan gum	7 mL
1½ tsp	bread machine or instant yeast	7 mL
½ tsp	salt	2 mL
1 tsp	dried oregano, basil, marjoram or thyme	5 mL
¾ cup	water	175 mL
1 tbsp	vegetable oil	15 mL
1 tsp	cider vinegar	5 mL
2 to 3 tbsp	sweet rice flour	30 to 45 mL

1. In a large bowl or plastic bag, combine brown rice flour, potato starch, sugar, xanthan gum, yeast, salt and oregano; mix well and set aside.

2. Pour water, oil and vinegar into the bread machine baking pan.

3. Select the **Dough Cycle**. As the bread machine is mixing, gradually add the dry ingredients, scraping bottom and sides of pan with a rubber spatula. Try to incorporate all the dry ingredients within 1 to 2 minutes. Stop bread machine as soon as the kneading portion of the cycle is complete. Do not let bread machine finish the cycle.

4. Using a moistened rubber spatula, scrape the very sticky dough into prepared pan, spreading out as much as possible. Generously sprinkle with sweet rice flour. With floured fingers, gently pat out dough to fill the pan evenly. Continue to sprinkle with sweet rice flour as needed. Form a rim of dough at the edge of pan. Let rise in a warm, draft-free place for 15 minutes. Meanwhile, preheat oven to 400°F (200°C).

5. Bake for 12 to 15 minutes or until bottom is golden and crust is partially baked.

Thin Pizza Crust

Try our version of right-to-the-edge thin-crust pizza.

Tips

To ensure success, see page 15 for information on using your bread machine and page 18 for general tips on bread machine baking.

To make pizza, add your favorite toppings (see recipes, pages 172–174) and bake until crust is brown and crisp and top is bubbly.

Yes, you're reading right: this dough is thin enough to pour.

Variation

Divide dough into equal portions to make eight 6-inch (15 cm) pizzas. Bake on greased baking sheets for 10 to 12 minutes.

NUTRITIONAL VALUES
per serving

Calories	68
Fat, total	2 g
Fat, saturated	0 g
Cholesterol	0 mg
Sodium	146 mg
Carbohydrate	11 g
Fiber	1 g
Protein	2 g
Calcium	9 mg
Iron	1 mg

◆ **Two 12-inch (30 cm) pizza pans, lightly greased**

1 cup	whole bean flour	250 mL
1 cup	sorghum flour	250 mL
1/3 cup	tapioca starch	75 mL
1 tsp	granulated sugar	5 mL
1/2 tsp	xanthan gum	2 mL
1 1/2 tsp	bread machine or instant yeast	7 mL
1 tsp	salt	5 mL
1 tsp	dried oregano (or 1 tbsp/15 mL fresh)	5 mL
1 3/4 cups	water	425 mL
2 tbsp	vegetable oil	30 mL
1 tsp	cider vinegar	5 mL

1. In a large bowl or plastic bag, combine whole bean flour, sorghum flour, tapioca starch, sugar, xanthan gum, yeast, salt and oregano; mix well and set aside.

2. Pour water, oil and vinegar into the bread machine baking pan.

3. Select the **Dough Cycle**. As the bread machine is mixing, gradually add the dry ingredients, scraping bottom and sides of pan with a rubber spatula. Try to incorporate all the dry ingredients within 1 to 2 minutes. Stop bread machine as soon as the kneading portion of the cycle is complete. Do not let bread machine finish the cycle.

4. Pour dough onto prepared pans and, using a moistened rubber spatula, spread evenly to the edges. Let rise in a warm, draft-free place for 15 minutes. Meanwhile, preheat oven to 400°F (200°C).

5. Bake for 12 to 15 minutes or until bottom is golden and crust is partially baked. (Don't worry about cracks on the surface of this crust — after 10 minutes of baking, they are gone. Expect slight shrinkage from the edges.)

Five-Cheese Pizza

**MAKES
8 SERVINGS**

We love cheese and couldn't decide which we like best on pizza — so we mixed five together. Which five do you like?

Tip

Check for gluten before you purchase a packaged shredded cheese mix.

Variations

Substitute your favorite cheese or cheeses, but keep the amount the same.

Replace the salsa with tomato sauce or GF pizza sauce.

◆ **Preheat oven to 400°F (200°C)**

1 to 2 oz	Asiago cheese, grated	30 to 60 g
1 to 2 oz	Cheddar cheese, shredded	30 to 60 g
1 to 2 oz	fontina cheese, shredded	30 to 60 g
1 to 2 oz	Gorgonzola cheese, crumbled	30 to 60 g
1 to 2 oz	Havarti cheese, shredded	30 to 60 g
1 cup	chunky salsa	250 mL
1	partially baked pizza crust (see recipes, pages 170 and 171)	1

1. In a small bowl, combine Asiago, Cheddar, fontina, Gorgonzola and Havarti cheese. Set aside.

2. Spread salsa over crust, then top with cheese mixture. Bake in preheated oven for 15 to 20 minutes or until crust is brown and crisp and cheese is lightly browned and bubbly. Transfer to a cutting board, let cool slightly, then cut into 8 pieces.

NUTRITIONAL VALUES
per serving (based on Plain Pizza Crust, page 170)

Calories	180
Fat, total	6 g
Fat, saturated	3 g
Cholesterol	18 mg
Sodium	454 mg
Carbohydrate	21 g
Fiber	2 g
Protein	6 g
Calcium	135 mg
Iron	1 mg

Roasted Vegetable Pizza

This one's for you if you like lots of topping with every bite.

Tip
Sprinkling some of the cheese on the crust before adding the other toppings helps the vegetables remain on the pizza.

Variations
Substitute GF salsa for the pizza sauce.

For a stronger cheese combination, try Asiago and Romano.

◆ **Preheat oven to 425°F (220°C)**
◆ **Roasting pan**

1 tbsp	extra virgin olive oil	15 mL
6	cloves garlic, minced	6
4	small zucchini, cut into ½-inch (1 cm) slices	4
2	small Italian eggplants, cut into ½-inch (1 cm) cubes	2
1	large red bell pepper, cut into ½-inch (1 cm) slices	1
1	large yellow bell pepper, cut into ½-inch (1 cm) slices	1
10 oz	portobello mushrooms, cut into ½-inch (1 cm) thick slices	300 g
½ cup	GF pizza sauce	125 mL
⅔ cup	shredded mozzarella cheese	150 mL
½ cup	freshly grated Parmesan cheese	125 mL
1	partially baked pizza crust (see recipes, pages 170 and 171)	1

1. Pour oil into roasting pan. Add garlic, zucchini, eggplants, red pepper, yellow pepper and mushrooms; toss to coat. Roast in preheated oven, turning once, for 10 to 15 minutes or until tender. Do not overcook. Set aside to cool. Reduce oven temperature to 400°F (200°C).

2. Spread pizza sauce over crust, then sprinkle with half the mozzarella. Top with roasted vegetables, the remaining mozzarella and Parmesan. Bake for 12 to 15 minutes or until crust is brown and crisp, topping is bubbly and cheese has melted. Transfer to a cutting board, let cool slightly, then cut into 8 pieces.

NUTRITIONAL VALUES
per serving (based on Plain Pizza Crust, page 170)

Calories	239
Fat, total	6 g
Fat, saturated	2 g
Cholesterol	10 mg
Sodium	317 mg
Carbohydrate	35 g
Fiber	7 g
Protein	10 g
Calcium	177 mg
Iron	1 mg

Leek-Mushroom Pizza

**MAKES
8 SERVINGS**

*Subtle leeks unite the
flavors of mushrooms and
pesto.*

Variations

Substitute extra Parmesan
for the Asiago.

Add strips of cooked chicken
to the leek mixture before
adding the cheeses.

◆ **Preheat oven to 400°F (200°C)**

1 tbsp	extra virgin olive oil	15 mL
2	leeks, white and light green parts only, cut into 1-inch (2.5 cm) pieces	2
2 cups	sliced cremini mushrooms	500 mL
½ cup	pesto sauce (store-bought or see recipe, page 226)	125 mL
⅔ cup	grated Asiago cheese	150 mL
⅓ cup	freshly grated Parmesan cheese	75 mL
1	partially baked pizza crust (see recipes, pages 170 and 171)	1

1. In a skillet, heat oil over medium-high heat. Add leeks and mushrooms; sauté for 3 to 5 minutes or until tender.
2. Spread pesto over crust. Top with leek mixture, Asiago and Parmesan. Bake in preheated oven for 15 to 20 minutes or until crust is brown and crisp and cheese is lightly browned and bubbly. Transfer to a cutting board, let cool slightly, then cut into 8 pieces.

NUTRITIONAL VALUES
per serving (based on Plain
Pizza Crust, page 170)

Calories	102
Fat, total	7 g
Fat, saturated	3 g
Cholesterol	13 mg
Sodium	140 mg
Carbohydrate	5 g
Fiber	1 g
Protein	6 g
Calcium	185 mg
Iron	1 mg

Oat Pizza Crust

MAKES 8 WEDGES
(1 per serving)

Beth Armour of Cream Hill Estates adapted this recipe from our Square Pizza Crust (page 176) and has given us permission to include it here so you can enjoy it too.

Tips

To ensure success, see page 15 for information on using your bread machine and page 18 for general tips on bread machine baking.

To make pizza, add your favorite topping ingredients and bake until crust is brown and crisp and top is bubbly.

Potato flour and potato starch are two completely different ingredients and cannot be substituted for one another.

NUTRITIONAL VALUES
per serving

Calories	144
Fat, total	3 g
Fat, saturated	0 g
Cholesterol	0 mg
Sodium	223 mg
Carbohydrate	19 g
Fiber	3 g
Protein	3 g
Calcium	15 mg
Iron	1 mg

◆ **Preheat oven to 400°F (200°C)**
◆ **12-inch (30 cm) pizza pan, lightly greased**

1¼ cups	GF oat flour	300 mL
¼ cup	potato flour (not potato starch)	60 mL
¼ cup	tapioca starch	60 mL
1 tsp	granulated sugar	5 mL
2 tsp	xanthan gum	10 mL
1 tbsp	bread machine or instant yeast	15 mL
¾ tsp	salt	3 mL
1¼ cups	water	300 mL
1 tbsp	extra virgin olive oil	15 mL
1 tsp	cider vinegar	5 mL

1. In a large bowl or plastic bag, combine oat flour, potato flour, tapioca starch, sugar, xanthan gum, yeast and salt; mix well and set aside.
2. Pour water, oil and vinegar into the bread machine baking pan.
3. Select the **Dough Cycle**. Gradually add the dry ingredients as the bread machine is mixing. Scrape with a rubber spatula while adding the dry ingredients. Try to incorporate all the dry ingredients within 1 to 2 minutes. Stop bread machine as soon as the kneading portion of the cycle is complete. Do not let bread machine finish the cycle.
4. Gently transfer dough to prepared pan and, using a moistened rubber spatula, spread evenly to the edges. Do not smooth top.
5. Bake in preheated oven for 12 minutes or until bottom is golden and crust is partially baked. Use right away or wrap airtight and freeze for up to 4 weeks. Thaw in the refrigerator overnight before using to make pizza.

Square Pizza Crust

Use this thin crust to make Florentine Pizza (page 177) or Sausage and Leek Pizza (page 178).

Tips

To ensure success, see page 15 for information on using your bread machine and page 18 for general tips on bread machine baking.

Pizza toppings stick better when you don't smooth the top of the crust.

Variation

Add 1 to 2 tsp (5 to 10 mL) dried or 1 to 2 tbsp (15 to 30 mL) chopped fresh rosemary, oregano, basil or thyme to the dry ingredients.

NUTRITIONAL VALUES per serving	
Calories	100
Fat, total	2 g
Fat, saturated	0 g
Cholesterol	0 mg
Sodium	178 mg
Carbohydrate	19 g
Fiber	2 g
Protein	2 g
Calcium	8 mg
Iron	1 mg

◆ **Preheat oven to 400°F (200°C)**
◆ **15- by 10-inch (40 by 25 cm) jelly roll pan, lightly greased**

⅔ cup	sorghum flour	150 mL
½ cup	quinoa flour	125 mL
⅓ cup	potato starch	75 mL
¼ cup	tapioca starch	60 mL
1 tsp	granulated sugar	5 mL
2 tsp	xanthan gum	10 mL
1 tbsp	bread machine or instant yeast	15 mL
¾ tsp	salt	3 mL
1¼ cups	water	300 mL
1 tbsp	extra virgin olive oil	15 mL
1 tsp	cider vinegar	5 mL

1. In a large bowl or plastic bag, combine sorghum flour, quinoa flour, potato starch, tapioca starch, sugar, xanthan gum, yeast and salt; mix well and set aside.
2. Pour water, oil and vinegar into the bread machine baking pan.
3. Select the **Dough Cycle**. Gradually add the dry ingredients as the bread machine is mixing. Scrape with a rubber spatula while adding the dry ingredients. Try to incorporate all the dry ingredients within 1 to 2 minutes. Stop bread machine as soon as the kneading portion of the cycle is complete. Do not let bread machine finish the cycle.
4. Gently transfer dough to prepared pan and, using a moistened rubber spatula, spread evenly to the edges. Do not smooth top.
5. Bake in preheated oven for 12 minutes or until bottom is golden and crust is partially baked. Use right away or wrap airtight and freeze for up to 4 weeks. Thaw in the refrigerator overnight before using to make pizza.

Florentine Pizza

**MAKES
10 SERVINGS**

This vegetarian Greek-style pizza has generous amounts of spinach, feta cheese and kalamata olives.

Tips

Drain spinach well in a colander before drying completely with paper towels.

Reheat leftover pizza under the broiler to enjoy crisp pizza.

Variations

For a stronger, more prominent garlic flavor, add an extra 1 to 2 cloves minced garlic.

Add ½ cup (125 mL) snipped sun-dried tomatoes.

Substitute Swiss chard or kale for the spinach and microwave until wilted.

NUTRITIONAL VALUES
per serving

Calories	174
Fat, total	7 g
Fat, saturated	3 g
Cholesterol	17 mg
Sodium	460 mg
Carbohydrate	18 g
Fiber	2 g
Protein	6 g
Calcium	187 mg
Iron	2 mg

◆ **Preheat oven to 400°F (200°C)**

1	package (10 oz/300 g) fresh baby spinach, washed and trimmed	1
1	partially baked Square Pizza Crust (page 176)	1
2	cloves garlic, minced	2
½ cup	freshly grated Parmesan cheese	125 mL
1 tbsp	extra virgin olive oil	15 mL
2 tsp	dried oregano	10 mL
1 cup	crumbled feta cheese	250 mL
½ cup	kalamata olives, sliced	125 mL

1. In a microwave-safe bowl, microwave spinach, uncovered, on High for 2 to 3 minutes or until wilted, stirring halfway through. Drain, place between layers of paper towels and pat dry. Spread over crust in a single layer to within ¼ inch (0.5 cm) of the edges.

2. In a small bowl, combine garlic, Parmesan, oil and oregano. Spread over spinach; sprinkle with feta and olives. Bake in preheated oven for 20 to 25 minutes or until spinach is crisp and top is golden. Transfer to a cutting board, let cool slightly, then cut into 10 pieces, each 5 by 3 inches (12.5 by 7.5 cm).

Sausage and Leek Pizza

**MAKES
10 SERVINGS**

This recipe is sure to fill up even the hungriest teen.

Tip

For information on cleaning leeks, see the Techniques Glossary, page 239.

Variations

Add ½ cup (125 mL) snipped sun-dried tomatoes with the mozzarella.

Try a mixture of Cheddar and mozzarella cheeses.

Substitute unsweetened apple juice for the wine.

◆ **Preheat oven to 400°F (200°C)**

1 lb	GF pork sausage, casings removed and meat crumbled	500 g
3	carrots, finely chopped	3
3	leeks, white and light green parts only, cut into ½-inch (1 cm) slices	3
1 cup	sliced mushrooms	250 mL
2 tbsp	crumbled dried rosemary	30 mL
2 tbsp	dry white wine	30 mL
1	partially baked Square Pizza Crust (page 176)	1
1 cup	shredded mozzarella cheese	250 mL

1. In a large skillet, over medium heat, brown sausage meat until no pink remains. Using a slotted spoon, remove to a plate and set aside. Drain off all but 1 tbsp (15 mL) fat from the skillet.

2. In the fat remaining in the skillet, over medium heat, cook carrots, leeks, mushrooms and rosemary, stirring, for 15 minutes or until carrots are tender. Drain off fat. Return browned sausage to skillet with wine; mix gently and set aside to cool slightly.

3. Spread filling over crust to within ¼ inch (0.5 cm) of the edges. Sprinkle with mozzarella. Bake in preheated oven for 20 to 25 minutes or until cheese is melted and top is golden. Transfer to a cutting board, let cool slightly, then cut into 10 pieces, each 5 by 3 inches (12.5 by 7.5 cm).

NUTRITIONAL VALUES
per serving

Calories	332
Fat, total	17 g
Fat, saturated	7 g
Cholesterol	37 mg
Sodium	509 mg
Carbohydrate	32 g
Fiber	7 g
Protein	11 g
Calcium	250 mg
Iron	5 mg

Herbed Square Pizza Crust

Here's another version of a square pizza crust, this one with plenty of fresh basil incorporated into the dough for extra flavor and crunch.

Tips

To ensure success, see page 15 for information on using your bread machine and page 18 for general tips on bread machine baking.

This is a thin crust. There is enough dough to cover the bottom of the pan evenly with a thin layer. Take your time.

Variation

Substitute an equal amount of chopped fresh rosemary for the basil.

NUTRITIONAL VALUES
per serving

Calories	99
Fat, total	2 g
Fat, saturated	0 g
Cholesterol	0 mg
Sodium	235 mg
Carbohydrate	16 g
Fiber	2 g
Protein	3 g
Calcium	18 mg
Iron	3 mg

◆ **Preheat oven to 400°F (200°C)**
◆ **15- by 10-inch (40 by 25 cm) jelly roll pan, greased and generously sprinkled with cornmeal**

¾ cup	amaranth flour	175 mL
½ cup	quinoa flour	125 mL
¼ cup	cornmeal	60 mL
¼ cup	cornstarch	60 mL
1 tsp	xanthan gum	5 mL
1 tbsp	bread machine or instant yeast	15 mL
1 tsp	salt	5 mL
¼ cup	snipped fresh basil	60 mL
1¼ cups	water	300 mL
1 tbsp	extra virgin olive oil	15 mL
1 tsp	cider vinegar	5 mL

1. In a large bowl or plastic bag, combine amaranth flour, quinoa flour, cornmeal, cornstarch, xanthan gum, yeast, salt and basil; mix well and set aside.

2. Pour water, oil and vinegar into the bread machine baking pan.

3. Select the **Dough Cycle**. Gradually add the dry ingredients as the bread machine is mixing. Scrape with a rubber spatula while adding the dry ingredients. Try to incorporate all the dry ingredients within 1 to 2 minutes. Stop bread machine as soon as the kneading portion of the cycle is complete. Do not let bread machine finish the cycle.

4. Gently transfer dough to prepared pan and, using a moistened rubber spatula, spread evenly to the edges. Do not smooth top.

5. Bake in preheated oven for 10 minutes or until bottom is golden and crust is partially baked.

Pizza Squares with Greek Topping

This vegetarian pizza is delicious served hot or at room temperature for a snack, lunch or brunch.

Tips

For information on roasting garlic, see the Techniques Glossary, page 238.

For fast, easy cutting, use a pizza wheel.

Variations

Substitute mozzarella, fontina or provolone cheese for the Monterey Jack.

Substitute an equal amount of chopped fresh rosemary for the basil.

Sprinkle some fresh baby spinach over the tomatoes before adding the remaining toppings.

Cut into bite-size appetizers for your next party.

◆ Preheat oven to 400°F (200°C)

1	partially baked Herbed Square Pizza Crust (page 179)	1
3	plum (Roma) tomatoes, thinly sliced	3
4	cloves garlic, roasted and chopped	4
⅔ cup	sliced black olives	150 mL
¼ cup	snipped fresh basil	60 mL
¼ tsp	freshly ground black pepper	1 mL
1 cup	shredded Monterey Jack cheese	250 mL
1 cup	crumbled feta cheese	250 mL

1. Arrange tomato slices over crust; sprinkle with garlic, olives, basil and pepper. Sprinkle with Monterey Jack and feta.

2. Bake in preheated oven for 20 to 25 minutes or until cheese is bubbly and crust is golden. Transfer to a cutting board, let cool slightly, then cut into 10 pieces, each 5 by 3 inches (12.5 by 7.5 cm). Transfer any squares you're not serving right away to a wire rack to prevent the crust from getting soggy.

NUTRITIONAL VALUES
per serving

Calories	197
Fat, total	10 g
Fat, saturated	5 g
Cholesterol	23 mg
Sodium	310 mg
Carbohydrate	19 g
Fiber	3 g
Protein	8 g
Calcium	189 mg
Iron	4 mg

Dessert Breads

Lemon Poppy Loaf

MAKES 15 SLICES
(1 per serving)

A perennial favorite flavor combination — poppy seeds and lemon.

Tips

To ensure success, see page 15 for information on using your bread machine and page 18 for general tips on bread machine baking.

Use a zester to make long, thin strips of lemon zest. Be sure to remove only the colored outer layer, avoiding the bitter white pith beneath.

Freshly squeezed lemon juice enhances the flavor. Roll the lemon on the counter or between your hands to loosen the juice.

Keep a lemon in the freezer. Zest while frozen, then juice after warming in the microwave.

NUTRITIONAL VALUES per serving	
Calories	167
Fat, total	6 g
Fat, saturated	1 g
Cholesterol	25 mg
Sodium	213 mg
Carbohydrate	26 g
Fiber	1 g
Protein	3 g
Calcium	54 mg
Iron	1 mg

1½ cups	brown rice flour	375 mL
⅔ cup	potato starch	150 mL
⅓ cup	arrowroot starch	75 mL
⅓ cup	granulated sugar	75 mL
1 tbsp	xanthan gum	15 mL
1¼ tsp	bread machine or instant yeast	6 mL
1¼ tsp	salt	6 mL
⅓ cup	poppy seeds	75 mL
1¼ cups	water	300 mL
2 tbsp	lemon zest (see tip, at left)	30 mL
¼ cup	freshly squeezed lemon juice	60 mL
¼ cup	vegetable oil	60 mL
2	eggs, lightly beaten	2
2	egg whites, lightly beaten	2

1. In a large bowl or plastic bag, combine brown rice flour, potato starch, arrowroot starch, sugar, xanthan gum, yeast, salt and poppy seeds; mix well and set aside.

2. Pour water, lemon zest, lemon juice and oil into the bread machine baking pan. Add eggs and egg whites.

3. Select the **Dough Cycle**. As the bread machine is mixing, gradually add the dry ingredients, scraping bottom and sides of pan with a rubber spatula. Try to incorporate all the dry ingredients within 1 to 2 minutes. When the mixing and kneading are complete, remove the kneading blade, leaving the bread pan in the bread machine. Quickly smooth the top of the loaf. Allow the cycle to finish. Turn off the bread machine.

4. Select the **Bake Cycle**. Set time to 60 minutes and temperature to 350°F (180°C). Allow the cycle to finish. Do not turn machine off before taking the internal temperature of the loaf with an instant-read thermometer. It should be 200°F (100°C). If it's between 180°F (85°C) and 200°F (100°C), leave machine on the **Keep Warm Cycle** until baked. If it's below 180°F (85°C), turn on the **Bake Cycle** and check the internal temperature every 10 minutes. (Some bread machines are automatically set for 60 minutes; others need to be set by 10-minute intervals.)

5. Once the loaf has reached 200°F (100°C), remove it from the pan immediately and let cool completely on a rack.

Variation
Substitute double the amount of orange zest for the lemon zest and use orange juice instead of lemon juice.

Gluten-Free Cycle

If your bread machine has a Gluten-Free Cycle, you will need to make these adjustments:

1. Decrease the yeast to ¾ tsp (3 mL).

2. Warm the water to between 110°F and 115°F (43°C and 46°C).

3. Warm the eggs and egg whites (see the Techniques Glossary, page 238).

4. Follow the recipe instructions, but select the **Gluten-Free Cycle** rather than the Dough Cycle and Bake Cycle.

5. At the end of the Gluten-Free Cycle, take the temperature of the loaf using an instant-read thermometer. It is baked at 200°F (100°C). If it's between 180°F (85°C) and 200°F (100°C), leave machine on the **Keep Warm Cycle** until baked. If it's below 180°F (85°C), turn on the **Bake Cycle** and check the internal temperature every 10 minutes. (Some bread machines are automatically set for 60 minutes; others need to be set by 10-minute intervals.)

Daffodil Loaf

Bring a little bit of springtime to your table! Enjoy this bread's light, pound cake–like texture, with its refreshing aroma and flavor of orange. Serve for a mid-morning coffee break.

Tips

To ensure success, see page 15 for information on using your bread machine and page 18 for general tips on bread machine baking.

For thin, even slices, use an electric knife for this and all breads.

For a stronger orange flavor, add 1 tbsp (15 mL) grated orange zest or 1 tsp (5 mL) pure orange extract with the liquids.

1½ cups	brown rice flour	375 mL
¾ cup	quinoa flour	175 mL
½ cup	arrowroot starch	125 mL
¼ cup	tapioca starch	60 mL
1 tbsp	xanthan gum	15 mL
1½ tsp	bread machine or instant yeast	7 mL
1¼ tsp	salt	6 mL
1 cup	water	250 mL
¼ cup	vegetable oil	60 mL
3 tbsp	frozen orange juice concentrate, thawed	45 mL
2	eggs, lightly beaten	2
½ cup	Orange Marmalade (page 229)	125 mL

1. In a large bowl or plastic bag, combine brown rice flour, quinoa flour, arrowroot starch, tapioca starch, xanthan gum, yeast and salt; mix well and set aside.

2. Pour water, oil and orange juice concentrate into the bread machine baking pan. Add eggs and marmalade.

3. Select the **Dough Cycle**. As the bread machine is mixing, gradually add the dry ingredients, scraping bottom and sides of pan with a rubber spatula. Try to incorporate all the dry ingredients within 1 to 2 minutes. When the mixing and kneading are complete, remove the kneading blade, leaving the bread pan in the bread machine. Quickly smooth the top of the loaf. Allow the cycle to finish. Turn off the bread machine.

4. Select the **Bake Cycle**. Set time to 60 minutes and temperature to 350°F (180°C). Allow the cycle to finish. Do not turn machine off before taking the internal temperature of the loaf with an instant-read thermometer. It should be 200°F (100°C). If it's between 180°F (85°C) and 200°F (100°C), leave machine on the **Keep Warm Cycle** until baked. If it's below 180°F (85°C), turn on the **Bake Cycle** and check the internal temperature every 10 minutes. (Some bread machines are automatically set for 60 minutes; others need to be set by 10-minute intervals.)

5. Once the loaf has reached 200°F (100°C), remove it from the pan immediately and let cool completely on a rack.

NUTRITIONAL VALUES
per serving

Calories	163
Fat, total	5 g
Fat, saturated	1 g
Cholesterol	25 mg
Sodium	205 mg
Carbohydrate	27 g
Fiber	2 g
Protein	3 g
Calcium	12 mg
Iron	1 mg

Variations

Substitute lime or three-fruit marmalade for the orange.

Gluten-Free Cycle

If your bread machine has a Gluten-Free Cycle, you will need to make these adjustments:

1. Warm the water to between 110°F and 115°F (43°C and 46°C).

2. Warm the eggs (see the Techniques Glossary, page 238).

3. Follow the recipe instructions, but select the **Gluten-Free Cycle** rather than the Dough Cycle and Bake Cycle.

4. At the end of the Gluten-Free Cycle, take the temperature of the loaf using an instant-read thermometer. It is baked at 200°F (100°C). If it's between 180°F (85°C) and 200°F (100°C), leave machine on the **Keep Warm Cycle** until baked. If it's below 180°F (85°C), turn on the **Bake Cycle** and check the internal temperature every 10 minutes. (Some bread machines are automatically set for 60 minutes; others need to be set by 10-minute intervals.)

Applesauce Apple Oatmeal Bread

This sweetly spiced loaf is flavored with apple cider and applesauce.

Tips

To ensure success, see page 15 for information on using your bread machine and page 18 for general tips on bread machine baking.

If you don't have apple pie spice, use ¾ tsp (3 mL) ground cinnamon, ½ tsp (2 mL) ground nutmeg and a pinch each of ground allspice and either ground cloves or ground ginger.

1⅓ cups	sorghum flour	325 mL
½ cup	GF oats	125 mL
½ cup	GF oat flour	125 mL
⅓ cup	tapioca starch	75 mL
3 tbsp	packed brown sugar	45 mL
1 tbsp	xanthan gum	15 mL
1 tbsp	bread machine or instant yeast	15 mL
1½ tsp	salt	7 mL
1½ tsp	apple pie spice	7 mL
¾ cup	unsweetened apple cider, at room temperature	175 mL
½ cup	unsweetened applesauce, at room temperature	125 mL
2 tbsp	vegetable oil	30 mL
2	eggs, lightly beaten	2

1. In a large bowl or plastic bag, combine sorghum flour, oats, oat flour, tapioca starch, brown sugar, xanthan gum, yeast, salt and apple pie spice; mix well and set aside.

2. Pour apple cider, applesauce and oil into the bread machine baking pan. Add eggs.

3. Select the **Dough Cycle**. As the bread machine is mixing, gradually add the dry ingredients, scraping bottom and sides of pan with a rubber spatula. Try to incorporate all the dry ingredients within 1 to 2 minutes. When the mixing and kneading are complete, remove the kneading blade, leaving the bread pan in the bread machine. Quickly smooth the top of the loaf. Allow the cycle to finish. Turn off the bread machine.

4. Select the **Bake Cycle**. Set time to 60 minutes and temperature to 350°F (180°C). Allow the cycle to finish. Do not turn machine off before taking the internal temperature of the loaf with an instant-read thermometer. It should be 200°F (100°C). If it's between 180°F (85°C) and 200°F (100°C), leave machine on the **Keep Warm Cycle** until baked. If it's below 180°F (85°C), turn on the **Bake Cycle** and check the internal temperature every 10 minutes. (Some bread machines are automatically set for 60 minutes; others need to be set by 10-minute intervals.)

NUTRITIONAL VALUES
per serving

Calories	132
Fat, total	3 g
Fat, saturated	0 g
Cholesterol	25 mg
Sodium	244 mg
Carbohydrate	22 g
Fiber	2 g
Protein	4 g
Calcium	15 mg
Iron	1 mg

Variation

For a tasty sandwich bread, omit the apple pie spice.

5. Once the loaf has reached 200°F (100°C), remove it from the pan immediately and let cool completely on a rack.

To make this recipe egg-free: Omit eggs from recipe. Combine $\frac{1}{3}$ cup (75 mL) flax flour or ground flaxseed with an additional $\frac{1}{2}$ cup (125 mL) warm apple cider. Set aside for 5 minutes. Add with the liquids.

Gluten-Free Cycle

If your bread machine has a Gluten-Free Cycle, you will need to make these adjustments:

1. Warm the apple cider and applesauce to between 110°F and 115°F (43°C and 46°C).
2. Warm the eggs (see the Techniques Glossary, page 238).
3. Follow the recipe instructions, but select the **Gluten-Free Cycle** rather than the Dough Cycle and Bake Cycle.
4. At the end of the Gluten-Free Cycle, take the temperature of the loaf using an instant-read thermometer. It is baked at 200°F (100°C). If it's between 180°F (85°C) and 200°F (100°C), leave machine on the **Keep Warm Cycle** until baked. If it's below 180°F (85°C), turn on the **Bake Cycle** and check the internal temperature every 10 minutes. (Some bread machines are automatically set for 60 minutes; others need to be set by 10-minute intervals.)

Oatmeal Date Loaf

This dessert bread reminds us of date squares. The rich, dark sweetness is so satisfying!

Tips

To ensure success, see page 15 for information on using your bread machine and page 18 for general tips on bread machine baking.

If you purchase chopped dates instead of whole ones, be sure to check the label for hidden gluten.

Instead of chopping with a knife, snip dates with kitchen shears. Dip the blades in hot water when they become sticky.

1¾ cups	sorghum flour	425 mL
½ cup	GF oats	125 mL
½ cup	GF oat flour	125 mL
½ cup	tapioca starch	125 mL
3 tbsp	packed brown sugar	45 mL
1 tbsp	xanthan gum	15 mL
2 tsp	bread machine or instant yeast	10 mL
1¼ tsp	salt	6 mL
1 tsp	ground nutmeg	5 mL
1 cup	snipped pitted dates	250 mL
1¼ cups	water	300 mL
¼ cup	vegetable oil	60 mL
2 tsp	cider vinegar	10 mL
2	eggs, lightly beaten	2
2	egg whites, lightly beaten	2

1. In a large bowl or plastic bag, combine sorghum flour, oats, oat flour, tapioca starch, brown sugar, xanthan gum, yeast, salt, nutmeg and dates; mix well and set aside.

2. Pour water, oil and vinegar into the bread machine baking pan. Add eggs and egg whites.

3. Select the **Dough Cycle**. As the bread machine is mixing, gradually add the dry ingredients, scraping bottom and sides of pan with a rubber spatula. Try to incorporate all the dry ingredients within 1 to 2 minutes. When the mixing and kneading are complete, remove the kneading blade, leaving the bread pan in the bread machine. Quickly smooth the top of the loaf. Allow the cycle to finish. Turn off the bread machine.

4. Select the **Bake Cycle**. Set time to 60 minutes and temperature to 350°F (180°C). Allow the cycle to finish. Do not turn machine off before taking the internal temperature of the loaf with an instant-read thermometer. It should be 200°F (100°C). If it's between 180°F (85°C) and 200°F (100°C), leave machine on the **Keep Warm Cycle** until baked. If it's below 180°F (85°C), turn on the **Bake Cycle** and check the internal temperature every 10 minutes. (Some bread machines are automatically set for 60 minutes; others need to be set by 10-minute intervals.)

NUTRITIONAL VALUES per serving	
Calories	191
Fat, total	5 g
Fat, saturated	1 g
Cholesterol	25 mg
Sodium	211 mg
Carbohydrate	33 g
Fiber	3 g
Protein	5 g
Calcium	20 mg
Iron	2 mg

Variation

For a subtle orange flavor, add 2 tbsp (30 mL) grated orange zest with the dry ingredients.

5. Once the loaf has reached 200°F (100°C), remove it from the pan immediately and let cool completely on a rack.

Gluten-Free Cycle

If your bread machine has a Gluten-Free Cycle, you will need to make these adjustments:

1. Warm the water to between 110°F and 115°F (43°C and 46°C).

2. Warm the eggs and egg whites (see the Techniques Glossary, page 238).

3. Follow the recipe instructions, but select the **Gluten-Free Cycle** rather than the Dough Cycle and Bake Cycle.

4. At the end of the Gluten-Free Cycle, take the temperature of the loaf using an instant-read thermometer. It is baked at 200°F (100°C). If it's between 180°F (85°C) and 200°F (100°C), leave machine on the **Keep Warm Cycle** until baked. If it's below 180°F (85°C), turn on the **Bake Cycle** and check the internal temperature every 10 minutes. (Some bread machines are automatically set for 60 minutes; others need to be set by 10-minute intervals.)

Honey Fig Loaf

MAKES 15 SLICES
(1 per serving)

This sweet loaf is delicious spread with applesauce for a light dessert.

Tips

To ensure success, see page 15 for information on using your bread machine and page 18 for general tips on bread machine baking.

If using apple cider and applesauce from the refrigerator, warm them each in the microwave for 1 minute on High before measuring.

Snip the figs with sharp kitchen shears. When the blades become sticky, dip them in warm water.

1⅔ cups	sorghum flour	400 mL
½ cup	pea flour	125 mL
½ cup	tapioca starch	125 mL
1 tbsp	xanthan gum	15 mL
1 tbsp	bread machine or instant yeast	15 mL
1½ tsp	salt	7 mL
1 tsp	ground cardamom	5 mL
1 cup	dried figs, snipped	250 mL
1 cup	unsweetened apple cider, at room temperature	250 mL
¾ cup	unsweetened applesauce, at room temperature	175 mL
2 tbsp	vegetable oil	30 mL
2 tbsp	liquid honey	30 mL
2	eggs, lightly beaten	2
1	egg white, lightly beaten	1

1. In a large bowl or plastic bag, combine sorghum flour, pea flour, tapioca starch, xanthan gum, yeast, salt, cardamom and figs; mix well and set aside.

2. Pour cider, applesauce, oil and honey into the bread machine baking pan. Add eggs and egg white.

3. Select the **Dough Cycle**. As the bread machine is mixing, gradually add the dry ingredients, scraping bottom and sides of pan with a rubber spatula. Try to incorporate all the dry ingredients within 1 to 2 minutes. When the mixing and kneading are complete, remove the kneading blade, leaving the bread pan in the bread machine. Quickly smooth the top of the loaf. Allow the cycle to finish. Turn off the bread machine.

4. Select the **Bake Cycle**. Set time to 60 minutes and temperature to 350°F (180°C). Allow the cycle to finish. Do not turn machine off before taking the internal temperature of the loaf with an instant-read thermometer. It should be 200°F (100°C). If it's between 180°F (85°C) and 200°F (100°C), leave machine on the **Keep Warm Cycle** until baked. If it's below 180°F (85°C), turn on the **Bake Cycle** and check the internal temperature every 10 minutes. (Some bread machines are automatically set for 60 minutes; others need to be set by 10-minute intervals.)

NUTRITIONAL VALUES
per serving

Calories	170
Fat, total	3 g
Fat, saturated	0 g
Cholesterol	25 mg
Sodium	252 mg
Carbohydrate	33 g
Fiber	4 g
Protein	5 g
Calcium	31 mg
Iron	2 mg

Tip

If only sweetened apple cider and applesauce are available, decrease the honey to 1 tbsp (15 mL). If you can't find apple cider at all, purchase high-quality unsweetened apple juice, not sweetened apple drink.

5. Once the loaf has reached 200°F (100°C), remove it from the pan immediately and let cool completely on a rack.

Gluten-Free Cycle

If your bread machine has a Gluten-Free Cycle, you will need to make these adjustments:

1. Warm the apple cider and applesauce to between 110°F and 115°F (43°C and 46°C).

2. Warm the eggs and egg white (see the Techniques Glossary, page 238).

3. Follow the recipe instructions, but select the **Gluten-Free Cycle** rather than the Dough Cycle and Bake Cycle.

4. At the end of the Gluten-Free Cycle, take the temperature of the loaf using an instant-read thermometer. It is baked at 200°F (100°C). If it's between 180°F (85°C) and 200°F (100°C), leave machine on the **Keep Warm Cycle** until baked. If it's below 180°F (85°C), turn on the **Bake Cycle** and check the internal temperature every 10 minutes. (Some bread machines are automatically set for 60 minutes; others need to be set by 10-minute intervals.)

Cranberry Orange Bread

MAKES 15 SLICES
(1 per serving)

You can make this tart but sweet loaf any time of the year — no need to wait for fresh cranberries in the fall.

Tips

To ensure success, see page 15 for information on using your bread machine and page 18 for general tips on bread machine baking.

Choose only unsweetened fruit juices. Fruit drinks or sweetened fruit juices will result in a less than perfect loaf.

1⅓ cups	brown rice flour	325 mL
1 cup	amaranth flour	250 mL
½ cup	tapioca starch	125 mL
¼ cup	granulated sugar	60 mL
2½ tsp	xanthan gum	12 mL
2 tsp	bread machine or instant yeast	10 mL
1½ tsp	salt	7 mL
1 cup	dried cranberries	250 mL
2 tbsp	grated orange zest	30 mL
1 cup	water	250 mL
¼ cup	unsweetened cranberry juice (not cranberry cocktail)	60 mL
¼ cup	vegetable oil	60 mL
2 tsp	cider vinegar	10 mL
2	eggs, lightly beaten	2
2	egg whites, lightly beaten	2

1. In a large bowl or plastic bag, combine brown rice flour, amaranth flour, tapioca starch, sugar, xanthan gum, yeast, salt, cranberries and orange zest; mix well and set aside.

2. Pour water, cranberry juice, oil and vinegar into the bread machine baking pan. Add eggs and egg whites.

3. Select the **Dough Cycle**. As the bread machine is mixing, gradually add the dry ingredients, scraping bottom and sides of pan with a rubber spatula. Try to incorporate all the dry ingredients within 1 to 2 minutes. When the mixing and kneading are complete, remove the kneading blade, leaving the bread pan in the bread machine. Quickly smooth the top of the loaf. Allow the cycle to finish. Turn off the bread machine.

4. Select the **Bake Cycle**. Set time to 60 minutes and temperature to 350°F (180°C). Allow the cycle to finish. Do not turn machine off before taking the internal temperature of the loaf with an instant-read thermometer. It should be 200°F (100°C). If it's between 180°F (85°C) and 200°F (100°C), leave machine on the **Keep Warm Cycle** until baked. If it's below 180°F (85°C), turn on the **Bake Cycle** and check the internal temperature every 10 minutes. (Some bread machines are automatically set for 60 minutes; others need to be set by 10-minute intervals.)

NUTRITIONAL VALUES per serving	
Calories	181
Fat, total	5 g
Fat, saturated	1 g
Cholesterol	25 mg
Sodium	249 mg
Carbohydrate	30 g
Fiber	2 g
Protein	4 g
Calcium	18 mg
Iron	2 mg

Variation

Try one of the other flavors of cranberry juice, such as cran-raspberry.

5. Once the loaf has reached 200°F (100°C), remove it from the pan immediately and let cool completely on a rack.

Gluten-Free Cycle

If your bread machine has a Gluten-Free Cycle, you will need to make these adjustments:

1. Warm the water and cranberry juice to between 110°F and 115°F (43°C and 46°C).

2. Warm the eggs and egg whites (see the Techniques Glossary, page 238).

3. Follow the recipe instructions, but select the **Gluten-Free Cycle** rather than the Dough Cycle and Bake Cycle.

4. At the end of the Gluten-Free Cycle, take the temperature of the loaf using an instant-read thermometer. It is baked at 200°F (100°C). If it's between 180°F (85°C) and 200°F (100°C), leave machine on the **Keep Warm Cycle** until baked. If it's below 180°F (85°C), turn on the **Bake Cycle** and check the internal temperature every 10 minutes. (Some bread machines are automatically set for 60 minutes; others need to be set by 10-minute intervals.)

Cranberry Raisin Bread

This recipe was inspired by a request for a GF raisin bread that is not too sweet.

Tips

To ensure success, see page 15 for information on using your bread machine and page 18 for general tips on bread machine baking.

Don't omit the xanthan gum, as it gives structure to the bread. The loaf is more apt to collapse without it.

1¼ cups	sorghum flour	300 mL
¾ cup	amaranth flour	175 mL
½ cup	brown rice flour	125 mL
½ cup	tapioca starch	125 mL
¼ cup	packed brown sugar	60 mL
2½ tsp	xanthan gum	12 mL
1½ tsp	bread machine or instant yeast	7 mL
1½ tsp	salt	7 mL
½ cup	dried cranberries	125 mL
½ cup	raisins	125 mL
1½ tsp	ground cardamom	7 mL
1¼ cups	water	300 mL
¼ cup	vegetable oil	60 mL
2 tsp	cider vinegar	10 mL
2	eggs, lightly beaten	2
2	egg whites, lightly beaten	2

1. In a large bowl or plastic bag, combine sorghum flour, amaranth flour, brown rice flour, tapioca starch, brown sugar, xanthan gum, yeast, salt, cranberries, raisins and cardamom; mix well and set aside.

2. Pour water, oil and vinegar into the bread machine baking pan. Add eggs and egg whites.

3. Select the **Dough Cycle**. As the bread machine is mixing, gradually add the dry ingredients, scraping bottom and sides of pan with a rubber spatula. Try to incorporate all the dry ingredients within 1 to 2 minutes. When the mixing and kneading are complete, remove the kneading blade, leaving the bread pan in the bread machine. Quickly smooth the top of the loaf. Allow the cycle to finish. Turn off the bread machine.

NUTRITIONAL VALUES
per serving

Calories	185
Fat, total	5 g
Fat, saturated	0 g
Cholesterol	25 mg
Sodium	251 mg
Carbohydrate	31 g
Fiber	2 g
Protein	4 g
Calcium	23 mg
Iron	2 mg

Variation

Substitute chocolate chips for half the raisins.

4. Select the **Bake Cycle**. Set time to 60 minutes and temperature to 350°F (180°C). Allow the cycle to finish. Do not turn machine off before taking the internal temperature of the loaf with an instant-read thermometer. It should be 200°F (100°C). If it's between 180°F (85°C) and 200°F (100°C), leave machine on the **Keep Warm Cycle** until baked. If it's below 180°F (85°C), turn on the **Bake Cycle** and check the internal temperature every 10 minutes. (Some bread machines are automatically set for 60 minutes; others need to be set by 10-minute intervals.)

5. Once the loaf has reached 200°F (100°C), remove it from the pan immediately and let cool completely on a rack.

Gluten-Free Cycle

If your bread machine has a Gluten-Free Cycle, you will need to make these adjustments:

1. Warm the water to between 110°F and 115°F (43°C and 46°C).

2. Warm the eggs and egg whites (see the Techniques Glossary, page 238).

3. Follow the recipe instructions, but select the **Gluten-Free Cycle** rather than the Dough Cycle and Bake Cycle.

4. At the end of the Gluten-Free Cycle, take the temperature of the loaf using an instant-read thermometer. It is baked at 200°F (100°C). If it's between 180°F (85°C) and 200°F (100°C), leave machine on the **Keep Warm Cycle** until baked. If it's below 180°F (85°C), turn on the **Bake Cycle** and check the internal temperature every 10 minutes. (Some bread machines are automatically set for 60 minutes; others need to be set by 10-minute intervals.)

Stollen

Stollen is a traditional German Christmas bread with a very dark, rich-colored crust and a domed top. It is served on Christmas Eve, when families gather to celebrate before going to church.

Tips

To ensure success, see page 15 for information on using your bread machine and page 18 for general tips on bread machine baking.

It is important to tent this bread with foil, as otherwise the crust becomes very dark and the raisins peeking out the top could burn.

◆ **9-inch (23 cm) round baking pan, lightly greased**

1 cup	brown rice flour	250 mL
1/3 cup	quinoa flour	75 mL
1/4 cup	almond flour	60 mL
1/3 cup	arrowroot starch	75 mL
1/4 cup	tapioca starch	60 mL
1 tbsp	xanthan gum	15 mL
1 tbsp	bread machine or instant yeast	15 mL
1 tsp	salt	5 mL
3/4 tsp	ground cardamom	3 mL
3/4 cup	chopped mixed candied fruit	175 mL
3/4 cup	raisins	175 mL
1 cup	water	250 mL
3 tbsp	vegetable oil	45 mL
2	eggs, lightly beaten	2
1/2 cup	marmalade	125 mL

Orange Glaze

1 cup	GF confectioner's (icing) sugar, sifted	250 mL
1 to 2 tbsp	frozen orange juice concentrate, thawed	15 to 30 mL

1. In a large bowl or plastic bag, combine brown rice flour, quinoa flour, almond flour, arrowroot starch, tapioca starch, xanthan gum, yeast, salt, cardamom, candied fruit and raisins; mix well and set aside.

2. Pour water and oil into the bread machine baking pan. Add eggs and marmalade.

3. Select the **Dough Cycle**. As the bread machine is mixing, gradually add the dry ingredients, scraping bottom and sides of pan with a rubber spatula. Try to incorporate all the dry ingredients within 1 to 2 minutes. Stop bread machine as soon as the kneading portion of the cycle is complete. Do not let bread machine finish the cycle.

NUTRITIONAL VALUES per serving	
Calories	198
Fat, total	5 g
Fat, saturated	1 g
Cholesterol	23 mg
Sodium	165 mg
Carbohydrate	37 g
Fiber	2 g
Protein	3 g
Calcium	24 mg
Iron	1 mg

Variation

For a more traditional presentation, omit the orange glaze and dust cooled stollen with GF confectioner's (icing) sugar to resemble a light covering of snow.

4. Gently transfer dough to prepared pan and smooth top. Let rise, uncovered, in a warm, draft-free place for 45 minutes or until risen almost to the top of pan. Meanwhile, preheat oven to 350°F (180°C).

5. Bake for 40 to 45 minutes, tenting with foil after 25 minutes, until internal temperature of loaf registers 200°F (100°C) on an instant-read thermometer. Remove from the pan immediately and let cool completely on a rack.

6. *For the glaze:* In a small bowl, combine confectioner's sugar and enough orange juice concentrate to make a thin glaze. Drizzle over cooled stollen.

Fruited Barm Brack

*Barm brack, meaning
"yeast bread" in Gaelic, is
an Irish bread with raisins
or currants and candied
fruit peel. Try our fruited
version, made with tea,
apricots and cranberries.
Perfect with an entrée
or dessert!*

Tips

To ensure success, see
page 15 for information on
using your bread machine
and page 18 for general tips
on bread machine baking.

Powdered ice tea mixes are
too sweet and too strongly
flavored with lemon to be
substituted for the tea in
this recipe.

NUTRITIONAL VALUES
per serving

Calories	135
Fat, total	3 g
Fat, saturated	0 g
Cholesterol	21 mg
Sodium	210 mg
Carbohydrate	25 g
Fiber	2 g
Protein	4 g
Calcium	28 mg
Iron	2 mg

◆ **Three 5³⁄₄- by 3¹⁄₄-inch (14 by 8 cm) loaf pans,
lightly greased**

1¹⁄₃ cups	sorghum flour	325 mL
½ cup	amaranth flour	125 mL
½ cup	teff flour	125 mL
½ cup	tapioca starch	125 mL
¼ cup	packed brown sugar	60 mL
1 tbsp	xanthan gum	15 mL
1 tbsp	bread machine or instant yeast	15 mL
1½ tsp	salt	7 mL
1½ tsp	ground cinnamon	7 mL
½ tsp	ground nutmeg	2 mL
½ cup	snipped dried apricots	125 mL
½ cup	currants	125 mL
½ cup	dried cranberries	125 mL
1¹⁄₃ cups	strong brewed black tea, at room temperature	325 mL
2 tbsp	vegetable oil	30 mL
1 tsp	cider vinegar	5 mL
2	eggs, lightly beaten	2
2	egg whites, lightly beaten	2

1. In a large bowl or plastic bag, combine sorghum flour, amaranth flour, teff flour, tapioca starch, brown sugar, xanthan gum, yeast, salt, cinnamon, nutmeg, apricots, currants and cranberries; mix well and set aside.

2. Pour tea, oil and vinegar into the bread machine baking pan. Add eggs and egg whites.

3. Select the **Dough Cycle**. As the bread machine is mixing, gradually add the dry ingredients, scraping bottom and sides of pan with a rubber spatula. Try to incorporate all the dry ingredients within 1 to 2 minutes. Stop bread machine as soon as the kneading portion of the cycle is complete. Do not let bread machine finish the cycle.

Tip
We allow our tea to steep longer than normal to make it extra strong for this recipe.

Variation
Try replacing one or more of the fruits with an equal quantity of snipped dried cherries, dried apples or dates.

4. Spoon batter into prepared pans, dividing evenly. Let rise, uncovered, in a warm, draft-free place for 70 minutes. Meanwhile, preheat oven to 350°F (180°C).

5. Bake for 33 to 38 minutes or until internal temperature of loaf registers 200°F (100°C) on an instant-read thermometer. Remove from the pan immediately and let cool completely on a rack.

Apricot Pecan Loaf

This nutritious, warm, dark teff loaf with contrasting chunks of golden apricots is a delicious snack for your coffee break.

Tips

To ensure success, see page 15 for information on using your bread machine and page 18 for general tips on bread machine baking.

Instead of chopping dried apricots with a knife, snip them with kitchen shears. Dip the blades in hot water when they become sticky.

1¼ cups	sorghum flour	300 mL
1 cup	teff flour	250 mL
½ cup	amaranth flour	125 mL
½ cup	tapioca starch	125 mL
1 tbsp	xanthan gum	15 mL
1¾ tsp	bread machine or instant yeast	8 mL
1¼ tsp	salt	6 mL
1 cup	snipped dried apricots	250 mL
1 cup	chopped pecans	250 mL
1¼ cups	water	300 mL
¼ cup	vegetable oil	60 mL
¼ cup	liquid honey	60 mL
2 tsp	cider vinegar	10 mL
2	eggs, lightly beaten	2
2	egg whites, lightly beaten	2

1. In a large bowl or plastic bag, combine sorghum flour, teff flour, amaranth flour, tapioca starch, xanthan gum, yeast, salt, apricots and pecans; mix well and set aside.

2. Pour water, oil, honey and vinegar into the bread machine baking pan. Add eggs and egg whites.

3. Select the **Dough Cycle**. As the bread machine is mixing, gradually add the dry ingredients, scraping bottom and sides of pan with a rubber spatula. Try to incorporate all the dry ingredients within 1 to 2 minutes. When the mixing and kneading are complete, remove the kneading blade, leaving the bread pan in the bread machine. Quickly smooth the top of the loaf. Allow the cycle to finish. Turn off the bread machine.

4. Select the **Bake Cycle**. Set time to 60 minutes and temperature to 350°F (180°C). Allow the cycle to finish. Do not turn machine off before taking the internal temperature of the loaf with an instant-read thermometer. It should be 200°F (100°C). If it's between 180°F (85°C) and 200°F (100°C), leave machine on the **Keep Warm Cycle** until baked. If it's below 180°F (85°C), turn on the **Bake Cycle** and check the internal temperature every 10 minutes. (Some bread machines are automatically set for 60 minutes; others need to be set by 10-minute intervals.)

NUTRITIONAL VALUES	
per serving	
Calories	217
Fat, total	7 g
Fat, saturated	2 g
Cholesterol	25 mg
Sodium	212 mg
Carbohydrate	35 g
Fiber	3 g
Protein	5 g
Calcium	38 mg
Iron	3 mg

Replace half the apricots with quartered figs.

5. Once the loaf has reached 200°F (100°C), remove it from the pan immediately and let cool completely on a rack.

Gluten-Free Cycle

If your bread machine has a Gluten-Free Cycle, you will need to make these adjustments:

1. Warm the water to between 110°F and 115°F (43°C and 46°C).
2. Warm the eggs and egg whites (see the Techniques Glossary, page 238).
3. Follow the recipe instructions, but select the **Gluten-Free Cycle** rather than the Dough Cycle and Bake Cycle.
4. At the end of the Gluten-Free Cycle, take the temperature of the loaf using an instant-read thermometer. It is baked at 200°F (100°C). If it's between 180°F (85°C) and 200°F (100°C), leave machine on the **Keep Warm Cycle** until baked. If it's below 180°F (85°C), turn on the **Bake Cycle** and check the internal temperature every 10 minutes. (Some bread machines are automatically set for 60 minutes; others need to be set by 10-minute intervals.)

Dried Apple Nut Bread

MAKES 15 SLICES
(1 per serving)

This rich, dark dessert bread is flecked with white dots of dried apple.

Tips

To ensure success, see page 15 for information on using your bread machine and page 18 for general tips on bread machine baking.

Use either dried apple rings or dried apple slices.

1⅓ cups	sorghum flour	425 mL
⅓ cup	GF oat flour	75 mL
⅓ cup	teff flour	75 mL
½ cup	tapioca starch	125 mL
¼ cup	packed brown sugar	60 mL
1 tbsp	xanthan gum	15 mL
2 tsp	bread machine or instant yeast	10 mL
1¼ tsp	salt	6 mL
2 tsp	ground cinnamon	10 mL
1 cup	chopped dried apples	250 mL
⅓ cup	chopped pecans	75 mL
1¼ cups	water	300 mL
2 tbsp	vegetable oil	30 mL
1 tsp	cider vinegar	5 mL
2	eggs, lightly beaten	2
2	egg whites, lightly beaten	2

1. In a large bowl or plastic bag, combine sorghum flour, oat flour, teff flour, tapioca starch, brown sugar, xanthan gum, yeast, salt, cinnamon, apples and pecans; mix well and set aside.

2. Pour water, oil and vinegar into the bread machine baking pan. Add eggs and egg whites.

3. Select the **Dough Cycle**. As the bread machine is mixing, gradually add the dry ingredients, scraping bottom and sides of pan with a rubber spatula. Try to incorporate all the dry ingredients within 1 to 2 minutes. When the mixing and kneading are complete, remove the kneading blade, leaving the bread pan in the bread machine. Quickly smooth the top of the loaf. Allow the cycle to finish. Turn off the bread machine.

NUTRITIONAL VALUES per serving	
Calories	152
Fat, total	5 g
Fat, saturated	1 g
Cholesterol	25 mg
Sodium	215 mg
Carbohydrate	24 g
Fiber	3 g
Protein	4 g
Calcium	24 mg
Iron	2 mg

Variation
Substitute dried apricots
for the apples and walnuts
for the pecans.

4. Select the **Bake Cycle**. Set time to 60 minutes and temperature to 350°F (180°C). Allow the cycle to finish. Do not turn machine off before taking the internal temperature of the loaf with an instant-read thermometer. It should be 200°F (100°C). If it's between 180°F (85°C) and 200°F (100°C), leave machine on the **Keep Warm Cycle** until baked. If it's below 180°F (85°C), turn on the **Bake Cycle** and check the internal temperature every 10 minutes. (Some bread machines are automatically set for 60 minutes; others need to be set by 10-minute intervals.)

5. Once the loaf has reached 200°F (100°C), remove it from the pan immediately and let cool completely on a rack.

Gluten-Free Cycle

If your bread machine has a Gluten-Free Cycle, you will need to make these adjustments:

1. Warm the water to between 110°F and 115°F (43°C and 46°C).

2. Warm the eggs and egg whites (see the Techniques Glossary, page 238).

3. Follow the recipe instructions, but select the **Gluten-Free Cycle** rather than the Dough Cycle and Bake Cycle.

4. At the end of the Gluten-Free Cycle, take the temperature of the loaf using an instant-read thermometer. It is baked at 200°F (100°C). If it's between 180°F (85°C) and 200°F (100°C), leave machine on the **Keep Warm Cycle** until baked. If it's below 180°F (85°C), turn on the **Bake Cycle** and check the internal temperature every 10 minutes. (Some bread machines are automatically set for 60 minutes; others need to be set by 10-minute intervals.)

Date Nut Loaf

MAKES 15 SLICES
(1 per serving)

This moist, dark, sweet loaf is delicious spread with cream cheese.

Tips

To ensure success, see page 15 for information on using your bread machine and page 18 for general tips on bread machine baking.

If you purchase chopped dates instead of whole ones, be sure to check the label for hidden gluten.

1½ cups	sorghum flour	375 mL
¾ cup	whole bean flour	175 mL
½ cup	tapioca starch	125 mL
1 tbsp	xanthan gum	15 mL
2½ tsp	bread machine or instant yeast	12 mL
1¼ tsp	salt	6 mL
1 cup	snipped pitted dates	250 mL
⅓ cup	chopped walnuts	75 mL
1¼ cups	water	300 mL
¼ cup	vegetable oil	60 mL
3 tbsp	light (fancy) molasses	45 mL
2 tsp	cider vinegar	10 mL
2	eggs, lightly beaten	2
2	egg whites, lightly beaten	2

1. In a large bowl or plastic bag, combine sorghum flour, whole bean flour, tapioca starch, xanthan gum, yeast, salt, dates and walnuts; mix well and set aside.

2. Pour water, oil, molasses and vinegar into the bread machine baking pan. Add eggs and egg whites.

3. Select the **Dough Cycle**. As the bread machine is mixing, gradually add the dry ingredients, scraping bottom and sides of pan with a rubber spatula. Try to incorporate all the dry ingredients within 1 to 2 minutes. When the mixing and kneading are complete, remove the kneading blade, leaving the bread pan in the bread machine. Quickly smooth the top of the loaf. Allow the cycle to finish. Turn off the bread machine.

4. Select the **Bake Cycle**. Set time to 60 minutes and temperature to 350°F (180°C). Allow the cycle to finish. Do not turn machine off before taking the internal temperature of the loaf with an instant-read thermometer. It should be 200°F (100°C). If it's between 180°F (85°C) and 200°F (100°C), leave machine on the **Keep Warm Cycle** until baked. If it's below 180°F (85°C), turn on the **Bake Cycle** and check the internal temperature every 10 minutes. (Some bread machines are automatically set for 60 minutes; others need to be set by 10-minute intervals.)

5. Once the loaf has reached 200°F (100°C), remove it from the pan immediately and let cool completely on a rack.

NUTRITIONAL VALUES
per serving

Calories	179
Fat, total	6 g
Fat, saturated	1 g
Cholesterol	25 mg
Sodium	211 mg
Carbohydrate	28 g
Fiber	3 g
Protein	5 g
Calcium	25 mg
Iron	1 mg

Gluten-Free Cycle

If your bread machine has a Gluten-Free Cycle, you will
need to make these adjustments:

1. Warm the water to between 110°F and 115°F (43°C
   and 46°C).
2. Warm the eggs and egg whites (see the Techniques
   Glossary, page 238).
3. Follow the recipe instructions, but select the
   Gluten-Free Cycle rather than the Dough Cycle
   and Bake Cycle.
4. At the end of the Gluten-Free Cycle, take the
   temperature of the loaf using an instant-read
   thermometer. It is baked at 200°F (100°C). If it's
   between 180°F (85°C) and 200°F (100°C), leave
   machine on the **Keep Warm Cycle** until baked. If it's
   below 180°F (85°C), turn on the **Bake Cycle** and check
   the internal temperature every 10 minutes. (Some bread
   machines are automatically set for 60 minutes; others
   need to be set by 10-minute intervals.)

Chocolate Hazelnut Dessert Bread

MAKES 15 SLICES
(1 per serving)

Plan to eat this one warm from the bread machine, as that's when the chocolate flavor is strongest.

Tips

To ensure success, see page 15 for information on using your bread machine and page 18 for general tips on bread machine baking.

You can use mini or jumbo chocolate chips, or just stick with the regular size.

See the Techniques Glossary, page 240, for information on toasting hazelnuts. For this recipe, there's no need to remove the skin after toasting them.

1½ cups	sorghum flour	375 mL
¾ cup	whole bean flour	175 mL
½ cup	tapioca starch	125 mL
¼ cup	granulated sugar	60 mL
1 tbsp	xanthan gum	15 mL
2½ tsp	bread machine or instant yeast	12 mL
1¼ tsp	salt	6 mL
¼ cup	unsweetened cocoa powder, sifted	60 mL
¾ cup	semisweet or bittersweet (dark) chocolate chips	175 mL
½ cup	toasted hazelnuts, coarsely chopped	125 mL
1⅔ cups	milk, warmed to room temperature	400 mL
¼ cup	vegetable oil	60 mL
2 tsp	cider vinegar	10 mL
2	eggs, lightly beaten	2
2	egg whites, lightly beaten	2

1. In a large bowl or plastic bag, combine sorghum flour, whole bean flour, tapioca starch, sugar, xanthan gum, yeast, salt, cocoa, chocolate chips and hazelnuts; mix well and set aside.

2. Pour milk, oil and vinegar into the bread machine baking pan. Add eggs and egg whites.

3. Select the **Dough Cycle**. As the bread machine is mixing, gradually add the dry ingredients, scraping bottom and sides of pan with a rubber spatula. Try to incorporate all the dry ingredients within 1 to 2 minutes. When the mixing and kneading are complete, remove the kneading blade, leaving the bread pan in the bread machine. Quickly smooth the top of the loaf. Allow the cycle to finish. Turn off the bread machine.

NUTRITIONAL VALUES	
per serving	
Calories	211
Fat, total	10 g
Fat, saturated	2 g
Cholesterol	26 mg
Sodium	224 mg
Carbohydrate	28 g
Fiber	3 g
Protein	6 g
Calcium	54 mg
Iron	2 mg

Variations

For a stronger hazelnut flavor, add 1 tbsp (15 mL) hazelnut liqueur (such as Frangelico) with the liquids.

For a stronger chocolate flavor, increase the cocoa to ⅓ cup (75 mL).

4. Select the **Bake Cycle**. Set time to 60 minutes and temperature to 350°F (180°C). Allow the cycle to finish. Do not turn machine off before taking the internal temperature of the loaf with an instant-read thermometer. It should be 200°F (100°C). If it's between 180°F (85°C) and 200°F (100°C), leave machine on the **Keep Warm Cycle** until baked. If it's below 180°F (85°C), turn on the **Bake Cycle** and check the internal temperature every 10 minutes. (Some bread machines are automatically set for 60 minutes; others need to be set by 10-minute intervals.)

5. Once the loaf has reached 200°F (100°C), remove it from the pan immediately and let cool completely on a rack.

Gluten-Free Cycle

If your bread machine has a Gluten-Free Cycle, you will need to make these adjustments:

1. Warm the eggs and egg whites (see the Techniques Glossary, page 238).

2. Follow the recipe instructions, but select the **Gluten-Free Cycle** rather than the Dough Cycle and Bake Cycle.

3. At the end of the Gluten-Free Cycle, take the temperature of the loaf using an instant-read thermometer. It is baked at 200°F (100°C). If it's between 180°F (85°C) and 200°F (100°C), leave machine on the **Keep Warm Cycle** until baked. If it's below 180°F (85°C), turn on the **Bake Cycle** and check the internal temperature every 10 minutes. (Some bread machines are automatically set for 60 minutes; others need to be set by 10-minute intervals.)

Hot Cross Buns

MAKES 10 BUNS
(1 per serving)

Before its significance for Christians, the cross symbolized the four quarters of the lunar cycle. So ancient Aztecs, Egyptians and Saxons all enjoyed hot cross buns. They have been served on Easter since the early days of the Church.

Tips

To ensure success, see page 15 for information on using your bread machine and page 18 for general tips on bread machine baking.

Confectioner's (icing) sugar may contain up to 5% starch, which could be from wheat, so make sure to look for a GF brand.

Use a pastry bag and tip to pipe the icing onto the crosses.

NUTRITIONAL VALUES
per serving

Calories	211
Fat, total	4 g
Fat, saturated	1 g
Cholesterol	38 mg
Sodium	258 mg
Carbohydrate	42 g
Fiber	2 g
Protein	4 g
Calcium	52 mg
Iron	2 mg

◆ **Baking sheet, lightly greased**

¾ cup	sorghum flour	175 mL
½ cup	whole bean flour	125 mL
⅓ cup	potato starch	75 mL
¼ cup	tapioca starch	60 mL
1 tbsp	xanthan gum	15 mL
2 tsp	bread machine or instant yeast	10 mL
1 tsp	salt	5 mL
1¼ tsp	ground cinnamon	6 mL
¼ tsp	ground cloves	1 mL
¼ tsp	ground nutmeg	1 mL
¾ cup	milk, warmed to room temperature	175 mL
⅓ cup	liquid honey	75 mL
2 tbsp	vegetable oil	30 mL
1 tbsp	light (fancy) molasses	15 mL
1 tsp	cider vinegar	5 mL
2	eggs, lightly beaten	2
1 cup	raisins	250 mL

Icing

¾ cup	sifted GF confectioner's (icing) sugar	175 mL
1 tbsp	milk	15 mL
¼ tsp	almond extract	1 mL

1. In a large bowl or plastic bag, combine sorghum flour, whole bean flour, potato starch, tapioca starch, xanthan gum, yeast, salt, cinnamon, cloves and nutmeg; mix well and set aside.

2. Pour milk, honey, oil, molasses and vinegar into the bread machine baking pan. Add eggs.

3. Select the **Dough Cycle**. As the bread machine is mixing, gradually add the dry ingredients, scraping bottom and sides of pan with a rubber spatula. Try to incorporate all the dry ingredients within 1 to 2 minutes. Add raisins. Stop bread machine as soon as the kneading portion of the cycle is complete. Do not let bread machine finish the cycle.

Variations

To prepare California-style buns, decrease the raisins to 1/3 cup (75 mL) and add 1/3 cup (75 mL) each dates and mixed candied peel.

Replace the milk in the icing with thawed frozen orange juice concentrate.

4. Drop 10 heaping spoonfuls of batter onto prepared baking sheet. Using the handle of a wooden spoon or a rubber spatula, make two indents 1/8 inch (3 mm) deep in the shape of a cross on the top of each bun. Let rise, uncovered, in a warm, draft-free place for 60 to 75 minutes or until dough has doubled in volume. Meanwhile, preheat oven to 350°F (180°C).

5. Bake for 20 to 25 minutes or until internal temperature of buns registers 200°F (100°C) on an instant-read thermometer. Remove from the pan immediately and let cool on a rack.

6. *For the icing:* In a small bowl, combine confectioner's sugar, milk and almond extract. Drizzle the crosses of warm buns with icing.

Cinnamon Buns

You asked us for a cinnamon bun you could roll out and pull apart to eat. Well, here it is! The assembly can be a bit tricky, but the dough is less sticky if kept cold.

Tips

To ensure success, see page 15 for information on using your bread machine and page 18 for general tips on bread machine baking.

We don't recommend using a springform pan unless you want to clean your oven and test your smoke alarm battery — ours leaked! You can use a regular metal 9-inch (23 cm) round cake pan as long as the sides are at least 2 inches (5 cm) high.

NUTRITIONAL VALUES	
per serving	
Calories	422
Fat, total	13 g
Fat, saturated	2 g
Cholesterol	31 mg
Sodium	314 mg
Carbohydrate	74 g
Fiber	5 g
Protein	7 g
Calcium	64 mg
Iron	3 mg

◆ **9-inch (23 cm) round silicone baking pan with 2-inch (5 cm) sides**

1½ to 1⅔ cups	sorghum flour, divided	375 to 400 mL
¾ cup	whole bean flour	175 mL
⅔ cup	tapioca starch	150 mL
½ cup	cornstarch	125 mL
2 tbsp	potato flour (not potato starch)	30 mL
½ cup	granulated sugar	125 mL
1 tbsp	xanthan gum	15 mL
4 tsp	bread machine or instant yeast	20 mL
1¼ tsp	salt	6 mL
1 cup	milk, warmed to room temperature	250 mL
2 tbsp	vegetable oil	30 mL
1 tsp	cider vinegar	5 mL
2	eggs, lightly beaten	2

Pecan Pan Glaze

⅓ cup	packed brown sugar	75 mL
⅓ cup	butter, melted	75 mL
⅓ cup	corn syrup	75 mL
24	pecan halves	24

Raisin Pecan Filling

1½ cups	raisins	375 mL
¾ cup	chopped pecans	175 mL
⅓ cup	packed brown sugar	75 mL
⅓ cup	butter, softened	75 mL
1½ tsp	ground cinnamon	7 mL

1. In a large bowl or plastic bag, combine 1 cup (250 mL) of the sorghum flour, whole bean flour, tapioca starch, cornstarch, potato flour, sugar, xanthan gum, yeast and salt; mix well and set aside.

2. Pour milk, oil and vinegar into the bread machine baking pan. Add eggs.

Tips

Be sure to prepare both the pan glaze and the filling before removing the first square of dough from the refrigerator. Work quickly when rolling out the dough and assembling the buns. Return the dough to the refrigerator for a few minutes if it becomes sticky.

We prefer to cut the dough into buns with a pizza wheel; however, kitchen shears or a sharp knife work well too. You may have to dip the cutter in hot water between cuts.

Freeze wrapped squares of dough for up to 1 month. Defrost overnight in the refrigerator.

Cinnamon buns can be frozen, individually wrapped, for up to 2 weeks. Defrost in the microwave.

Variations

Substitute ¾ cup (175 mL) chopped pecans and ½ cup (125 mL) pure maple syrup or pancake syrup for the pan glaze.

Divide pecan pan glaze evenly among the cups of a lightly greased 12-cup muffin tin. Place a bun, cut side up, in each cup. Reduce baking time to 20 to 25 minutes.

3. Select the **Dough Cycle**. As the bread machine is mixing, gradually add the dry ingredients, scraping bottom and sides of pan with a rubber spatula. Try to incorporate all the dry ingredients within 1 to 2 minutes. Stop bread machine as soon as the kneading portion of the cycle is complete. Do not let bread machine finish the cycle.

4. Generously coat two large sheets of plastic wrap with some of the remaining sorghum flour. Divide dough in half and place each half on a sheet of plastic wrap. Generously dust each with sorghum flour. Fold plastic wrap to cover dough and pat out to a square about ½ inch (1 cm) thick. Wrap airtight and refrigerate for at least 2 hours, until chilled, or overnight.

5. *For the glaze:* In a bowl, combine brown sugar, butter and corn syrup. Spread evenly on bottom of pan. Arrange pecan halves, flat side up, over glaze. Set aside.

6. *For the filling:* In a bowl, combine raisins, pecans, brown sugar, butter and cinnamon. Set aside.

7. Remove one square of dough from the refrigerator. Place on a sheet of parchment paper generously dusted with sorghum flour. Generously dust dough with sorghum flour and cover with another sheet of parchment paper. Lightly roll out to a 9-inch (23 cm) square, about ¼ inch (0.5 cm) thick. Remove top sheet of parchment paper.

8. Sprinkle half the filling over the dough. Beginning at one side, roll up like a jelly roll, lifting the parchment paper to help the dough form a roll. Using your fingers, brush off excess sorghum flour. Using a pizza wheel dipped in hot water, cut into 6 equal pieces; place cut side up, fairly close together, in prepared pan. Repeat with second square of dough.

9. Let rise, uncovered, in a warm, draft-free place for 60 to 75 minutes or until doubled in volume. Meanwhile, preheat oven to 350°F (180°C).

10. Bake for 50 to 60 minutes, tenting with foil after 40 minutes, until internal temperature of buns registers 200°F (100°C) on an instant-read thermometer. Immediately invert onto a serving platter. Let stand for 5 minutes before removing pan. Serve warm.

Banana Raisin Sticky Buns

This recipe is a bit tricky, so don't try it first if you've never baked gluten-free before. However, the results are worth the effort and time it takes.

Tips

To ensure success, see page 15 for information on using your bread machine and page 18 for general tips on bread machine baking.

We don't recommend using a springform pan unless you want to clean your oven and test your smoke alarm battery — ours leaked!

♦ 9-inch (23 cm) round silicone baking pan with 2-inch (5 cm) sides

1¼ cups	sorghum flour	300 mL
⅓ cup	whole bean flour	75 mL
¼ cup	almond flour	60 mL
½ cup	tapioca starch	125 mL
⅓ cup	cornstarch	75 mL
2 tbsp	potato flour (not potato starch)	30 mL
¼ cup	packed brown sugar	60 mL
1 tbsp	xanthan gum	15 mL
2 tbsp	bread machine or instant yeast	30 mL
1 tsp	salt	5 mL
⅓ cup	water	75 mL
¼ cup	vegetable oil	60 mL
1 tsp	cider vinegar	5 mL
1 cup	mashed ripe bananas	250 mL
3	eggs, lightly beaten	3
⅓ to ½ cup	sweet rice flour	75 to 125 mL

Pan Glaze

⅓ cup	packed brown sugar	75 mL
¼ cup	butter, melted	60 mL

Filling

1⅔ cups	raisins	400 mL
¼ cup	packed brown sugar	60 mL
½ tsp	ground cinnamon	2 mL
2 tbsp	butter, melted	30 mL

1. In a large bowl or plastic bag, combine sorghum flour, whole bean flour, almond flour, tapioca starch, cornstarch, potato flour, brown sugar, xanthan gum, yeast and salt. Mix well and set aside.

2. Pour water, oil and vinegar into the bread machine baking pan. Add bananas and eggs.

NUTRITIONAL VALUES per serving	
Calories	354
Fat, total	13 g
Fat, saturated	4 g
Cholesterol	62 mg
Sodium	277 mg
Carbohydrate	57 g
Fiber	3 g
Protein	6 g
Calcium	45 mg
Iron	2 mg

Tips

Be sure to prepare both the pan glaze and the filling before removing the first square of dough from the refrigerator. Work quickly when rolling out the dough and assembling the buns. Return the dough to the refrigerator for a few minutes if it becomes sticky.

We prefer to cut the dough into buns with a pizza wheel; however, kitchen shears or a sharp knife work well too. You may have to dip the cutter in hot water between cuts.

Because it is cold, this dough takes longer to rise than most.

To safely turn a silicone baking pan upside down, first place it on a cooling rack, then, using the ends of the rack as handles, invert it over a serving platter.

The wrapped squares of dough can be frozen for up to 1 month. Defrost overnight in the refrigerator.

Baked sticky buns can be frozen, individually wrapped, for up to 2 weeks. Defrost in the microwave.

Variation

Divide pan glaze evenly among the cups of a lightly greased 12-cup muffin tin. Place a bun, cut side up, in each cup. Reduce the baking time to 20 to 25 minutes.

3. Select the **Dough Cycle**. As the bread machine is mixing, gradually add the dry ingredients, scraping bottom and sides of pan with a rubber spatula. Try to incorporate all the dry ingredients within 1 to 2 minutes. Stop bread machine as soon as the kneading portion of the cycle is complete. Do not let bread machine finish the cycle.

4. Generously coat two large sheets of plastic wrap with some of the sweet rice flour. Divide dough in half and place each half on a sheet of plastic wrap. Generously dust each with sweet rice flour. Top with another sheet of plastic wrap and pat out to a square about $1/2$ inch (1 cm) thick. Wrap airtight and refrigerate for at least 2 hours, until chilled, or overnight.

5. *For the pan glaze:* In baking pan, combine brown sugar and butter; spread evenly over bottom of pan. Set aside.

6. *For the filling:* In a bowl, combine raisins, brown sugar, cinnamon and butter. Set aside.

7. Remove one square of dough from the refrigerator. Place on a sheet of parchment paper generously dusted with sweet rice flour. Generously dust dough with sweet rice flour and cover with another sheet of parchment paper. Lightly roll out to a 9-inch (23 cm) square, about $1/4$ inch (0.5 cm) thick. Remove top sheet of parchment paper. With your fingers or a pastry brush, brush off excess flour.

8. Sprinkle half the filling over the dough. Roll up dough like a jelly roll, lifting the parchment paper to help the dough form a roll. Using a pizza wheel dipped in hot water, cut into 6 equal pieces. Place cut side up, fairly close together, in prepared pan. Repeat with the remaining dough and filling.

9. Let rise, uncovered, in a warm, draft-free place for $1^1/2$ to 2 hours or until doubled in volume. Meanwhile, preheat oven to 350°F (180°C).

10. Bake for 40 to 45 minutes, tenting with foil after 25 minutes, until internal temperature of buns registers 200°F (100°C) on an instant-read thermometer. Immediately invert onto a serving platter. Let stand for 5 minutes before removing pan. Serve warm.

Orange Breakfast Danish

MAKES 12 DANISH
(1 per serving)

Easier to make than traditional Danish, these cream cheese–filled rounds will be a hit with your family.

Tips

To ensure success, see page 15 for information on using your bread machine and page 18 for general tips on bread machine baking.

To ensure that the Danish are exactly the same size, and are kept at least 2 inches (5 cm) apart, draw 4½-inch (11 cm) circles on the parchment paper, then flip the paper over onto the baking sheets.

◆ **Two baking sheets, lightly greased and lined with parchment paper**

1½ cups	amaranth flour	375 mL
¾ cup	almond flour	175 mL
½ cup	tapioca starch	125 mL
½ cup	cornstarch	125 mL
½ cup	granulated sugar	125 mL
1 tbsp	xanthan gum	15 mL
4 tsp	bread machine or instant yeast	20 mL
1¼ tsp	salt	6 mL
1 tbsp	grated orange zest	15 mL
⅔ cup	water	150 mL
⅓ cup	frozen orange juice concentrate, thawed	75 mL
2 tbsp	vegetable oil	30 mL
1 tsp	cider vinegar	5 mL
2	eggs, lightly beaten	2

Orange Filling

1	package (8 oz/250 g) light or regular brick cream cheese, softened	1
½ cup	granulated sugar	125 mL
1 tbsp	frozen orange juice concentrate, thawed	15 mL
½ cup	raspberry jam	125 mL

1. In a large bowl or plastic bag, combine amaranth flour, almond flour, tapioca starch, cornstarch, sugar, xanthan gum, yeast, salt and orange zest; mix well and set aside.
2. Pour water, orange juice concentrate, oil and vinegar into the bread machine baking pan. Add eggs.
3. Select the **Dough Cycle**. As the bread machine is mixing, gradually add the dry ingredients, scraping bottom and sides of pan with a rubber spatula. Try to incorporate all the dry ingredients within 1 to 2 minutes. Stop bread machine as soon as the kneading portion of the cycle is complete. Do not let bread machine finish the cycle.

NUTRITIONAL VALUES per serving	
Calories	357
Fat, total	15 g
Fat, saturated	5 g
Cholesterol	54 mg
Sodium	323 mg
Carbohydrate	51 g
Fiber	3 g
Protein	7 g
Calcium	67 mg
Iron	5 mg

Tip

When using two baking sheets, place them in the upper and lower thirds of the oven. For even baking, switch their positions and rotate them from back to front halfway through the baking time.

Variations

In place of the jam, sprinkle the filling with chopped pecans.

Try a different jam or applesauce for the Danish centers.

4. Using a $\frac{1}{4}$-cup (60 mL) scoop, drop 6 scoops of dough at least 3 inches (7.5 cm) apart onto each prepared baking sheet. Using a moistened rubber spatula, spread each scoop into a $4\frac{1}{2}$-inch (11 cm) circle, keeping the circles 2 inches (5 cm) apart. Let rise, uncovered, in a warm, draft-free place for 60 minutes or until doubled in volume. Meanwhile, preheat oven to 350°F (180°C).

5. *For the filling:* In a small bowl, beat together cream cheese, sugar and orange juice concentrate. Spread a generous 2 tbsp (30 mL) filling on top of each dough circle and spoon 2 tsp (10 mL) jam in the center.

6. Bake in preheated oven (see tip, at left) for 15 to 20 minutes or until edges are lightly browned. Remove from the pan immediately and let cool completely on a rack.

Chop Suey Loaf

This old standby is chock full of mixed candied fruit. Keep one loaf for yourself and share the others.

Tips

To ensure success, see page 15 for information on using your bread machine and page 18 for general tips on bread machine baking.

For a lighter, less sweet loaf, rinse the fruit under cold water and dry well before adding to the baking pan.

Variation

Kulich: Substitute raisins for some of the candied fruit.

NUTRITIONAL VALUES
per serving

Calories	174
Fat, total	4 g
Fat, saturated	0 g
Cholesterol	21 mg
Sodium	211 mg
Carbohydrate	30 g
Fiber	2 g
Protein	4 g
Calcium	23 mg
Iron	11 mg

◆ **Three 5¾- by 3¼-inch (14 by 8 cm) loaf pans, lightly greased**

1½ cups	amaranth flour	375 mL
1¼ cups	brown rice flour	300 mL
½ cup	potato starch	125 mL
1 tbsp	xanthan gum	15 mL
1¾ tsp	bread machine or instant yeast	8 mL
1½ tsp	salt	7 mL
1 cup	chopped mixed candied fruit	250 mL
¼ cup	slivered almonds	60 mL
1¼ cups	water	300 mL
2 tbsp	vegetable oil	30 mL
3 tbsp	liquid honey	45 mL
1 tsp	cider vinegar	5 mL
2 tsp	almond extract	10 mL
2	eggs, lightly beaten	2
2	egg whites, lightly beaten	2

1. In a large bowl or plastic bag, combine amaranth flour, brown rice flour, potato starch, xanthan gum, yeast, salt, candied fruit and almonds; mix well and set aside.

2. Pour water, oil, honey, vinegar and almond extract into the bread machine baking pan. Add eggs and egg whites.

3. Select the **Dough Cycle**. As the bread machine is mixing, gradually add the dry ingredients, scraping bottom and sides of pan with a rubber spatula. Try to incorporate all the dry ingredients within 1 to 2 minutes. Stop bread machine as soon as the kneading portion of the cycle is complete. Do not let bread machine finish the cycle.

4. Spoon batter into prepared pans, dividing evenly. Let rise, uncovered, in a warm, draft-free place for 75 minutes. Meanwhile, preheat oven to 350°F (180°C).

5. Bake for 38 to 42 minutes or until internal temperature of loaf registers 200°F (100°C) on an instant-read thermometer. Remove from the pan immediately and let cool completely on a rack.

Beyond Breads

French Toast

MAKES 2 SLICES
(1 per serving)

Quick, easy, traditional breakfast fare. Makes good use of leftover breads.

Tip
We like to use Ancient Grains Bread (page 62) or Cinnamon Raisin Bread (page 38) for this recipe.

Variation
Sprinkle with ground cinnamon and GF confectioner's (icing) sugar just before serving.

◆ 8-inch (20 cm) skillet

2	eggs	2
2 tbsp	milk	30 mL
2	slices GF bread	2
1 tsp	butter	5 mL
	Maple syrup, honey yogurt or fresh fruit	

1. In a shallow bowl or pie plate, whisk together eggs and milk. Add bread slices and let soak for 1 minute. Turn and soak for 1 minute.
2. In the skillet, melt butter over medium heat, Add soaked bread and cook for 2 minutes or until bottom is deep golden. Turn and cook for 2 minutes or until bottom is golden. Serve immediately with your choice of topping.

NUTRITIONAL VALUES
per serving

Calories	273
Fat, total	13 g
Fat, saturated	5 g
Cholesterol	228 mg
Sodium	373 mg
Carbohydrate	28 g
Fiber	2 g
Protein	10 g
Calcium	63 mg
Iron	3 mg

Christmas Morning Strata

**MAKES
6 SERVINGS**

Busy enough on Christmas morning? Assemble this the night before. All you need to add is fresh fruit, and breakfast is ready.

Tips

Choose portobello, cremini or button mushrooms, or a mixture.

Try Swiss, sharp (old) Cheddar, Monterey Jack or a Tex-Mex mixture for the cheese.

Variations

Use GF salami or GF prosciutto instead of the GF ham.

Try rosemary, dill or marjoram in place of the basil.

◆ **8-inch (20 cm) square baking pan, lightly greased**

1 tbsp	butter	15 mL
1	small onion, chopped	1
8 oz	mushrooms (see tip, at left), sliced	250 g
4 oz	GF ham, cut into 1/2-inch (1 cm) cubes	125 g
2 tbsp	snipped fresh parsley	30 mL
1 tbsp	snipped fresh basil	15 mL
3 cups	cubed GF bread (1/2-inch/1 cm cubes)	750 mL
2 cups	shredded cheese (see tip, at left)	500 mL
4	eggs	4
1 cup	milk	250 mL
1 tbsp	Dijon mustard	15 mL

1. In a large skillet, melt butter over medium heat. Sauté onion and mushrooms for 4 to 6 minutes or until tender. Remove from heat and stir in ham, parsley and basil.
2. Arrange half of the bread cubes in prepared pan. Top with half the ham mixture and half the cheese. Repeat layers.
3. In a small bowl, whisk together eggs, milk and mustard until blended. Pour over strata. Cover with foil and refrigerate overnight.
4. Preheat oven to 350°F (180°C). Bake, covered with foil, for 20 minutes. Remove foil and bake for 30 to 35 minutes or until center is set and top is golden.

NUTRITIONAL VALUES per serving	
Calories	480
Fat, total	22 g
Fat, saturated	11 g
Cholesterol	181 mg
Sodium	1040 mg
Carbohydrate	45 g
Fiber	2 g
Protein	25 g
Calcium	470 mg
Iron	5 mg

Poultry Stuffing Bread

The flavor of the herbs bakes right into each bite of this loaf. It's perfect to use in stuffing for Cornish game hens or turkey (see Poultry Stuffing, page 222).

Tips

To ensure success, see page 15 for information on using your bread machine and page 18 for general tips on bread machine baking.

This is an excellent loaf for making croutons and bread crumbs. See the Techniques Glossary, page 237, for information about bread crumbs.

1½ cups	sorghum flour	375 mL
¾ cup	brown rice flour	175 mL
½ cup	potato starch	125 mL
¼ cup	tapioca starch	60 mL
2 tbsp	granulated sugar	30 mL
1 tbsp	xanthan gum	15 mL
2 tsp	bread machine or instant yeast	10 mL
1½ tsp	salt	7 mL
¼ cup	snipped fresh parsley	60 mL
3 tbsp	minced dried onion	45 mL
3 tbsp	dried rubbed sage	45 mL
3 tbsp	dried savory	45 mL
1½ tsp	celery seeds	7 mL
1¼ cups	water	300 mL
⅓ cup	vegetable oil	75 mL
1 tsp	cider vinegar	5 mL
2	eggs	2

1. In a large bowl or plastic bag, combine sorghum flour, brown rice flour, potato starch, tapioca starch, sugar, xanthan gum, yeast, salt, parsley, dried onion, sage, savory and celery seeds; mix well and set aside.

2. Pour water, oil and vinegar into the bread machine baking pan. Add eggs.

3. Select the **Dough Cycle**. As the bread machine is mixing, gradually add the dry ingredients, scraping bottom and sides of pan with a rubber spatula. Try to incorporate all the dry ingredients within 1 to 2 minutes. When the mixing and kneading are complete, remove the kneading blade, leaving the bread pan in the bread machine. Quickly smooth the top of the loaf. Allow the cycle to finish. Turn off the bread machine.

NUTRITIONAL VALUES
per serving

Calories	177
Fat, total	7 g
Fat, saturated	1 g
Cholesterol	25 mg
Sodium	245 mg
Carbohydrate	27 g
Fiber	3 g
Protein	3 g
Calcium	43 mg
Iron	2 mg

4. Select the **Bake Cycle**. Set time to 60 minutes and temperature to 350°F (180°C). Allow the cycle to finish. Do not turn machine off before taking the internal temperature of the loaf with an instant-read thermometer. It should be 200°F (100°C). If it's between 180°F (85°C) and 200°F (100°C), leave machine on the **Keep Warm Cycle** until baked. If it's below 180°F (85°C), turn on the **Bake Cycle** and check the internal temperature every 10 minutes. (Some bread machines are automatically set for 60 minutes; others need to be set by 10-minute intervals.)

5. Once the loaf has reached 200°F (100°C), remove it from the pan immediately and let cool completely on a rack.

Gluten-Free Cycle

If your bread machine has a Gluten-Free Cycle, you will need to make these adjustments:

1. Warm the water to between 110°F and 115°F (43°C and 46°C).

2. Warm the eggs (see the Techniques Glossary, page 238).

3. Follow the recipe instructions, but select the **Gluten-Free Cycle** rather than the Dough Cycle and Bake Cycle.

4. At the end of the Gluten-Free Cycle, take the temperature of the loaf using an instant-read thermometer. It is baked at 200°F (100°C). If it's between 180°F (85°C) and 200°F (100°C), leave machine on the **Keep Warm Cycle** until baked. If it's below 180°F (85°C), turn on the **Bake Cycle** and check the internal temperature every 10 minutes. (Some bread machines are automatically set for 60 minutes; others need to be set by 10-minute intervals.)

Poultry Stuffing

Traditional flavor with a modern twist! We introduced the idea of making stuffing that begins with poultry-seasoned bread crumbs when we first started developing bread machine recipes.

Tip

Allow 1 cup (250 mL) of stuffing for each 1 lb (500 g) raw poultry.

Variation

If you want softer, moister stuffing, add ½ cup (125 mL) water or extra GF chicken broth in step 2.

◆ **3-quart (3 L) casserole dish**

1	loaf Poultry Stuffing Bread (page 220), torn into chunks	1
2 cups	chopped celery	500 mL
1 cup	chopped onions	250 mL
½ cup	pan juices or GF chicken broth	125 mL

1. In a food processor fitted with a metal blade, pulse bread into coarse crumbs. Transfer to a large bowl and stir in celery and onions.
2. Place stuffing in casserole dish and stir in pan juices. Cover and bake beside the bird at 350°F (180°C) for the last hour of roasting.

Caution

The United States Department of Agriculture (USDA) and Agriculture Canada both recommend baking stuffing separately, not inside the bird. If you do stuff the bird, loosely fill the cavity and immediately put bird in the oven to roast. Remove the stuffing as soon as the bird is done. Refrigerate leftovers immediately.

NUTRITIONAL VALUES
per serving

Calories	98
Fat, total	4 g
Fat, saturated	0 g
Cholesterol	13 mg
Sodium	139 mg
Carbohydrate	15 g
Fiber	2 g
Protein	2 g
Calcium	28 mg
Iron	1 mg

Whole-Grain Croutons

**MAKES 4 DOZEN
CROUTONS**
(6 per serving)

*Here's a healthy version
of croutons to top
off a salad.*

Tip

Use an electric knife or a
knife with a serrated edge
to cube bread slices.

Variation

Use any other leftover
day-old GF bread.

◆ **Preheat oven to 375°F (190°C)**
◆ **Rimmed baking sheet**

4	slices day-old Historic Grains Bread (page 64), cut into 1-inch (2.5 cm) cubes	4
1 tbsp	extra virgin olive oil	15 mL
2 tbsp	dried tarragon	30 mL

1. In a bowl, toss bread cubes with oil and tarragon. Spread in a single layer on baking sheet. Bake in preheated oven, turning often, for 10 to 15 minutes or until crisp and golden. Let cool completely on baking sheet.

2. Use immediately or store in an airtight container at room temperature for up to 3 weeks.

NUTRITIONAL VALUES per serving	
Calories	103
Fat, total	4 g
Fat, saturated	1 g
Cholesterol	13 mg
Sodium	107 mg
Carbohydrate	14 g
Fiber	2 g
Protein	3 g
Calcium	32 mg
Iron	2 mg

Garlic Croutons

MAKES 4 DOZEN CROUTONS
(6 per serving)

This is a good way to use up GF bread you found in the freezer!

Tips

You can make croutons from any of the bread recipes in this book.

Watch the croutons carefully while they're in the oven; some breads brown more quickly than others.

Variation

Add 2 tbsp (30 mL) dried herbs.

◆ **Preheat oven to 375°F (190°C)**
◆ **Rimmed baking sheet**

4	slices day-old GF bread, cut into 1-inch (2.5 cm) cubes	4
1 tbsp	extra virgin olive oil	15 mL
2	cloves garlic, minced	2

1. In a bowl, toss bread cubes with oil and garlic. Spread on a single layer on baking sheet. Bake in preheated oven, turning often, for 10 to 15 minutes or until crisp and golden. Let cool completely on baking sheet.

2. Use immediately or store in an airtight container at room temperature for up to 3 weeks.

NUTRITIONAL VALUES
per serving (based on White Bread, page 28)

Calories	73
Fat, total	3 g
Fat, saturated	0 g
Cholesterol	0 mg
Sodium	99 mg
Carbohydrate	10 g
Fiber	1 g
Protein	2 g
Calcium	11 mg
Iron	1 mg

Blue Cheese Croutons

MAKES 2 CUPS (500 ML) (¼ cup/60 mL per serving)

Add tang to any soup or salad with these delightful cheesy croutons.

Tips

Two slices of bread will yield about 2 cups (500 mL) bread cubes.

The baking time depends on how dry the bread cubes are.

Variation

Substitute finely chopped walnuts for the parsley.

- **Preheat oven to 375°F (190°C)**
- **Rimmed baking sheet**

2 cups	cubed GF bread	500 mL
2 tbsp	crumbled GF blue cheese	30 mL
1 tbsp	finely snipped fresh parsley	15 mL
2 tbsp	red wine vinegar	30 mL
1 tbsp	extra virgin olive oil	15 mL
1 tbsp	Dijon mustard	15 mL

1. Spread bread cubes in a single layer on baking sheet. Bake in preheated oven, turning often, for 15 minutes or until crisp.
2. Meanwhile, in a bowl, whisk together blue cheese, parsley, vinegar, oil and mustard. Add warm croutons and toss to coat.
3. Return to baking sheet and bake, turning often, for 10 to 15 minutes or until deep golden and crisp. Let cool completely on baking sheet.
4. Use immediately or store in an airtight container in the refrigerator for up to 2 days.

NUTRITIONAL VALUES
per serving (based on White Bread, page 28)

Calories	42
Fat, total	3 g
Fat, saturated	0 g
Cholesterol	1 mg
Sodium	97 mg
Carbohydrate	4 g
Fiber	0 g
Protein	1 g
Calcium	14 mg
Iron	0 mg

Pesto Sauce

**MAKES 1 CUP
(250 ML)
(1/2 cup/125 mL
per serving)**

*When fresh basil is
plentiful, make lots of
pesto sauce and freeze it
to use in the winter.*

2	large cloves garlic	2
1 cup	fresh basil leaves	250 mL
1/4 cup	fresh parsley leaves	60 mL
1/4 cup	freshly grated Parmesan cheese	60 mL
1 tbsp	extra virgin olive oil	15 mL
1/4 to 1/3 cup	GF vegetable broth	60 to 75 mL

1. With the motor of a food processor running, drop garlic through the feed tube and process until chopped. Add basil, parsley, Parmesan and oil; process until well mixed, stopping once or twice to scrape down the sides of the bowl with a rubber spatula. With the motor running, add broth through the feed tube and process until blended.

2. Store in an airtight container in the refrigerator for up to 3 days or in the freezer for up to 1 month.

NUTRITIONAL VALUES
per serving

Calories	131
Fat, total	11 g
Fat, saturated	3 g
Cholesterol	10 mg
Sodium	272 mg
Carbohydrate	3 g
Fiber	1 g
Protein	6 g
Calcium	221 mg
Iron	1 mg

Honey Butter

**MAKES
6 SERVINGS**

*We like to spread this
butter on toasted English
Muffins (page 148).*

Tips

This recipe can be doubled
or tripled.

Be sure to use a pasteurized
creamed honey, not a
liquid honey.

Variations

Spice up this recipe with
a pinch of ground allspice,
cinnamon or cloves.

Substitute lemon zest for
the orange zest.

⅓ cup	butter, softened	75 mL
2 tbsp	creamed honey	30 mL
1 tsp	grated orange zest	5 mL

1. In a small bowl, cream together butter, honey and orange zest.
2. Store in an airtight container in the refrigerator for up to 2 weeks. Let warm to room temperature before spreading.

NUTRITIONAL VALUES
per serving

Calories	106
Fat, total	10 g
Fat, saturated	6 g
Cholesterol	26 mg
Sodium	97 mg
Carbohydrate	6 g
Fiber	0 g
Protein	0 g
Calcium	4 mg
Iron	0 mg

Apple Jelly

**MAKES 2½ CUPS
(625 ML)
(2 tbsp/30 mL per
serving)**

*You don't need fresh
fruit to make this
jelly — it's easy to
prepare all year round.*

Tip

The jelly will appear very
thin at first. But don't
worry — it will thicken as it
cools in the refrigerator.

Variation

Substitute white grape
juice or any other type of
unsweetened fruit juice for
the apple juice.

3 cups	unsweetened apple juice	750 mL
1 cup	granulated sugar	250 mL
2 tbsp	unflavored gelatin powder	30 mL
1 tbsp	freshly squeezed lemon juice	15 mL

1. Pour apple juice, sugar, gelatin and lemon juice into the bread machine baking pan. Insert pan into oven chamber and select the **Jam Cycle**. At the end of the cycle, wearing oven mitts, carefully open the lid; let baking pan remain in the machine for 30 minutes.

2. Remove baking pan carefully and ladle jelly into sterilized jars, leaving ¼ inch (0.5 cm) headspace.

3. Store in the refrigerator for up to 3 weeks, freeze for up to 4 months or process in a boiling water canner for 10 minutes to preserve jelly so it is shelf-stable (see the Techniques Glossary, page 237).

Tips for Making Jelly and Marmalade

- Before attempting this recipe and the one on page 229, read your bread machine manual for information about making jelly and marmalade. Follow any instructions carefully.

- To prevent jelly and marmalade from boiling over, don't exceed the quantities given in the recipes.

- Wear oven mitts when handling hot jelly or marmalade — it's hotter than the fat used in deep-frying!

NUTRITIONAL VALUES per serving	
Calories	59
Fat, total	0 g
Fat, saturated	0 g
Cholesterol	0 mg
Sodium	3 mg
Carbohydrate	14 g
Fiber	1 g
Protein	1 g
Calcium	2 mg
Iron	0 mg

Orange Marmalade

MAKES 4 CUPS (1 L)
(2 tbsp/30 mL
per serving)

Looking for a change of spreads for your morning toast? You'll want to make extra so you can take a jar of this delicious marmalade with you the next time you visit friends.

Tip

If you don't have a Jam Cycle on your bread machine, try mixing ingredients for 5 to 6 minutes on the Basic Cycle. Turn off the bread machine, then restart it and select the Bake Cycle.

Variation

For thicker marmalade, add 2 to 3 tsp (10 to 15 mL) "light" or "for less sugar" pectin crystals with the fruit.

2	oranges (Seville or Valencia)	2
1	lemon	1
½ cup	water	125 mL
2½ cups	granulated sugar	625 mL
1½ cups	grated carrots (2 to 3 medium)	375 mL

1. Wash and scrub the peels of oranges and lemon. Cut each into 8 pieces and remove tough center membranes and seeds.

2. In a food processor fitted with a metal blade, pulse oranges and lemon until coarsely chopped.

3. Pour water into the bread machine baking pan. Add sugar, carrots, oranges and lemon. Insert pan into oven chamber and select the **Jam Cycle**. At the end of the cycle, wearing oven mitts, carefully open the lid; let baking pan remain in the machine for 30 minutes.

4. Remove baking pan carefully and ladle marmalade into sterilized jars, leaving ¼ inch (0.5 cm) headspace. Handle the marmalade carefully — it is still extremely hot after cooling for 30 minutes in the bread machine.

5. Store in the refrigerator for up to 3 weeks, freeze for up to 4 months or process in a water bath for 10 minutes to preserve marmalade so it is shelf-stable (see the Techniques Glossary, page 237).

NUTRITIONAL VALUES per serving	
Calories	216
Fat, total	0 g
Fat, saturated	0 g
Cholesterol	0 mg
Sodium	6 mg
Carbohydrate	56 g
Fiber	2 g
Protein	1 g
Calcium	20 mg
Iron	0 mg

Equipment Glossary

Baguette pan. A metal baking pan divided into two sections shaped like long, thin loaves. The bottom surface may be perforated with small holes to produce a crisp crust and reduce the baking time.

Colander. A bowl-shaped utensil with many holes, used to drain liquids from solids.

Cooling rack. Parallel and perpendicular thin bars of metal at right angles, with feet attached, used to hold hot baking off the surface to allow cooling air to circulate.

Hamburger bun pan. A baking pan that makes six 4-inch (10 cm) hamburger buns.

Instant-read thermometer. See page 20.

Loaf pan. Container used for baking loaves. Common pan sizes are 9 by 5 inches (23 by 12.5 cm) and 8 by 4 inches (20 by 10 cm).

Parchment paper. Heat-resistant paper similar to waxed paper, usually coated with silicon on one side; used with or as an alternative to other methods (such as applying vegetable oil or spray) to prevent baked goods from sticking to the baking pan.

Pastry brush. Small brush with nylon or natural bristles used to apply glazes or egg washes to dough. Wash thoroughly after each use. To store, lay flat or hang on a hook through the hole in the handle.

Pizza wheel. A sharp-edged wheel (without serrations) anchored to a handle.

Portion scoop. A utensil similar to an ice cream scoop, used to measure equal amounts of batter. Cookie scoops come in different sizes, for 2-inch (5 cm), $2\frac{1}{2}$-inch (6 cm) and $3\frac{1}{4}$-inch (8 cm) cookies. Muffin scoops have a $\frac{1}{4}$-cup (50 mL) capacity.

Rolling pin. A smooth cylinder of wood, marble, plastic or metal; used to roll out dough.

Sieve. A bowl-shaped utensil with many holes, used to drain liquids from solids.

Spatula. A utensil with a handle and a blade that can be long or short, narrow or wide, flexible or inflexible. It is used to spread, lift, turn, mix or smooth foods. Spatulas are made of metal, rubber, plastic or silicone.

Zester. A tool used to cut very thin strips of outer peel from citrus fruits. One type has a short, flat blade tipped with five small holes with sharp edges. Another style of zester that is popular is made of stainless steel and looks like a tool used for planing wood in a workshop.

Ingredient Glossary

Almond flour (almond meal). See Nut flours and meals on page 23.

Almonds. An ivory-colored nut with a pointed oval shape and a smooth texture. Almonds have a thin, medium brown skin that adheres to the nut. Sweet almonds have a delicate taste that is delicious in breads, cookies, cakes, fillings and candies. Blanched (skin off) and natural (skin on) almonds are interchangeable in recipes. Almonds are available whole, sliced, slivered or ground.

Amaranth flour. See page 22.

Apricots. A small stone fruit with a thin, pale yellow to orange skin and meaty orange flesh. Dried unpeeled apricot halves are used in baking.

Arrowroot starch. Helps baked goods bind better, lightens the finished product and causes breads to rise higher.

Asiago cheese. A pungent hard cheese from northern Italy. Cured for more than 6 months, its texture is ideal for grating.

Baking powder. A chemical leavener, containing an alkali (baking soda) and an acid (cream of tartar), that gives off carbon dioxide gas under certain conditions. Select gluten-free baking powder.

Baking soda (sodium bicarbonate). A chemical leavener that gives off carbon dioxide gas in the presence of moisture — particularly acids such as lemon juice, buttermilk and sour cream. It is also one of the components of baking powder.

Balsamic vinegar. A dark Italian vinegar made from grape juice that has been cooked until the water content is reduced by half, then aged for several years in wooden barrels. It has a pungent sweetness and can be used to make salad dressings and marinades or drizzled over roasted or grilled vegetables.

Bean flours. See page 24.

Bell peppers. These sweet-flavored members of the capsicum family (which includes chile peppers) have a hollow interior lined with white ribs and seeds attached at the stem end. They are most commonly green, red, orange or yellow, but can also be white or purple.

Blueberries. Wild low-bush berries are smaller than the cultivated variety and more time-consuming to pick, but their flavor makes every minute of picking time worthwhile. Readily available year-round in the frozen fruit section of most grocery stores.

Brown rice flour. See page 24.

Brown sugar. A refined sugar with a coating of molasses. It can be purchased coarse or fine and comes in dark, golden and light.

Buckwheat flour. See page 22.

Cardamom. This popular spice is a member of the ginger family. A long green or brown pod contains the strong, spicy, lemon-flavored seed. Although native to India, cardamom is used in Middle Eastern, Indian and Scandinavian cooking — in the latter case, particularly for seasonal baked goods.

Cheddar cheese. Always select a sharp (old), good-quality Cheddar for baking recipes. (The flavor of mild or medium Cheddar is not strong enough for baking.) Weight/volume equivalents are:

> *4 oz (125 g) = 1 cup (250 mL) shredded*
> *2 oz (60 g) = 1/2 cup (125 mL) shredded*
> *1 1/2 oz (45 g) = 1/3 cup (75 mL) shredded*

Chickpea (garbanzo bean) flour. Interchangeable with whole bean flour in any of the recipes in this book.

Cilantro. See Coriander.

Confectioner's (icing) sugar. Granulated sugar that has been ground to a fine powder, then sifted. It usually contains 3% cornstarch as an anticaking agent, to prevent clumping. Canadian confectioner's sugar may contain wheat starch, so check the label. Always sift confectioner's sugar just before using. Also called powdered sugar and fondant sugar.

Coriander. These tiny, yellow-ridged seeds taste of cardamom, cloves, white pepper and orange. Coriander leaves (also known as cilantro) have a flavor reminiscent of lemon, sage and caraway. To increase flavor in a recipe, substitute cilantro for parsley.

Cornmeal. See page 22.

Cornstarch. Helps baked goods bind better, lightens the finished product and causes breads to rise higher.

Corn syrup. Made from cornstarch, corn syrup keeps foods moist and prevents them from spoiling quickly. It is common for corn syrup to be flavored with vanilla extract.

Cranberries. Grown in bogs on low vines, these sweet-tart berries are available fresh, frozen and dried. Fresh cranberries are available only in season — typically from mid-October until January — but can be frozen right in the bag. Substitute dried cranberries for sour cherries, raisins or currants.

Currants. Similar in appearance to small dark raisins, currants are made by drying a special seedless variety of grape. Not the same as a type of berry that goes by the same name.

Dates. The fruit of the date palm tree, dates are long and oval in shape, with a paper-thin skin that turns from green to dark brown when ripe. Eaten fresh or dried, dates have a very sweet, light brown flesh around a long, narrow seed.

Egg replacer. The egg substitutes sold in most supermarkets contain egg products and should not be confused with commercial egg replacer. Egg replacer is a white powder containing a combination of baking powder and starches. It is added with the dry ingredients so that it is well mixed in before it touches the liquids. The oil or other fat in the recipe may have to be increased slightly.

Eggs. Liquid egg products, such as Naturegg Simply Whites, Break-Free and Omega Pro liquid eggs and Just Whites, are available in the United States and Canada. Powdered egg whites, such as Just Whites, can be used by reconstituting with warm water or as a powder. A similar product is called meringue powder in Canada. Substitute ¼ cup (60 mL) liquid whole eggs for each large egg, and 2 tbsp (25 mL) liquid egg whites for each large egg white.

Fava bean flour. Interchangeable with whole bean flour in any of the recipes in this book.

Feta cheese. A crumbly white Greek-style cheese with a salty, tangy flavor. Store in the refrigerator, in its brine, and drain well before using. Traditionally made with sheep's or goat's milk in Greece and usually with cow's milk in Canada and the U.S. A lactose-free flavored soy product is also available.

Figs. Pear-shaped fruit with thick, soft skin, available in green and purple. Eaten fresh or dried, the tan-colored, sweet flesh contains many tiny edible seeds.

Flaxseed. See page 22.

Garbanzo bean flour. Interchangeable with whole bean flour in any of the recipes in this book.

Garfava (garbanzo-fava bean) flour. Interchangeable with whole bean flour in any of the recipes in this book.

Garlic. An edible bulb composed of several sections (cloves), each covered with a papery skin. An essential ingredient in many styles of cooking.

Gelatin, unflavored. A colorless, odorless, flavorless powder used as a thickener. When dissolved in hot liquid and then cooled, it forms a jelly-like substance.

Gingerroot. A bumpy rhizome, ivory to greenish yellow in color, with a tan skin. Fresh gingerroot has a peppery, slightly sweet flavor, similar to lemon and rosemary, and a pungent aroma. Ground ginger is made from dried gingerroot. It is spicier and not as sweet or as fresh. Crystallized, or candied, ginger is made from pieces of fresh gingerroot that have been cooked in sugar syrup and coated with sugar.

Gluten. A natural protein in wheat flour that becomes elastic with the addition of moisture and kneading. Gluten traps gases produced by leaveners inside the dough and causes it to rise.

Glutinous rice flour. See Sweet rice flour, page 24.

Golden raisins. See Raisins.

Granulated sugar. A refined, crystalline, white form of sugar that is also commonly called white sugar, table sugar or just sugar.

Guar gum. A white, flour-like substance made from an East Indian seed high in fiber, this vegetable substance contains no gluten. It may have a laxative effect for some people. It can be substituted for xanthan gum.

Hazelnut flour (hazelnut meal). See Nut flours and meals on page 23.

Hazelnuts. Slightly larger than filberts, hazelnuts have a weaker flavor. Both nuts have a round, smooth shell and look like small brown marbles. They have a sweet, rich flavor and are interchangeable in recipes.

Herbs. Plants whose stems, leaves or flowers are used as a flavoring, either dried or fresh. To substitute fresh herbs for dried, a good rule of thumb is to use three times the amount of fresh as dried. Taste and adjust the amount to suit your preference.

Honey. Sweeter than sugar, honey is available in liquid, honeycomb and creamed varieties. Use liquid honey for baking.

Kalamata olives. See Olives, kalamata.

Linseed. See Flaxseed, page 22.

Maple syrup. A very sweet, slightly thick brown liquid made by boiling the sap from North American maple trees. Use pure maple syrup, not pancake syrup, in baking.

Millet. See page 23.

Mixed candied fruit. A mixture of dried candied orange and lemon peel, citron and glazed cherries. Citron, which can be expensive, is often replaced in the mix by candied rutabaga.

Molasses. A by-product of refining sugar, molasses is a sweet, thick, dark brown (almost black) liquid. It has a distinctive, slightly bitter flavor. It is available in the United States in light, dark and blackstrap varieties. In Canada, these varieties are called fancy, cooking and blackstrap. Use light (fancy) molasses for baking unless blackstrap is specified. Store in the refrigerator if used infrequently.

Nut flour (nut meal). See page 23.

Oat bran. See page 24.

Oat flour. See page 24.

Oats. See page 24.

Olive oil. Produced from pressing tree-ripened olives. Extra virgin oil is taken from the first cold pressing; it is the finest and fruitiest, pale straw to pale green in color, with the least amount of acid, usually less than 1%. Virgin oil is taken from a subsequent pressing; it contains 2% acid and is pale yellow. Light oil comes from the last pressing; it has a mild flavor, light color and up to 3% acid. It also has a higher smoke point. Product sold as "pure olive oil" has been cleaned and filtered; it is very mild-flavored and has up to 3% acid.

Olives, kalamata. A large, flavorful variety of Greek olive, typically dark purple in color and pointed at one end.

Parsley. A biennial herb with dark green curly or flat leaves used fresh as a flavoring or garnish. It is also used dried in soups and other mixes. Substitute parsley for half the amount of a strong-flavored herb such as basil.

Pea flour. See page 24.

Pecan flour (pecan meal). See Nut flours and meals on page 23.

Pecans. This sweet, mellow nut is smooth and oval, golden brown on the outside and tan on the inside. You can purchase pecans whole, halved, chopped or in chips.

Peel (mixed, candied or glacé). This type of peel is crystallized in sugar.

Peppers. See Bell peppers.

Pinto bean flour. Interchangeable with whole bean flour in any of the recipes in this book.

Poppy seeds. These tiny, kidney-shaped seeds have a mild, sweet, nutty, dusty flavor. They are available whole or ground. They are most flavorful when roasted and crushed.

Potato flour. See page 23.

Potato starch (potato starch flour). See Starches on page 23.

Pumpkin seeds. These are available roasted or raw, salted or unsalted, and with or without hulls. Raw pumpkin seeds without hulls — often known as pepitas ("little seeds" in Spanish) — are a dull, dark olive green. Roasted pumpkin seeds have a rich, almost peanuty flavor.

Quinoa flour. See page 23.

Raisins. Dark raisins are sun-dried Thompson seedless grapes. Golden raisins are treated with sulfur dioxide and dried artificially, yielding a moister, plumper product.

Rice bran. See page 24.

Rice flours. See page 24.

Rice polish. See page 24.

Salt. See page 25.

Sesame seeds. These flat oval seeds, which can be ivory, red, brown, pale gold or black, have a nutty, slightly sweet flavor. Black sesame seeds have a more pungent flavor and bitter taste than white or natural sesame seeds.

Sorghum flour. See page 23.

Sour cream. A thick, smooth, tangy product made by adding bacterial cultures to pasteurized, homogenized cream containing varying amounts of butterfat. Check the label: some lower-fat and fat-free brands may contain gluten.

Soy flour. See page 24.

Starches. See page 23.

Sun-dried tomatoes. Available either dry or packed in oil, sun-dried tomatoes have a dark red color, a soft chewy texture and a strong tomato flavor. Use dry, not oil-packed, sun-dried tomatoes in recipes. Use scissors to snip. Oil-packed and dry are not interchangeable in recipes.

Sunflower seeds. These plump, nutlike kernels grow in teardrop shapes within gray-and-white shells. They are sold raw or roasted, and salted, seasoned or plain. Shelled sunflower seeds are sometimes labeled "sunflower kernels" or "nutmeats." When buying seeds in shell, look for clean, unbroken shells.

Sweet peppers. See Bell peppers.

Sweet rice flour. See page 24.

Tapioca starch. Helps baked goods bind better, lightens the finished product and causes breads to rise higher.

Tarragon. An herb with narrow, pointed, dark green leaves and a distinctive anise-like flavor with undertones of sage. Use fresh or dried.

Teff flour. See page 23.

Vegetable oil. Common oils used are canola, corn, sunflower, safflower, olive, peanut, soy and walnut.

Walnuts. Inside a tough shell, a walnut's curly nutmeat halves offer a rich, sweet flavor, and the edible, papery skin adds a hint of bitterness to baked goods. Walnuts are available whole (shelled and unshelled), halved and chopped.

White (navy) bean flour. Interchangeable with whole bean flour in any of the recipes in this book.

Whole bean flour. Made from Romano beans (also called cranberry beans or speckled sugar beans). The dried beans are cooked to help reduce flatulence, then stone-ground to a uniform, fine, dark, strong-tasting flour. If it's not available, substitute fava bean flour, chickpea (garbanzo bean) flour, garfava flour (sold as garbanzo-fava bean flour in Canada), white (navy) bean flour or pinto bean flour.

Wild rice. Not actually rice at all but a marsh grass seed. The long, shiny black or dark brown grains take longer to cook than white rice and triple or quadruple in size when cooked. In its natural state, wild rice is gluten-free, but when found in boxed wild rice/white rice mixes, it is best avoided.

Xanthan gum. See page 25.

Yeast. See page 26.

Yogurt. Made by fermenting cow's milk using a bacteria culture. Plain yogurt is gluten-free, but not all flavored yogurt is.

Zest. Strips from the outer layer of rind (colored part only) of citrus fruit. Avoid the bitter part underneath. Used for its intense flavor.

Techniques Glossary

Almond flour (almond meal). *To make:* See Nut flour. *To toast:* Spread in a 9-inch (23 cm) baking pan and bake at 350°F (180°C), stirring occasionally, for 8 minutes or until light golden.

Almonds. *To blanch:* Cover almonds with boiling water and let stand, covered, for 3 to 5 minutes. Drain. Grasp the almond at one end, pressing between your thumb and index finger, and the nut will pop out of the skin. Nuts are more easily chopped or slivered while still warm from blanching. *To toast:* see Nuts.

Baking pan. *To prepare, or to grease:* Either spray the bottom and sides of the baking pan with nonstick cooking spray or brush with a pastry brush or a crumpled-up piece of waxed paper dipped in vegetable oil or shortening.

Bananas. *To mash and freeze:* Select overripe fruit, mash and package in 1-cup (250 mL) amounts in freezer containers. Freeze for up to 6 months. Defrost and warm to room temperature before using. About 2 to 3 medium bananas yield 1 cup (250 mL) mashed.

Beat. To stir vigorously to incorporate air, using a spoon, whisk, handheld beater or electric mixer.

Bell pepper. *To roast:* Place whole peppers on a baking sheet, piercing each near the stem with a knife. Bake at 425°F (220°C) for 18 minutes. Turn and bake for 15 minutes or until the skins blister. (Or roast on the barbecue, turning frequently, until skin is completely charred.) Place in a paper or plastic bag. Seal and let cool for 10 minutes or until skin is loose. Peel and discard seeds.

Boiling water canner. Place filled jars, with finger-tightened lids, upright on a rack in a boiling water canner filled with enough boiling water so that jars are covered by at least 1 inch (2.5 cm) of hot water. Cover canner and return to a full, rolling boil. Boil for the time specified in the recipe.

Blueberries, frozen. *To partially defrost:* Place 1 cup (250 mL) frozen blueberries in a single layer on a microwave-safe plate and microwave on High for 80 seconds.

Bread crumbs. *To make fresh:* For best results, the GF bread should be at least 1 day old. Using the pulsing operation of a food processor or blender, process until crumbs are of the desired consistency. *To make dry:* Spread bread crumbs in a single layer on a baking sheet and bake at 350°F (180°C) for 6 to 8 minutes, shaking pan frequently, until lightly browned, crisp and dry. (Or microwave, uncovered, on High for 1 to 2 minutes, stirring every

30 seconds.) *To store:* Package in airtight containers and freeze for up to 3 months.

Combine. To stir two or more ingredients together for a consistent mixture.

Cream. To combine softened fat and sugar by beating to a soft, smooth, creamy consistency while trying to incorporate as much air as possible.

Digital instant-read thermometer. *To test baked goods for doneness:* Insert the metal stem of the thermometer at least 2 inches (5 cm) into the thickest part of baked good. Temperature should register 200°F (100°C).

Drizzle. To slowly spoon or pour a liquid (such as icing or melted butter) in a very fine stream over the surface of food.

Dust. To coat by sprinkling GF confectioner's (icing) sugar, unsweetened cocoa powder or any GF flour lightly over food or a utensil.

Eggs. *To warm to room temperature:* Place eggs in the shell from the refrigerator in a bowl of hot water and let stand for 5 minutes.

Egg whites. *To warm to room temperature:* Separate eggs while cold. Place bowl of egg whites in a larger bowl of hot water and let stand for 5 minutes. *To whip to soft peaks:* Beat to a thickness that comes up as the beaters are lifted and folds over at the tips. *To whip to stiff peaks:* Beat past soft peaks until the peaks remain upright when the beaters are lifted.

Flaxseed. *To grind:* Place whole seeds in a coffee grinder or blender. Grind only the amount required. If necessary, store extra ground flaxseed in the refrigerator. *To crack:* Pulse in a coffee grinder, blender or food processor just long enough to break the seed coat but not long enough to grind completely.

Garlic. *To peel:* Use the flat side of a large knife to flatten the clove of garlic. Skin can then be easily removed. *To roast:* Cut off top of head to expose clove tips. Drizzle with 1/4 tsp (1 mL) olive oil and microwave on High for 70 seconds, until fork-tender. Or bake in a pie plate or baking dish at 375°F (190°C) for 15 to 20 minutes, or until fork-tender. Let cool slightly, then squeeze cloves from skins.

Glaze. To apply a thin, shiny coating to the outside of a baked food to enhance the appearance and flavor.

Grease pan. See Baking pan.

Hazelnut flour (hazelnut meal). *To make:* See Nut flour. *To toast:* Spread in a 9-inch (23 cm) baking pan and bake at 350°F (180°C), stirring occasionally, for 8 minutes or until light golden. Let cool before using.

Hazelnuts. *To remove skins:* Place hazelnuts in a 350°F (180°C) oven for 15 to 20 minutes. Immediately place in a clean, dry kitchen towel. With your hands, rub the nuts against the towel.

Skins will be left in the towel. Be careful: hazelnuts will be very hot.

Herbs. *To store full stems:* Fresh-picked herbs can be stored for up to 1 week with stems standing in water. (Keep leaves out of water.) *To remove leaves:* Remove small leaves from stem by holding the top and running fingers down the stem in the opposite direction of growth. Larger leaves should be snipped off the stem using scissors. *To clean and store fresh leaves:* Rinse under cold running water and spin-dry in a lettuce spinner. If necessary, dry between layers of paper towels. Place a dry paper towel along with the clean herbs in a plastic bag in the refrigerator. Use within 2 to 3 days. Freeze or dry for longer storage. *To measure:* Pack leaves tightly into correct measure. *To snip:* After measuring, transfer to a small glass and cut using the tips of sharp kitchen shears/scissors to avoid bruising the tender leaves. *To dry:* Tie fresh-picked herbs together in small bunches and hang upside down in a well-ventilated location with low humidity and out of sunlight until the leaves are brittle and fully dry. If they turn brown (rather than stay green), the air is too hot. Once fully dried, strip leaves off the stems for storage. Store whole herbs in an airtight container in a cool, dark place for up to 1 year and crushed herbs for up to 6 months. (Dried herbs are stored in the dark to prevent the color from fading.) Before using, check herbs and discard any that have faded, lost flavor or smell old and musty. *To dry using a microwave:* Place $\frac{1}{2}$ to 1 cup (125 to 250 mL) herbs between layers of paper towels. Microwave on High for 3 minutes, checking often to be sure they are not scorched. Then microwave for 10-second periods until leaves are brittle and can be pulled from stems easily. *To freeze:* Lay whole herbs in a single layer on a flat surface in the freezer for 2 to 4 hours. Leave whole and pack in plastic bags. Herbs will keep in the freezer for 2 to 3 months. Crumble frozen leaves directly into the dish. Herb leaves are also easier to chop when frozen. Use frozen leaves only for flavoring and not for garnishing, as they lose their crispness when thawed. Some herbs, such as chives, have a very weak flavor when dried, and do not freeze well, but they do grow well inside on a windowsill.

Leeks. *To clean:* Trim roots and wilted green ends. Peel off tough outer layer. Cut leeks in half lengthwise and rinse under cold running water, separating the leaves so the water gets between the layers. Trim individual leaves at the point where they start to become dark in color and coarse in texture — this will be higher up on the plant the closer you get to the center.

Mix. To combine two or more ingredients uniformly by stirring or using an electric mixer on a low speed.

Nut flour (nut meal). *To make:* Toast nuts (see Nuts), cool to room temperature and grind in a food processor or blender to desired consistency. *To make using ground nuts:* Bake at 350°F (180°C) for 6 to 8 minutes, cool to room temperature and grind finer.

Nuts. *To toast:* Spread nuts in a single layer on a baking sheet and bake at 350°F (180°C) for 6 to 8 minutes, shaking the pan frequently, until fragrant and lightly browned. (Or microwave, uncovered, on High for 1 to 2 minutes, stirring every 30 seconds.) Nuts will darken upon cooling.

Oat flour. *To make:* In a food processor or blender, pulse oats until finely ground, or to desired consistency.

Olives. *To pit:* Place olives under the flat side of a large knife; push down on knife until pit pops out.

Onions. *To caramelize:* In a nonstick frying pan, heat 1 tbsp (15 mL) oil over medium heat. Add 2 cups (500 mL) sliced or chopped onions; cook slowly until soft and caramel-colored. If necessary, add 1 tbsp (15 mL) water or white wine to prevent sticking while cooking.

Pecan flour (pecan meal). *To make:* See Nut flour.

Pumpkin seeds. *To toast:* See Seeds.

Sauté. To cook quickly at high temperature in a small amount of fat.

Seeds. *To toast:* There are three methods you could use: 1) Spread seeds in a single layer on a baking sheet and bake at 350°F (180°C) for 6 to 10 minutes, shaking the pan frequently, until aromatic and lightly browned; 2) Spread seeds in a single layer in a large skillet and toast over medium heat for 5 to 8 minutes, shaking pan frequently; or 3) Microwave seeds, uncovered, on High for 1 to 2 minutes, stirring every 30 seconds. Seeds will darken upon cooling.

Sesame seeds. *To toast:* See Seeds.

Skillet. *To test for correct temperature:* Sprinkle a few drops of water on the surface. If the water bounces and dances across the pan, it is ready to use. If the drops of water evaporate, it is too hot.

Sunflower seeds. *To toast:* See Seeds.

Wild rice. *To cook:* Rinse 1 cup (250 mL) wild rice under cold running water. Add to a large saucepan, along with 6 cups (1.5 L) water. Bring to a boil and cook, uncovered, at a gentle boil for 35 minutes. Reduce heat, cover and cook for about 10 minutes or until rice is soft but not mushy. Makes about 3 cups (750 mL). Store in the refrigerator for up to 1 week.

Zest. *To zest:* Use a zester, the fine side of a box grater or a small sharp knife to peel off thin strips of the colored part of the skin of citrus fruits. Be sure not to remove the bitter white pith below.

About the Nutrient Analysis

The nutrient analysis done on the recipes in this book was derived from The Food Processor Nutrition Analysis Software, version 7.71, ESHA Research (2001).

Where necessary, data were supplemented using the following references:

1. Shelley Case, *Gluten-Free Diet: A Comprehensive Resource Guide*, Expanded Edition (Regina, SK: Case Nutrition Consulting, 2006).
2. Bob's Red Mill Natural Foods. Nutritional information product search. Retrieved April 15, 2009, from www.bobsredmill.com/catalog/index.php?action=search.
3. Gluten-free oats and oat flour from Cream Hill Estates (www.creamhillestates.com). Certificate of Analysis of Pure Oats (Lasalle, QC: Silliker Canada Co., 2005). Certificate of Analysis of Oat Flour (Lasalle, QC: Silliker Canada Co., 2006).
4. Flax Council of Canada. Nutritional information product search. Retrieved April 15, 2009, from www.flaxcouncil.ca.

Recipes were evaluated as follows:
- The larger number of servings was used where there is a range.
- Where alternatives are given, the first ingredient and amount listed were used.
- Optional ingredients and ingredients that are not quantified were not included.
- Calculations were based on imperial measures and weights.
- Nutrient values were rounded to the nearest whole number.
- Defatted soy flour, 25% reduced-sodium broth and brown rice flour were used, including where these ingredients are listed as soy flour, stock and rice flour.
- Calculations involving meat and poultry used lean portions without skin.
- Canola oil was used where the type of fat was not specified.
- Recipes were analyzed prior to cooking.

It is important to note that the cooking method used to prepare the recipe may alter the nutrient content per serving, as may ingredient substitutions and differences among brand-name products.

Index

S

Washburn, Donna
    125 best gluten-free bread machine recipes / Donna Washburn and Heather Butt.

Includes index.
ISBN 978-0-7788-0238-9

1. Gluten-free diet—Recipes. 2. Cookery (Bread). 3. Automatic bread machines.
I. Butt, Heather II. Title.
III. Title: One hundred twenty-five best gluten-free bread machine recipes.

RM237.86.W368 2010   641.5'638   C2009-906696-3

More Great Books
from Robert Rose

Appliance Cooking

- 200 Best Pressure Cooker Recipes
  by Cinda Chavich
- 200 Best Panini Recipes
  by Tiffany Collins
- The Juicing Bible, Second Edition
  by Pat Crocker
- The Smoothies Bible, Second Edition
  by Pat Crocker
- The Mixer Bible, Second Edition
  by Meredith Deeds and Carla Snyder
- The 150 Best Slow Cooker Recipes
  by Judith Finlayson
- Delicious & Dependable Slow Cooker Recipes
  by Judith Finlayson
- 175 Essential Slow Cooker Classics
  by Judith Finlayson
- The Healthy Slow Cooker
  by Judith Finlayson
- Slow Cooker Comfort Food
  by Judith Finlayson
- The Vegetarian Slow Cooker
  by Judith Finlayson
- The Dehydrator Bible
  by Jennifer MacKenzie, Jay Nutt & Don Mercer
- 300 Slow Cooker Favorites
  by Donna-Marie Pye

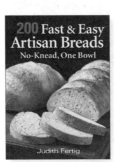

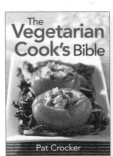

Baking

- 1500 Best Bars, Cookies, Muffins, Cakes & More
  by Esther Brody
- 200 Fast & Easy Artisan Breads
  by Judith Fertig
- The Complete Book of Pies
  by Julie Hasson
- 125 Best Chocolate Recipes
  by Julie Hasson
- 125 Best Cupcake Recipes
  by Julie Hasson
- Bars & Squares
  by Jill Snider
- Cookies
  by Jill Snider
- Complete Cake Mix Magic
  by Jill Snider

Healthy Cooking

- 125 Best Vegetarian Recipes
  by Byron Ayanoglu with contributions from Algis Kemezys
- 125 Best Vegan Recipes
  by Maxine Effenson Chuck and Beth Gurney
- The Vegetarian Cook's Bible
  by Pat Crocker
- The Vegan Cook's Bible
  by Pat Crocker
- 175 Natural Sugar Desserts
  by Angelina and Ari Dayan

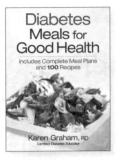

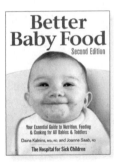

Also Available
by the same authors